Advance Praise for Leigh Eric Schmidt's
HEAVEN'S BRIDE

"The life and work of Ida C. Craddock show all the signs of a genuine erotic mysticism, as profound as any in the history of religions. Her attempts to express the full measure of this love—from secularism and religious liberalism, through psychical research, British occultism, and Indian Tantra, to marriage reform, sexology, and women's rights—were as diverse and as passionate as the censorship campaigns, familial condemnations, criminal prosecutions, and mental pathologizing that finally silenced her. Leigh Eric Schmidt, with his trademark erudition, balance, and humor, has effectively resurrected Ida for us from all of this cruelty. She speaks again. This is historical scholarship at its most liberating and most redeeming."

—JEFFREY J. KRIPAL, J. Newton Rayzor Professor of Religious Studies, Rice University, and author of *Authors of the Impossible: The Paranormal and the Sacred*

"Leigh Schmidt offers us a compulsively readable account of the tragic, fantastic, and utterly idiosyncratic life of Ira Craddock, self-taught scholar, mystic, sex reformer, and psychoanalytic subject. Sympathetic toward Craddock, yet even-handed in his treatment of both her admirers and her vehemently critical detractors, Schmidt opens a window on the fierce ideological cross-currents at the intersection of sexuality, psychology, and religion at the turn of the last century. This is serious scholarship in a form that everyone can enjoy."

—ANN TAVES, Professor of Religious Studies, University of California at Santa Barbara

"With a novelist's grace, Leigh Schmidt tells the absorbing, astonishing, and long-forgotten story of Ida C. Craddock, religious seeker and sex radical. Through Craddock's life, Schmidt restores the spiritual pulse to the sexual revolution of the early twentieth-century. *Heaven's Bride* is a masterful contribution to the entwined history of religion, sexuality, and American reform."

—KATHI KERN, author of *Mrs. Stanton's Bible*

more . . .

"Schmidt's lyrical, compelling, and captivating story of a truly unique American religious experimenter is a rare gift. In *Heaven's Bride*, Craddock's sometimes amusing, often tragic interactions with bellydancers, vice informants, the police, asylums, freethinkers, scholars, mystics (and even a disapproving mother and a range of spirit friends) come to life and provide a window into the unsettledness of American religious life one century ago. Yet Craddock's story is much more than an entertaining and tragic narrative. In Schmidt's story, Craddock's refusal to live within the social boundaries taking shape around her and the consequences that she suffered expose the enormous and often violent efforts that have been required to solidify the distinctions that modern Americans take to be self evident. For all those readers think they know the difference between science and religion, mysticism and sexuality, amateurs and experts, psychosis and devotion, Craddock's life—and Schmidt's analysis—presents perspicuous challenges. This enormously fascinating book inspires and unsettles, prompting 'curiosities and hopes and suspicions all in equal measure.' Miss Ida C. Craddock would be pleased."

—COURTNEY BENDER,
Associate Professor of Religion at Columbia University

"In *Heaven's Bride* Leigh Eric Schmidt has done an admirable job of rescuing the remarkable Ida C. Craddock from the ashes of history and places her before us in her full glory: a brilliant autodidact, a sexual researcher, writer of sex manuals, and wife of an angel named Soph. Craddock is a classic American iconoclast in the spirit of Walt Whitman and her fascinating story is far-reaching, touching on abuses of free speech, early feminism, and America's still-ongoing obsession with sex and purity."

—MARTIN GARBUS, First Amendment lawyer and
author of *The Next Twenty Five Years*

HEAVEN'S BRIDE

THE UNPRINTABLE LIFE
of IDA C. CRADDOCK, AMERICAN MYSTIC, SCHOLAR, SEXOLOGIST, MARTYR, *and* MADWOMAN

———◆———

LEIGH ERIC SCHMIDT

BASIC BOOKS
A Member of the Perseus Books Group
New York

Copyright © 2010 by Leigh Eric Schmidt

Published by Basic Books,
A Member of the Perseus Books Group

All rights reserved. Printed in the United States of America. No part of this book may be reproduced in any manner whatsoever without written permission except in the case of brief quotations embodied in critical articles and reviews. For information, address Basic Books, 387 Park Avenue South, New York, NY 10016–8810.

Books published by Basic Books are available at special discounts for bulk purchases in the United States by corporations, institutions, and other organizations. For more information, please contact the Special Markets Department at the Perseus Books Group, 2300 Chestnut Street, Suite 200, Philadelphia, PA 19103, or call (800) 810–4145, ext. 5000, or e-mail special.markets@perseusbooks.com.

Editorial production by the Book Factory.
Composition in 11 pt Adobe Caslon Pro by Cynthia Young.

A CIP catalog record for this book is available from the Library of Congress.

Library of Congress Control Number: 2010929343
ISBN: 978-0-465-00298-6

Phrases from "Margaret Sanger Addresses the Ghost of Ida Craddock," originally published in *Lizzie Borden in Love* by Julianna Baggott; Copyright © 2006 by Julianna Baggott; reproduced with permission of the publisher, Southern Illinois University Press.

10 9 8 7 6 5 4 3 2 1

For R. Marie Griffith,
my own educator in right marital living

CONTENTS

———•◆•———

PREFACE

———•◦•———

Setting out from Greenwich Village on a Saturday in late September 1997, a jovial group of sightseers embarked on an unconventional tour of New York City. Sponsored by *Playboy* magazine, the excursion offered aficionados a journey to the storied landmarks of the sexual revolution. A visit to Margaret Sanger's ground-breaking clinic paid homage to the birth-control campaign she spurred in the 1910s and 1920s; a stop at the Stonewall Inn recalled the famed riots of 1969 that catalyzed the gay rights movement; a pause at the New Amsterdam Theatre celebrated the high-kicking dancers of Ziegfeld's Follies, the risqué showgirls who opened on Broadway in 1913. It was an urban expedition, as Hugh Hefner imagined it, through "the first phase of the revolution," a period of heroic struggle for freedom of expression against an army of censors and prudes. For all their lightheartedness, these day-trippers were on a countercultural pilgrimage to memorialize and sanctify the history of American sexual liberation, the long and ongoing battle against the forces of "puritan repression."[1]

If the tour-goers imagined that they would mostly be traipsing through the bohemian precincts of Greenwich Village, *Playboy* senior editor James R. Petersen had a surprise for them: The "Century of Sex" did not actually begin with any of the familiar New York milestones or hot spots. Instead, the revolution could be traced to a small apartment on West 23rd Street, where a relatively unknown reformer, Ida C. Craddock, had taken refuge in 1902. So, off the group went to pay their respects to a largely forgotten forebear, a daring innovator whom the anarchist Emma Goldman had once eulogized as "one of the bravest champions of women's emancipation," but who had since slipped into obscurity.

The tribute that *Playboy*'s parade of libertarians, bohemians, and merrymakers offered Craddock was apt enough. A marriage reformer demonstrably concerned with free sexual expression, she no doubt deserved to be on the outing's itinerary, and yet that notice captured only a small fraction of her colorful and oddly consequential life. A secular freethinker, a bookish folklorist, a spiritual eclectic, a civil-liberties advocate, and a psychoanalytic case history, Craddock was a distinct American visionary whose story sweeps across a vast cultural and religious terrain.[2]

That *Playboy*'s tour director introduced the sightseers to Craddock's contribution was an unexpected twist, but that gesture was not half so unlikely as the historian's opportunity to craft Craddock's story from her own writings: Craddock was supposed to have been silenced, and a book like this made impossible to write. Between 1893 and 1902, Craddock produced six pamphlets offering frank advice to married couples, but all of these tracts were suppressed as obscene literature and thus turned into exceedingly scarce commodities. Having consigned Craddock to the mixed company of pornographers, birth-control proponents, and literary renegades such as Walt Whitman and George Bernard Shaw, America's moral guardsmen made it very difficult for her to print and circulate her views at all.

As a result of her recurrent legal jeopardy, almost all of Craddock's writings went unpublished. The bulk of her literary output existed only in manuscripts and typescripts, which were especially vulnerable to destruction. The danger came not only from the official censors—notably the New York Society for the Suppression of Vice, a government-backed organization dedicated to upholding public morality—but also from those nearer (if not always dearer) to Craddock. "I recalled what Mother had said," Craddock noted with despair in her diary in 1896, "that if I die before she does, she will burn every one of my manuscripts."³ Craddock's mother often threatened her, sometimes idly, usually not; so Craddock wisely took steps to safeguard her papers, including an intimate diary of her mystical experiences and several book drafts on subjects ranging from marriage reform to comparative mythology. She shipped off most of the manuscripts to a patron in England where they remained safely tucked away until after World War I out of reach of the censor's fire.

The retrieval of Craddock's life from the vaults of vice suppression offers an entryway into major social and political issues of her day—and, often enough, of our own as well. Foremost among these is the religious and moral character of the United States, the very durability of the country's Christian identity. No less an authority than the Supreme Court declared in a decision in 1892 that everywhere in American life there was "a clear recognition of the same truth": namely, "that this is a Christian nation." The ideal of a Christian America still holds sway with a significant portion of the American public—but, as a cultural standard, it was first seriously tested by religious and secular challenges posed during Craddock's lifetime.⁴

Ida Craddock's conflict-ridden story offers an opening to investigate some of the cracks in the declared consensus—that a fusion of evangelical Christianity and Anglo-Saxon civilization necessarily undergirded the nation's laws, civic customs, moral codes, and global enterprises. Her unmooring from her own Protestant upbringing provides a parable of a larger cultural transformation: the disruption of evangelical Christianity's power to define the nation's sexual taboos, artistic limits, and sacred canon. "I don't know about you," the novelist Kurt Vonnegut once remarked, "but I practice a disorganized religion." Craddock was part of an advanced band of troublemaking inquirers who helped propel that creative experimentation in American religious life. By 1925, America's God was less securely Christian, let alone firmly evangelical.⁵

Drifting away from her natal Protestant faith, Craddock pursued both secular activism and spiritual variety. As a leader of the American Secular Union, Craddock pushed that group's most uncompromising demands for church-state separation, including the purging of prayer and Bible reading from the public schools. She also pressed for a universal "sexual enlightenment" on medical, legal, and educational grounds that looked very much apiece with a secular agenda of advancing scientific knowledge against outworn superstition. Craddock, for instance, insisted that married couples deserved how-to guides—which often took the form of explicit sexual guidebooks—to help them navigate the bedroom. Those initiatives, though, were only half her program.

Unlike the secular revolutions of sexuality that Alfred Kinsey and Hugh Hefner subsequently advanced, Craddock was part of a larger circle of nineteenth-century marital innovators who imagined a sexual revolution in specifically sacred terms. Having no desire to blot out all religion as an infamy, Craddock and her associates yoked sexual enlightenment to spirituality, the marriage bed to the passions of mystical experience. That maneuver, however baffling it sounded to secular liberals, carried a silver lining for them in their opposition to Christian statecraft and moral crusading: Sex, like religion, was made an intimate affair of personal satisfaction and individual liberty, a private matter of the heart. Human sexuality, once redeemed by spiritual association, could shed the veil of censorship and don the halo of free expression.[6]

The cultural skirmishes involving religion, politics, and sex provided combat enough, but Craddock also had to negotiate her way through a rapidly changing intellectual landscape. At once scholar and seeker, she occupied an ambiguous position amid a series of newly demarcated fields of inquiry, including comparative religions, psychology, folklore, and sexology. Unlike William James at Harvard, Morris Jastrow at the University of Pennsylvania, or G. Stanley Hall at Clark University, Craddock never inhabited an ivory tower that raised her to the level of reputable academic observer. Instead, as a love-steeped mystic, adrift and exposed, she herself became the object of scientific scrutiny.

Craddock, a skilled shape-shifter, always remained hard to pin down, but that elusiveness seemed only to intensify the desire to categorize her. Was she merely one more case history who could be pigeonholed by the new psychological and neurological sciences—an erotomaniac, nymphomaniac, or hysteric, a victim of an insane delusion of one diagnostic type or another? Or, was she a latter-day visionary, a weirdly American Teresa of Avila, "the madwoman," as Hélène Cixous put it, "who knew more than all the men"? In other words, had Craddock mastered the new disciplines for her own self-making, or did they ultimately master her? The scales were inevitably weighted against her— she would lobby hard, and unsuccessfully, to open the liberal arts at the University of Pennsylvania to women. Thanks, in part, to that early frustration of her collegiate ambitions, Craddock had to make her way as a thinly credentialed amateur in a world increasingly controlled by professionals and specialists.[7]

Kept on the intellectual margins, Craddock often delighted in her own unconventionality, well aware that her very edginess allowed her to enter one cultural fray after another: How much muscle would evangelical Protestantism have to define and enforce the norms of American literary, sexual, and religious expression? Would women be able to claim academic standing, spiritual authority, and social equality in American public life? Was visionary experience an empowering capacity or a debilitating clinical symptom? Was the erotic redeemable, a grace rather than a curse, a spiritual yearning as much an animal appetite? Those questions are the durable refrains of Craddock's story, but the answers come through the particularities of her unfamiliar life, not apart from them. "I am poet of the Body and I am poet of the Soul," Walt Whitman had proclaimed in *Leaves of Grass*, "The pleasures of heaven are with me and the pains of hell are with me." Craddock, as much as anyone of her era, revealed the force of those doubled passions.[8]

Ida C. Craddock—her very name had the homophonous ring of *idiosyncratic*, and that fluke of christening ended up pitch perfect for her. A talented eccentric, she was one of Whitman's unbound wayfarers, those bold swimmers who, no longer willing to wade timidly "holding a plank by the shore," jump off "in the midst of the sea." To write a cultural biography of her—a woman "very clever but queer," as one contemporary described Craddock—is to dignify the ramblings of a social, religious, and intellectual drifter. It is to write with, rather than against, the grain of American dissent—with "mind and heart wide open," as George Santayana said of his mentor William James, to the "odd, personal, or visionary in religion," to all those "spiritually disinherited, passionately hungry individuals of which America is full." Greatness, after all, is not what distinguishes Craddock's story; she is by no means an old-fashioned worthy. Instead hers is a tale of the obscure and the obscured; to tell it is to recover a dangerous and difficult woman from prearranged disappearance. *Heaven's Bride* makes legible a heretofore unprintable life.[9]

The story begins with Craddock's out-of-the-blue defense of belly dancing—an exotic art that had caused a furor at the World's Fair in Chicago in 1893. That hullabaloo managed to condense, in a single episode, all the controversies that eventually raged around her. Organized around Craddock's successive self-inventions, *Heaven's Bride* next explores her efforts to claim the mantles of freethinker and scholar, her determination to be taken seriously as a student of the sexual history of religion. It then tracks her increasingly eclectic religious fascinations—curiosities that included everything from the Ouija board to new meditative techniques to the supposed Tantric secrets of Hindu yogis. Scholar and mystic—those incarnations were plenty controversial—but then there was Craddock's professed expertise as a sexologist and marriage counselor, her insistence that couples could benefit from her intimate advice on love and sex. Her labors on behalf of marriage reform—and the repeated arrests for obscenity that resulted thereby—created yet another identity for Craddock: a martyr for civil liberties. Even then, Craddock still had one last role to play. Latched onto by Theodore Schroeder, a free-speech lawyer turned Freudian theorist, she looked like the epitome of religious and sexual manias. Ida C became, in due time, Schroeder's Anna O.

CHAPTER ONE

Belly-Dancing's Defender

———•◦•———

Fᴏʀ ʏᴇᴀʀs sʜᴇ ʜᴀᴅ ʀᴇꜰᴇʀʀᴇᴅ ᴛᴏ ᴛʜᴇᴍ ᴀs "the Holy Fathers of
the American Inquisition." When Anthony Comstock, head of the
New York Society for the Suppression of Vice, and three of his deputies
arrived at her Manhattan apartment in February 1902, Ida Craddock
was not surprised. She had long anticipated a last-ditch showdown with
Comstock, America's most formidable censor, and his smut-fighting
organization. About a week earlier Comstock had warned her directly
against any further violation of federal and state anti-obscenity laws,
and, as a repeat offender, she was well aware of her vulnerability. So when
Comstock and his fellow inspectors showed up at her cramped residence
on West 23rd Street with a warrant for her arrest, Craddock steeled
herself anew. "I wish to fight right through to a finish," she wrote her
lawyer shortly afterward. "All I ask is that you use me in the most
effective way possible." As an unabashed sex reformer and a mystic
founder of her own Church of Yoga, Craddock was to Comstock a
twice-damned purveyor of obscenity and blasphemy. He wanted to shut
down her whole operation—the distribution of her pamphlets, the
delivery of her lectures, even her face-to-face counseling sessions. "I am
taking my stand on the First Amendment to the Constitution of the
United States," Craddock countered, "guaranteeing me religious
freedom, freedom of speech and freedom of the press."[1]

Craddock could do little more than watch as Comstock conducted
his raid. Scanning the shelves of her private library, he found sixty-one
books and 536 circulars worthy of removal, all of which he could use as

evidence against her before once again pulping such filth. A heavy-set man with mutton-chop sideburns and creased blue eyes, Comstock had been at this for a while, having led the New York Society for the Suppression of Vice since its incorporation in 1873. For three decades now he had been frustrating the designs of shady booksellers, sketchy impresarios, dime novelists, condom distributors, abortion providers, birth-control advocates, and taboo-breaking artists. Imbued with a strong sense of Christian discipline from his Connecticut youth, he had further honed his self-control through prayerfully resisting the temptations of army life during the Civil War—the whiskey drinking, coarse language, and tobacco chewing that marked the camaraderie of his fellow soldiers. "Boys got very drunk," Comstock noted of his army mates at one point in his diary. "I did not drink a drop. . . . Touch not. Taste not. Handle not."[2]

After the war Comstock had settled in New York City where he got a job working as a clerk in a dry goods store. Still in his early twenties, he navigated his way through the urban streets with the moral compass of the Young Men's Christian Association. Metropolitan leisure looked, if anything, even worse than army unruliness; the snares of the city, Comstock decided, required systematic efforts at vice suppression. He soon formed a local obscenity-busting committee, and, with the help of well-heeled allies in the Protestant business community, he built it into one of the most powerful agencies of evangelical reform in the country's history. Shrewdly targeting the U.S. mails as the chief conduit for the national dissemination of printed matter, Comstock established himself as a special agent of the U.S. Post Office, a role that gave him far-reaching authority to monitor and control the circulation of any and all indecent materials. The federal postal system, with its transcontinental reach, became his ticket for limiting the flow of objectionable media. By the close of 1903, he calculated that his vice society had obtained 2,712 arrests and 2,009 convictions through its inspective vigilance. He also proudly tabulated the seizure and destruction of thirty-eight tons of obscene books, pamphlets, and periodicals, not to mention 1,023,655 lewd pictures and photographs. Adding a few pounds of contraband from Craddock's shelves hardly looked like much of a haul in light of Comstock's weighty caseload.[3]

The zealousness of Comstock's campaign for moral purity made him an outsized figure in Victorian America. To his evangelical admirers, he was a broad-shouldered, sinewy hero; to his lusty caricaturists, he was a corpulent, greasy villain. Few looked on his two-hundred-and-ten-pound frame with indifference: Was that a fighter's build or a Falstaff's belly? From one side, Comstock appeared a godsend to a Christian nation, the great protector of American family values; from the other, he looked like the joyless face of an evangelical theocracy, the destroyer of American liberties. Craddock was only one among thousands of his targets, and yet her case ended up giving this cultural divide an almost mythic cast. "[Miss] Craddock was a surprisingly lovely woman," one observer sympathetic to her plight noted. "She and Comstock were the Beauty and the Beast."[4]

Craddock's pretty lady-like exterior never fooled Comstock. She always stood out in his mind as a particularly repulsive troublemaker: "I do not know of any obscene book . . . that contains matters more dangerous to the young, than the matters this woman has published," Comstock wrote at the time of her arrest. "It is not a question of sympathy, or lack of sympathy for this poor woman. But it is a question of preventing the youth of this great country, from being debauched in mind, body and soul." In the Society's *Annual Report* for 1902, which detailed the group's usual successes against America's "Moral-Cancer-Planters," the coverage of Craddock's indictment far outstripped that of all other cases. For a group that combated everything from bawdy plays and gambling dens to contraceptive devices and indecent pictures on the walls of saloons, Craddock had somehow become the focal point in Comstock's crusade against obscenity and vice. The author of "indescribably nasty books" and the purveyor of "outrageous blasphemy,"

Anthony Comstock, standing in his office of the New York Society for the Suppression of Vice, has the look of a man grown weary—if no less determined—through the ceaseless combat of sin and sleaze. WHi-4495, Wisconsin Historical Society.

During her battle with Comstock in New York City in 1902, Craddock became an icon among social radicals. This particular photograph, inscribed with the notation "Ida Craddock Comstock Victim," was likely used as part of efforts to generate money to support her legal defense. Labadie Collection, University of Michigan.

she was, Comstock swore, "a disgrace to her sex" and a danger to the public peace.[5]

Having already been arrested in Philadelphia, Chicago, and Washington, DC, on similar charges, Craddock well knew that Comstock and his three deputies had come to her apartment to take her into custody. All were playing their expected parts, but, as Craddock stood waiting for Comstock to finish inspecting her belongings, she heard the great "apostle of purity," as she wryly called him, whistling a tune with a peculiarly composed and calm air. Craddock took it to be a sign that his imagination, so prone in her view to salacious and even sadistic fantasies, was drifting off into its favored territory of erotic reverie. With a disturbing coolness, the federally appointed protector of innocent youth was humming the music of "the Koochy-Koochy Dance," a notorious form of belly dancing only recently introduced to American audiences and one that had quickly become a byword for sensually charged dancing, the Hootchy-Kootchy or Danse du Ventre.[6]

Perhaps, as Comstock inspected her bookshelves, he had alighted on a stray copy of the second edition of Craddock's own *Danse du Ventre*, "revised and enlarged, bound in yellow," a remarkable defense of just such hip-shaking performances. Craddock certainly made that connection herself; shortly after her arrest she sent a copy of the pamphlet to her lawyer, marking it as "especially important . . . because Anthony evidently objects to pelvic movements being written about," despite, she noted bitterly, having had belly dancing very much on his mind as he rummaged through her office. Or, perhaps Comstock, a man who definitely liked to keep close count of his wins and losses, had not drifted into erotic fantasy at all, but was whistling a premeditated victory song. Perhaps he was taunting Craddock, shaming her by scandalous association—just as he did later in taking her to jail aboard the elevated train, loudly calling attention to her with "opprobrious epithets" about the filth and blasphemy of her writings. No doubt he wanted to bring her to justice, but even more he wished to bring her into disgrace. After all, with this search-and-seizure operation, he was evening an old score, one that went back at least a decade to the World's Fair in Chicago in 1893 and one that would come to a crushing end in October 1902 eight months after this raid.[7]

———•—•———

CHICAGO HAD MADE A manifesto of the 1893 World's Fair, conjuring up a vision of triumphal progress on the shore of Lake Michigan. Dubbed the Columbian Exposition in honor of the four-hundredth anniversary of Columbus's globe-altering voyage, the fair declared the nation's achievements through an array of giant pavilions dedicated to American plenty and ingenuity. A sequence of sixty different statues of Abundance adorned Agricultural Hall, and nearby at the Electricity Building, a heroic sculpture of Benjamin Franklin paid him the tribute (in Latin) of having stolen heaven's thunderbolt and broken the tyrant's scepter. Not to be outshone, the Palace of Mechanic Arts contained a vast twenty-three acres of floor space for displaying the prodigious machinery of American industry—the cranes, forges, pumps, boilers, and furnaces that fueled the country's economic growth and material prosperity. Westinghouse, for example, exhibited thirteen of its latest and most powerful engines, while the country's vast textile mills flaunted their ever-improving technologies for the mass production of consumer goods, a nonstop stream of readymade mittens, jeans, hosiery, and handkerchiefs. Fittingly enough, winged angels carrying laurel victory wreaths crowned the palace's soaring towers.

Even more than serving as a showcase for the country's commercial and industrial accomplishments, this "Dream City," as it was celebrated at the time, was America's claim to cultural prestige on a transatlantic level. Many of the other grand expositions of the nineteenth century had been held in such European hubs as London, Paris, and Vienna; while the United States had hosted a variety of international fairs, only the nation's Centennial Exhibition in Philadelphia in 1876 had rivaled those Old World stages. For the gleaming design of Chicago's fair, the planners drew on the most renowned architectural firms from across the country, enlisting the talents of such giants as Frederick Law Olmsted and Louis Sullivan. The monumental statuary, stately colonnades, cascading fountains, great domes, spacious rotundas, and colossal art galleries—all announced America's own full-blown renaissance. Chicago was presented as an American Venice, and, thanks to Olmsted's architectural landscaping, the fair's meticulously sculpted grounds possessed the canals, lagoons, and gondolas to make that comparison quite literal.[8]

The Columbian Exposition's grand staging radiated both a boastful chauvinism and a bracing cosmopolitanism. That was nowhere more apparent than in the World's Parliament of Religions, a much watched assembly convened during the final weeks of the fair in September 1893. The exposition generated a plethora of auxiliary congresses dedicated to almost every conceivable subject—from astronomy to psychology to folklore to woman's suffrage to peace arbitration to meteorology. None of these gatherings created a greater buzz than this seventeen-day parliament of faiths. To most Protestant observers, the convention looked like a prime opportunity to dramatize the superiority of Christian civilization, the crown jewel of the world's religions and cultures. In the eyes of many religious liberals, by contrast, the parliament appeared the advance wave of a more cosmopolitan tide of interfaith exchange and solidarity.

From whatever angle Americans viewed it, the World's Parliament of Religions presented a spectacle unlike any they had witnessed before. With Buddhist, Muslim, Jewish, Hindu, Shinto, Zoroastrian, Jain, Confucian, Roman Catholic, and Unitarian representatives, it offered an unusually broad platform for religious plurality. More than a few of the parliament's participants imagined themselves as harbingers of a resplendent universal faith. They were builders of the new temple that the British poet Alfred Lord Tennyson had envisaged just the year before:

"Neither Pagod[a], Mosque, nor Church,/ But loftier, simpler, always open-doored/ To every breath from heaven." In a city of magical dreams, that vision of religious concord and openness was among the most dazzling. Whether listening to the addresses of Swami Vivekananda, the Buddhist monk Anagarika Dharmapala, or the Muslim convert Alexander Russell Webb, many Americans were drawn for the first time to the new spiritual possibilities that the parliament disclosed.[9]

For all of its scientific, artistic, and religious ambitions, the Columbian Exposition very much indulged as well the country's fondness for the showman, huckster, and carnival barker. The fair's most reliable product was not cultural renaissance or spiritual uplift, but popular amusement, the well-hyped road that ran from P. T. Barnum's American Museum to Buffalo Bill Cody's Wild West shows. The Midway Plaisance was the fair's three-ring circus. A boulevard of curiosities, it included a panorama of a Hawaiian volcano, a Javanese village, an ostrich farm, an American Indian pageant, a Moorish palace, and a model of St. Peter's Basilica in Rome. The Midway also boasted the debut of the Ferris wheel, which carried visitors more than 250 feet into the air and turned on a seventy-ton axle, "the largest piece of steel ever forged," its promoters bragged. In the wheel's gargantuan shadow was Cairo Street, where tourists could watch the reenactment of a wedding procession that included bejeweled camels, "donkey boys," and "tom-tom beaters." As if that were not enough to leave spectators awestruck, there followed impersonators of the "priests of Luxor," staging the semblance of ancient pagan mysteries, "the rites of Ammon-Ra, Mout, and Chons." At the end of it all, some lucky visitors were afforded their own precarious camel ride, a sight that the rest of the crowd found wildly amusing.[10]

Cairo Street's open-air spectacles made it a very popular destination, but what sealed its fame were the performers of the Danse du Ventre at the Egyptian Theatre. A dozen or so young women, usually taking the stage one at a time, swayed their hips to the accompaniment of tambourines, flutes, drums, and castanets. With "numerous bangles and

The Ferris wheel, "the chief wonder of the Fair of 1893," loomed over the international exposition. Its popularity among sightseers—27 million of whom visited this magic city—became legendary. Halsey C. Ives, The Dream City: A Portfolio of Photographic Views of the World's Columbian Exposition *(St. Louis: Thompson, 1893), n.p.*

Among the most discussed sites at the fair was Cairo Street with its exotic staging of the Orient. A popular destination on the Midway Plaisance, it combined Egyptian gods, faux mosques, and ornamented camels. Halsey C. Ives, The Dream City: A Portfolio of Photographic Views of the World's Columbian Exposition *(St. Louis: Thompson, 1893), n.p.*

neck chains" accentuating their chests and with tassels adorning their waists, the dancers displayed "powerful contortions of the abdomen" to the wonderment of the spectators. Not surprisingly, this scandalously exotic exhibition held the rapt attention of the country's journalists as much as it did other fairgoers. The dancer "commences to sway her body in a dreamy way," one typical account related, "while a turbaned Turk in the background strikes a throbbing, whirring monotone from a one-stringed instrument. . . . The mind is thus prepared for a dance quite as un-American as the surroundings." By the end of 1893, the media's excited coverage had effectively introduced the belly dance to the American public on a national scale.[11]

The newspaper reports on this "astonishing anatomical exercise" offered at the same time a fine miniature of how the American imperial imagination worked in the late nineteenth century. Predictably belly dancing conjured up fantasies of harems and seraglios, exotic Oriental worlds made especially vivid in the West through the colonial enterprises of Britain and France. But those foreign climes were not all the Danse du Ventre evoked for American journalists. Some quickly linked the performances in the Egyptian Theatre to the dances of American Indians, noting a parallel between the "vulgar" rites of the Oklahoma territory and these "writhing exponents of African barbarism" on the Midway. A particularly troubling association in that regard was the Ghost Dance, a pan-Indian movement of the late nineteenth century centered on the performance of a prophetic spirit dance. Deeply linked to Lakota Sioux resistance, the Ghost Dance had been a factor in the massacre at Wounded Knee in 1890. That was not the only native ceremony, though, under federal ban at the time: Indian dances across the board were routinely subject to policies of suppression and reform— as if any unregulated form of indigenous dance was inimical to the progress of American empire. Red versus white, primitive versus civilized, immoral versus moral, Orient versus Occident, the Danse du Ventre managed to stir up a series of free-associated images, variations on the dangers and occasional allures of striking cultural difference. The media, not surprisingly, thrived on such spectacular comparisons and multiplied them with gusto.[12]

All the sensationalism helped engender a considerable public debate over this exotic new dance. Were the Cairo Street dancers presenting a program that was safe for public consumption, or were they instead purveyors of a barbarous vice that required suppression? Could the performance be "tolerated in a civilized and Christian community"? Was this "heathen show" simply "so demoralizing, and so disgusting" that it had to be shuttered? Or might it somehow prove a useful lesson in social evolution, if not cultural variety? The Harvard ethnologist Frederic

A group of tourists pose with "natives" in Cairo Street in front of the "Dancing Theatre," which became a focal point of controversy and fascination. Halsey C. Ives, The Dream City: A Portfolio of Photographic Views of the World's Columbian Exposition *(St. Louis: Thompson, 1893), n.p.*

Ward Putnam, a chief planner of the exposition's archaeological and anthropological exhibits, argued for leniency. Every nation has its own curious dance forms, he insisted: "Is it not probable," he asked, "that our waltz would seem equally strange to these dusky women of Egypt?" Putnam had to concede, though, that many Americans regarded the Dance du Ventre as "low and repulsive" and feared any exposure whatsoever to such base exhibitions. Putnam's highbrow curiosity hardly stilled those deeper cultural apprehensions: Why risk contaminating the country with the waste of "Oriental slums"?[13]

Protestant moralists, in particular, wanted the "horrible orgie" closed down, and they instinctively called on the most powerful and determined inspector of the day, Anthony Comstock, for help. By no means confining himself to his headquarters in New York City,

FRANK LESLIE'S
ILLUSTRATED
WEEKLY

NEW YORK, AUGUST 10, 1893.   Price, 10 Cents.

SEE "A TRIP IN A GONDOLA AT THE WORLD'S COLUMBIAN EXPOSITION" ON PAGES 90 AND 91.

THE WORLD'S COLUMBIAN EXPOSITION AT CHICAGO.

DANCING GIRLS IN THE EGYPTIAN THEATRE ON THE MIDWAY PLAISANCE.—Drawn by B. West Clinedinst.—[See Page 89.]

In the summer of 1893 the Danse du Ventre took hold of the media's imagination as much as it did the tourists who frequented its performance. Frank Leslie's Illustrated Weekly, *Aug. 10, 1893, cover.*

The scene, as Craddock actually witnessed it in the Egyptian Theatre, partook more of an ethnological display of folk dance than of the darkened nightclub and libidinous carnival evoked in the press's sensationalized coverage. The caption to this souvenir photograph nonetheless recalled that it was "a matter of serious public debate in the councils of the Exposition whether the customs of Cairo should be faithfully reproduced, or the morals of the public faithfully protected." Halsey C. Ives, The Dream City: A Portfolio of Photographic Views of the World's Columbian Exposition *(St. Louis: Thompson, 1893), n.p.*

Comstock commonly logged thousands of miles a year in tracking obscenity to its source. (It helped that his commission as a special agent of the Post Office Department afforded him free travel by rail, steamboat, and stage all across the country.) With a keen sense of civic and religious duty, he quickly headed to Chicago in late July 1893 to tour the theaters of the Midway. Leading an investigative entourage, Comstock predictably discovered a scene of dance-crazed debauchery. He wasted no time in rallying the faithful to clean up these "indecent exhibitions" and to rout the "shameless women" who were degrading true womanhood. As one member of his inspection team professed, "I would sooner lay my two boys in their graves than that they should look upon the sights I saw." Or, as another despaired upon exiting the show, "I have been to the mouth of hell to-day."[14]

Despite the protests (and in part because of them), the Cairo Street dancers triumphed in the court of popular appeal and public voyeurism. The fair's organizers, acutely aware of the bottom line, had little interest in discouraging tourist fascination. They made a few modest concessions with the dancers' costuming and then let the show go on. In another battle already fought out in court, Protestant moral reformers had failed to keep the fairgrounds closed on Sundays in deference to the Christian Sabbath, and now they had to endure this slight as well. The exposition's management, for all its professed decency and respectability, was showing little remorse. Sol Bloom, the illustrious promoter of the Midway's entertainments, exulted in all the controversy and attention that the Danse du Ventre was generating: "I had a gold mine."[15]

Comstock was dumbfounded over this flouting of his moral ideals. Returning to New York in early August 1893, he continued to shake his head at the Chicago spectacle he had witnessed the month before. He announced that "the very lowest places of public amusement" on his home turf would not tolerate the Danse du Ventre for a moment. (He seemed to be trying to prove that point when he subsequently had three of these "heathen" dancers arrested and fined when they ventured to

A NEW COLUMBUS.

Comstock, an object of satire as much as heroic celebration, often saw his vice campaigns turned into cartoons. In this one—captioned "New York's Great Viceologist on a Voyage of Discovery to Chicago"—he sets sail to discover the sins of the Columbian Exposition, specifically those on the Midway's minaret-marked "Street in Cairo." St. Louis Post-Dispatch, *Aug. 6, 1893, 18.*

New York with their "obscene & indecent exhibition.") In the immediate battle over the Midway performances, however, Comstock could only express bewilderment that the young women were allowed to "go on every day defiling the magnificence of that Columbian Exhibition with [their] nastiness."[16]

Exasperated with the country's lack of moral clarity over the Danse du Ventre, Comstock tried to pull off a bit of didactic theater for a reporter—his own "imitation" of the dance. Rising from his office chair, he arched his arms over his head and shook his own imposing midsection. "Of course I can't do it exactly as they did," he lamely explained. "I am not as little as they are." Comstock's vice-fighting career was spotted with moments of public ridicule (he was, for example, later lampooned for raiding the Art Students' League over a brochure that contained nude sketches). Here was another incident—a stout rendition of what he had witnessed on the Midway—in which he left himself wide open for caricature, a buffoonish stunt that undercut his larger effort to dim the spectacle of the culture's burgeoning sex industries. Over the course of a lifetime of chasing down smutty publishers and booksellers, Comstock considered himself (as did his Protestant benefactors) a heroic fighter with far more victories than defeats, but the Danse du Ventre was proving surprisingly hard to suppress. "The most shameless exhibition of depravity" continued unabated in Chicago, while Comstock's flamboyant outrage had itself become an object of satire.[17]

———————

AMID THE HUBBUB, little more than a week after Comstock's ill-fated simulation, belly dancing gained a new and unexpected defender in Ida C. Craddock, an unmarried thirty-six-year-old freethinker, an advocate for women's rights, and a teacher of stenography. On August 13, 1893, Craddock published a lengthy defense of the Danse du Ventre in the Sunday pages of Joseph Pulitzer's *New York World*, an immensely popular paper with a famously sharp eye for controversy. At the same time she sent a long defense of the show to one of the fair's managing boards, urging its leadership to stand strong against the censoring impulse of "Anthony Comstock and his helpers." Craddock's apologia for belly dancing came without warning, and her ideas flew in the face of everything the vice reformer believed about what he had seen on the Midway.[18]

In Craddock's opinion, the Danse du Ventre was not at all scandalous or disgusting. It was also far more than another diverting museum exhibit to take in once one had ridden the Ferris wheel or visited the ostrich farm. It was actually a "religious memorial" that offered a venerable, edifying, and much needed blend of sexuality and spirituality. Here, in the agitation of hips and abdomen, in the snapping of castanets and shaking of tassels, was "a most valuable object lesson," a performance that managed to combine "the apotheosis of female passion" with graceful self-control. Instead of warranting suppression, the Danse du Ventre, Craddock argued, should be "performed far and wide through our country"—and not for mature audiences only. It would prove an excellent "pre-nuptial educator of our young people," a valuable introduction to both the sensual and the sacred dimensions of marital relations. In Craddock's estimation, the show was worth seeing for the good of body and soul.[19]

Craddock's perspective was so deeply at odds with Comstock's evangelical sensibilities as to be almost unintelligible in its offensiveness. It was a standing conviction among the devout that dancing feet (let alone undulating hips) placed praying knees in serious jeopardy. Nineteenth-century evangelicals often banned dance entirely from their lives as part of stringent codes of holiness—alongside other vices like card-playing, drinking, smoking, swearing, theater-going, and immodest dress. Not all American Protestants, of course, were so rigorous, but the two largest and most influential denominational groups, the Baptists and Methodists, regularly made such rules a constitutive part of the

Christian life. Even those ministers who wanted to distance themselves from the "squeamish class" thought the Danse du Ventre crossed the line. As one prominent Episcopal clergyman reminded the faithful at the height of the controversy, "We must remember after all that Terpsichore was a heathen divinity, and that, taken as whole, dancing is a heathen institution," holding a prominent place in "the Sodoms and Gomorrahs" of idolaters. "In a word, knowing as I do the story of ancient heathenism," he continued, with a direct blast at Craddock's position, "this plea itself that the Midway Plaisance dance is 'a religious dance' appears in my eyes simply as the sentence of its condemnation. Indeed, the plea affords a powerful and all-sufficient reason for its banishment not only from the World's Fair but from the face of God's earth."[20]

To say the very least, Craddock had a tough sell on her hands to make this idolatrous art palatable to a Christian nation. Was it any wonder that both Isadora Duncan and Loie Fuller, American innovators in modern dance, found it advantageous to leave the country later in the decade to join the French avant-garde? In a religious culture so suspicious of the sensuousness of dance, there was little breathing room for the creative license associated with its contemporary elaboration— let alone for the dancers themselves. In another decade or two, choreographer Ruth St. Denis would redeem the art and spiritual exoticism of "Oriental dance" for her bohemian American audiences, but Craddock's exploratory efforts in the early 1890s looked to the nation's Protestant opinion-makers like no more than a tawdry burlesque.[21]

Having stirred up the fire-and-brimstone element with her defense of libidinous heathenism at the expense of Christian civilization, Craddock would have been well advised to let the matter rest. "No ordinary Western woman looked on these performances with anything but horror," a popular souvenir volume had warned in prescribing disgust as the only appropriate response of white women to the Cairo Street dancers. These were strong stipulations—of race, religion, and gender—

A souvenir volume from the World's Fair juxtaposed a "frightful" Cairo Street performer of the Danse du Ventre with the "Western beauty and grace" of a European dancer. "Only Darwin could expatiate impartially on the variations of taste in the human kind," the caption insisted. Halsey C. Ives, The Dream City: A Portfolio of Photographic Views of the World's Columbian Exposition *(St. Louis: Thompson, 1893), n.p.*

and, yet instead of letting the controversy quiet down, Craddock decided to broaden her defense of the Danse du Ventre. She expanded her essay into a stand-alone pamphlet, began circulating it for fifty cents a copy, and offered to take up the subject on the lecture circuit of freethinking clubs.[22]

Craddock also sent the piece to Moses Harman, activist editor of *Lucifer the Light-Bearer: A Journal of Investigation and Reform Devoted to the Emancipation of Woman from Sex Slavery.* That December Harman, the granddaddy of marriage reformers who himself had been in and out of the Kansas penitentiary for violating Comstock's anti-obscenity laws, published a substantial excerpt from Craddock's essay under the title "Sex Modesty—The True and the False." The appearance of her work in Harman's infamous journal served, in effect, as public notice that Craddock was joining the ranks of unbuttoned radicals. Hitherto she had been seen as an up-and-comer among liberals and freethinkers: A Unitarian "of the most advanced kind," she had been elected an officer of the American Secular Union, a group promoting strict church-state separation, and had actively campaigned for women's equal access to higher education. Still, she had hardly been a wild-eyed dissenter, definitely not a sex radical. The brouhaha over belly dancing was the hinge: "I have come to stay in the reform work of which my essay treats," she now told Harman proudly.[23]

Making the Danse du Ventre the occasion for coming out as a marriage reformer was a quirky decision on Craddock's part. No two ways about that. She was nonetheless quick to point out that her ideas actually derived from a large body of learning focused on ancient "Sex Worship." The Midway exhibition, Craddock insisted, looked vastly different once one had digested the writings of antiquarians, historians, and ethnologists on "phallic" rites, symbols, and traditions. Having taken stock of those quasi-academic investigations, she saw how deeply and thoroughly religion was entwined with fertility and sexual reproduction. "We have traveled fast and far since those old uplifting days of Phallic or Sex Worship," she observed, but we have "lost something" important in that evolutionary process: namely, "the recognition of sex as the chief educator of the human race in things material and in things spiritual." Primeval forms of worship, Craddock was sure, offered not a lesson in fetishistic depravity, but a vehicle of erotic redemption. Free sexual expression was potentially retrievable through the bookish pursuit of archaeology, folklore, anthropology, and comparative religions. Once Americans learned about the sexual history of religion, they would see more clearly the liberties they had forfeited through the ages of Christian repression. We still have much "to learn from heathen nations," Craddock concluded, "and I, for one, rejoice that this Danse du Ventre should have been one of the appointed means of grace."[24]

Whether the Danse du Ventre really served Craddock's emancipationist purposes remained, of course, an open question. On this much, at least, Comstock and company were correct: Such routines easily became the stuff of nightclub revues, stag parties, and peep shows, a staple in the various haunts of sporting men. In March 1894 the *National Police Gazette*, a sensationalist rag of its day, pictured on its cover a performance of the Danse du Ventre in Brooklyn with "A CROWD OF SPORTS" gaping at the "FASCINATING EXHIBITION." The accompanying story, with its account of strip-teasing flirtations and roguish howls, left little doubt about the kind of attention this exotic entertainment was arousing. Even Craddock had to admit that some ogling men at the Egyptian Theatre had "looks on their faces" that they would have been "ashamed to have their mothers or sisters see." She also explicitly criticized one of the dancers in Cairo Street for smiling coquettishly at the crowd rather than treating the performance with the solemnity that the rest of the company did. Perhaps that "would-be cajoler" proved the exception at the World's Fair, but Craddock was nonetheless on treacherous ground. As shrewd impresarios turned the Danse du Ventre to their own lucrative purposes, her claims about its liberating potential looked all the more dubious.[25]

Much to Craddock's chagrin, belly dancing's standing as a lewd entertainment soon seemed everywhere in the ascendancy. By September 1894, slightly over a year after Craddock's initial published defense of the dance, a columnist in Milwaukee was complaining of the "latest fad" to be taken up by the worldly youth of that city—"private subscription dances" at shadowy roadhouses where "a young woman named Habeebe" performed "the danse-du-ventre in all of its oriental splendor, appearing entirely naked!" Craddock had no desire to clothe such strip shows in a feminist covering, but it certainly looked, thirteen months on, like her defense of women's sexual expression had simply been absorbed into the larger commercialization of female sexuality. Within another year or so, even Thomas Edison had gotten into the act of exploiting belly dancing's titillation, making the Danse du Ventre the subject of two of his earliest moving pictures. Concocting these silent shorts for the new kinetoscope parlors just coming into urban fashion, he cheekily offered at least one of them in censored and uncensored versions.[26]

Despite the imposing hurdles, Craddock wanted to save the Danse du Ventre from Christian indignation, stag-party voyeurism, and commercial exploitation. She herself loved to dance and had fond memories of the graceful movement of her own body as a young woman, shorn of corsets and the encumbering constraints of Victorian fashions. "I am accustomed to the various swayings and balancings of a person who rises on the ball of the foot as a dancer," she recalled in her diary in 1894. "For three years, I stood head of the class at [the] dancing-school of the leading dancing-master of Philadelphia. . . . I know every phase of the balancing of a dancer's body in ordinary good dancing. I have several times danced . . . such dances as the Spanish cachuca, requiring swaying, passionate movement." In watching the young women who performed at the Egyptian Theatre, Craddock had been reminded of her own youthful pursuits, the hours she had spent bending and balancing "from sheer love of the movements."[27]

THE NATIONAL POLICE GAZETTE

THE LEADING ILLUSTRATED SPORTING JOURNAL IN AMERICA

Copyrighted for 1894 by the Proprietor, Richard K. Fox, Franklin Square Publishing, Printing and Engraving House, New York City.

RICHARD K. FOX, Editor and Proprietor.

NEW YORK, SATURDAY, MARCH 31, 1894.

VOLUME LXIII.—No. 865. Price 10 Cents.

DANSE DU VENTRE IN BROOKLYN, N. Y.
A CROWD OF SPORTS PAY A BIG PRICE TO SEE FATIMA GIVE A FASCINATING EXHIBITION.

The Danse du Ventre was soon being fully exploited as a form of nightclub entertainment. The National Police Gazette *captured the lurid spectacle with the journal's typical flair for the scandalous with this cover in March 1894.*

The satisfactions she took from dance came not from the stares of spectators, male or otherwise, but from the liberty and the discipline of her own body in such practiced motion. Not surprisingly, in those instances in which she noted in her diary attempting to perform the Danse du Ventre herself, she did so in the privacy of her own room, intentionally trying to remain out of sight and earshot of anyone else. Once she reported happily, for example, that she was looking forward to her mother being out for the evening, since "when she is home, I don't feel like performing a very vigorous Danse du Ventre, lest she hear me." A few years later in 1898 the sexologist Havelock Ellis, whose work Craddock admired, invented the designation "auto-erotism" as an elastic term that potentially included everything from sexual fantasy to artistic daydreaming to mystical experience. "Auto-erotic phenomena," by Ellis's account, went far beyond the old moral hobgoblin of masturbation. In making the Danse du Ventre her own personal affair, Craddock offered a striking embodiment of such intimate and fanciful self-exploration. Sensually charged—she said it gave her a "delicious" feeling—the Danse du Ventre allowed Craddock to relish her undulating physique wholly apart from her mother's eavesdropping and the lothario's leer.[28]

Craddock was attracted to dance not only for its bodily pleasure, but also as a religious exercise. In the aftermath of the uproar over the Midway performances, her spiritual curiosities had intensified, and she had started dancing again as part of that metaphysical turn. To Craddock, nimbleness of body and vivacity of soul were joined together, and she even started to dream of "being levitated," of being lifted off the ground in a moment of perceptible spiritual elevation. Those extravagant hopes, too, were nurtured through dance. After a particularly exhilarating practice session Craddock confided in her diary in 1894 that she had sensed, at least hazily, an "unseen force" moving with her as she swept up onto the ball of her feet and held one supple pose. Not exactly a glittering epiphany, but it was indicative of where she was headed with dancing—and everything else. Though she had so far kept the news mostly to herself, Craddock, the amateur scholar and active freethinker, was also a budding mystic. Those spiritual aspirations would give her sexual politics an increasingly visionary cast and make her a dual threat to Comstock's Christian America: both shameless marriage reformer and brash religious innovator.[29]

Craddock's potential as a double menace was already well foreshadowed in the Danse du Ventre episode. Viewing that performance as a kind of marital aid, she saw in belly dancing a brilliant fusion of spiritual idealism and erotic abandon. Her conviction that married couples needed to bring a mood of religious aspiration into the bedroom grew more detailed over the years, but the outlines of it were clearly present in her defense of belly dancing. Without an ambiance of religious longing, sexual partners would not experience "complete satisfaction"; they would fail to become "one in flesh and one in spirit." Craddock was quick to add that those who found such pious talk off-putting need not worry: Ecstatic union could be achieved by partners of any religious affiliation—or none. Her cosmopolitan openness was of a variety that would have made most of the delegates at the World's Parliament of Religions blush. "If you believe in Jesus, aspire to be in unison with His will from the moment the [sex] ecstasy sets in;" she advised in her *Danse du Ventre* pamphlet, "if you believe only in God the Father, aspire in joy and thankfulness to him; if you are an Atheist, aspire to be in harmony with the law of the Universe." Religiously inclusive and sexually explicit at the same time, Craddock laid the gauntlet down for Comstock and his fellow backers of a Christian America.[30]

In deriving such theologically promiscuous claims from the Egyptian Theatre exhibition, Craddock knew that she was very likely to damage her own womanly reputation. To be above moral reproach, as a single woman, she was expected to have remained chaste through the years and to be without firsthand sexual knowledge. Certainly all her clever talk about phallic symbols and ancient sex worship was bad enough, but how had she gained so much familiarity with the "supreme moments" of sexual ecstasy, "this final quivering of passion"? Why was she able to comment so knowingly on the erotic mastery of the Cairo Street performers? "The Danse du Ventre," she insisted in a manner that served only to confirm such suspicions, "trains the muscles of the woman in the endurance desirable in the wife . . . and therefore increases her capacity, not only for receiving, but also for conferring pleasure." Even her friends and admirers had to admit that Craddock often did herself no favors in getting carried away with her own candor.[31]

There were certainly modest ways of defending the Danse du Ventre, but Craddock's approach was not one of them. The journalist Kate Field claimed such abdominal gyrations would make an excellent cure for American invalidism and would be a good gymnastic training for giving birth. The performer Loie Fuller, already famous for her serpentine skirt dances, made instead a purely aesthetic appeal, arguing that belly dancing appeared indecent only to those who lost sight of its artistic grace and beauty. "People of that sort," she said, would be scandalized by the Venus de Milo or would find "something suggestive" in a dainty minuet. Craddock's argument, by contrast, lacked even the veneer of well-tempered discretion and good taste. She seemed to know far too much about sex, especially for an unwed woman associated with boisterous liberals and freethinkers.[32]

Craddock had a rationale for this sexual knowledge that sounded tame and respectable enough, and yet this was precisely where her account became even more fantastic, if not hallucinatory: "I would say that I speak from the standpoint of a wife," she wrote in a "little paragraph" that she added to her Danse du Ventre essay when she began circulating it in typescript to friends and colleagues in late 1893, only to drop the point when she printed the revised edition in 1897. There was, though, a small problem with that conjugal explanation: Craddock had never been married in any conventional civic, religious, or, for that matter, terrestrial sense. "My husband," she reported, "is in the world beyond the grave, and had been for many years previous to our union, which took place in October, 1892." Being curious about spiritualism and psychical research was perfectly common among liberals and agnostics, but there was no way for Craddock to make this claim about a heavenly marriage anything but a bombshell. "Let the dead marry the dead," freethinker George Macdonald scoffed at Craddock in an editorial in December 1893. He suggested that she find herself a real husband in order to put an end to a fantasy worthy only of a medieval convent, not modern America.[33]

Before late 1893, when she revealed that she had an angelic husband, Craddock had never had her sanity questioned; after that, it would never go unquestioned. She had been well aware that this fantastic conjugal assertion would raise serious doubts about her mental state. But, as she explained in that "little paragraph" attached to her limited-circulation typescript, the relevant question was not so much the source but the content of her experience. Hallucination or not, she now saw marriage and sexuality differently:

> How far the reader may value my testimony as being the result of my personal experience, he will of course decide according to his bias for or against the possibility of communication with our deceased friends beyond the grave. However, whether my psychical experience be a fact or an hallucination, I can truthfully say that I have gained from it a knowledge of sex relations which many years of reading and discussions with other people never brought me.

In a heavily Christian culture, it would have been one thing, of course, for Craddock to describe herself as a bride of Christ, to have taken Jesus as her husband, and to have surrendered herself—body and soul—to him. Here was another kind of spiritual betrothal, a very different sort of conjugal tie to an angelic specter, an experience that allowed her to speak openly and authoritatively about the relationship between religion and sex.[34]

That her angelic intimacies marked her, in legal and medical terms, as an insane person was not an accusation that Craddock ever took lying down on a couch. Her mother viewed the whole Danse du Ventre episode as a sure sign that her daughter had "gone crazy" and quickly enlisted two physicians in an effort to commit her to a hospital for the insane. That plot initially failed, and Craddock simply scoffed when one of the doctors reported: "Had that essay been written by a man, by a physician or by any other scientist (and the paragraph about the spirit husband omitted) it would have been alright; but coming from an unmarried woman, neither a physician or a scientist, and with that claim of a spirit husband, there is no explanation possible but (1) illicit experience, which is denied by all who know her, or (2) insanity." As Craddock understood the physician's logic, her "worst offense" seemed to be "that, as a woman, I was out of my province in openly preaching marital reform" and thus needed to be confined in an asylum "until I should recant my heresy."[35]

Whether or not Craddock's religious experiences proved her a madwoman, they certainly changed the course of her life work and transformed her reputation. Her religious dreams allowed clinicians to stamp her as a delusional nymphomaniac and would eventually make her a case history in psychoanalytic theorizing about the sexual origins of religion. But, her fantasies also emboldened her to make marriage reform the substance of her labors and offered her the clarity of vision to challenge skeptical physicians, prosecuting attorneys, postal inspectors, and vice crusaders as they sought to suppress her teachings. Ida Craddock's legacy, for better or for worse, would be irrevocably joined to a private, ghostly romance.

———•◦•———

CRADDOCK HAD BEEN taken aback when Comstock started whistling the music of "the Koochy-Koochy Dance" as he prepared to arrest her in February 1902, but was it any wonder that he seemed, just then, to be meditating on belly dancing? For the better part of a decade Craddock had been performing her own dangerous and increasingly scandalous dance, riling moral watchdogs across the country. In the process she had moved back and forth between courtroom and asylum, visionary excess and restrained secularism, madness and rationality, spirituality and sexuality. Working along the intensely policed borders of obscenity and free speech as well as blasphemy and religious liberty, Craddock had become in the eyes of her opponents the very embodiment of the lewd and the sacrilegious. To Anthony Comstock and the New York Society for the Suppression of Vice, Craddock's literary exhibition had proven more abominable than the World Fair's Danse du Ventre had ever been. "Vile books and papers are branding-irons heated in the fires of hell," Comstock fumed, "and used by Satan to sear the highest life of the soul." Few influences were as diabolical as "EVIL READING," and Craddock had proven a particularly recalcitrant purveyor of such polluting materials. She was, in Comstock's view, one of "the devil's sharpshooters"; she had to be stopped once and for all. The fragile and threatened innocence of America's youth demanded it.[36]

The more that Comstock reviled Craddock, the more useful her case became for defenders of civil and religious liberties. How, she wanted to know, could Comstock deprive her of the constitutional guarantees to freedom of religion, speech, and expression? Had not his censorship campaign overreached its mark and endangered fundamental American liberties? Craddock and her backers remained incredulous that Comstock possessed the legal authority to close down her educational enterprise and prevent people from receiving frank instruction about the sexual functions of their own bodies. Hell, he had not just seized "the printing-press of the man who printed my pamphlets," Craddock vented; he had even confiscated "my type-writer . . . as contraband." Would this crackdown ever let up? "In this fight, I stand for the right of the common people to sexual enlightenment, in print, sent through the mails to whomsoever wishes it, without molestation by Anthony Comstock or anybody else," Craddock vowed.[37]

A few years earlier when facing federal trial in Philadelphia, Craddock had written physician Edward Bond Foote, a leading birth-control and free-speech advocate, to underline her all-out commitment to their shared work: "I would lay down my life for the cause of sex reform," she had pledged, "but I don't want to be swept away, a useless sacrifice. I want to make a breach in the enemy's lines before I pass in my checks." She had experienced few moments of peace in the four years since that indictment in Philadelphia, and so by the time Comstock and his agents came knocking at her New York apartment in early 1902, enough was enough. "Use me as a battering-ram against Comstock," she now exhorted her latest lawyer, Hugh Pentecost. "Pour out my life like water, relentlessly, in this fight." The slamming of Comstock had already begun, but the spilling out of her life, in blood, still seemed unnecessary and far from inevitable.[38]

CHAPTER TWO

Not an Infidel,
But a Freethinker and a Scholar

⬥⬥⬥

CRADDOCK HAD ADVANCED MANY PECULIAR claims in her slim treatise on belly dancing, but perhaps the most outrageous was her self-presentation as "a student of Phallic antiquities." Not that the knowledge she gained from that research sounded wildly surprising: "The serpent is a well-known Phallic symbol of the male organ," she casually remarked; or, the dancer's castanets, "a symbol recognizable by any Phallic student," typified female passion. The astonishing part was that she dared to represent herself as an expert on this subject at all. Since the end of the eighteenth century, a good number of freethinkers had seen such fertility symbolism as a rich lode to mine for anticlerical nuggets, but no woman had ever joined this particular fraternity of gentlemanly dilettantes and antiquarians. That exclusion seemed only to energize Craddock. As she informed the leader of the Manhattan Liberal Club in late 1893 in hopes of lining up a public lecture before that society, "I have given the subject of folklore in its reference to Christian theology considerable study for a number of years past; and I can say, without egotism, that this study has qualified me to speak with some authority as a specialist on Phallic Worship."[1]

In offering her services as a public lecturer to the Manhattan Liberal Club, Craddock had picked her potential audience wisely—and a little audaciously. That organization, inaugurated in 1869, provided a weekly forum dedicated to the discussion of new ideas, whether in science, religion, or politics. It was, one enthusiast remarked, New York's preeminent gathering place for "intellectual athletes": "On its platform were the most brilliant thinkers, scholars, writers, orators, poets, in the city." Not at all afraid of controversy, the club embraced "the choice revolutionary spirits of the day"; the anarchist Emma Goldman, the muckraking journalist Lincoln Steffens, and the civil-liberties lawyer Thaddeus B. Wakeman all congregated there.[2]

The president of the Manhattan Liberal Club did not immediately leap at Craddock's offer. Hesitating, he pointed her to the Brooklyn Philosophical Association and the Newark Liberal League instead. Perhaps the recent Danse du Ventre episode, along with her proposed lecture topic, made her sound too eccentric and high risk even for this "congregation of 'cranks' of the first order." Craddock strongly emphasized, though, that she very much shared the club's liberal outlook and was right now in the thick of the intellectual fray. "I have been writing up a book on the Origin of the Devil, from a folklore standpoint," she explained, "which I trust will strike some telling blows in behalf of Freethought." In other words, she had trained her attention on scholarly pursuits and was now ready to share the results of her research on the public lecture circuit. For a fee of ten dollars, she would hold forth on the history of phallic worship and its relevance for marriage reform.[3]

Craddock's explanation worked. She maneuvered her way onto the lecture platform of the Manhattan Liberal Club for a Friday evening the next February. She titled her address "Survivals of Sex Worship in Christianity and in Paganism," and the announced lecture certainly caught people's notice. Held in the German Masonic Temple on East Fifteenth Street, the meeting was crowded, a mixed audience with "at least thirty women" on hand. At the close of Craddock's lecture, the presiding moderator emphasized that the subject was delicate and urged respectful caution in the customary discussion period.

The moderator's plea went completely unheeded. One woman, an officer of the club, quickly "marched to the front, flushed and excited," and moved that the meeting immediately adjourn "for the sake of the good name of the Liberal Club." Craddock's paper, she claimed, was indecent and improper; it should never have been presented to the group and was certainly unfit to be discussed. "We are all ladies and gentlemen here, and it is not for us to listen to any talk of this sort," she argued, invoking the demands of class-based decorum. In its report on the evening—"A Very Shocking Time: Miss Craddock's Talk Caused Blushes"—the *New York World* concurred. The paper reminded its readers of Craddock's outlandish defense of the Danse du Ventre the previous summer and declared this latest lecture "unprintable."[4]

The motion to adjourn provoked much confusion within the ranks of the Manhattan Liberal Club, a ruckus of name-calling and finger-pointing, but the consensus was nonetheless to go forward with the discussion. "It is fair to say that no such debate ever before followed a lecture delivered before a mixed audience in this town," the *World* concluded. Despite the proposed bow to propriety, the club had again fulfilled its promise to serve as an unusually free platform—one that was open even to a lecturer as heterodox as Craddock. The group proudly claimed that in its twenty-five-year history only one speaker had ever been blackballed, a Protestant minister who had violated "the hearty co-operative respect" that formed a cornerstone of the group's intellectual give-and-take. Craddock did not become a second outcast, but she certainly pushed at the club's limits. Even in this liberal hotbed, the very notion of a woman lecturing on the history of sex worship tested the underlying bounds of decency and order. She had eluded the muzzle of premature adjournment, but she had hardly won everyone over. Freethinker George Macdonald, a prominent editor in these intellectual circles, offered her only a sardonic compliment: "An opportunity as Miss Craddock's lecture affords cannot be lost, I fear, without deplorably lessening the sum total of human cussedness."[5]

Despite the storm at the Manhattan Liberal Club, a squall was not inevitable when Craddock took the platform. The next Sunday she lectured on the same subject at the Brooklyn Philosophical Association, and things reportedly went fine. Her "plea for more enlightenment on sexual matters," heard by a "most attentive" audience, caused no hubbub there. Things had gone even better a couple of months earlier when she appeared at the Ladies' Liberal League of Philadelphia. Her discourse on "Survivals of Sex Worship" filled the house, even on a very rainy night, and met with warm applause and lively discussion. "Some of the members expressed themselves as considering it one of the best lectures ever given before them," Craddock proudly reported.[6]

The Ladies' Liberal League, anything but matronly, was the perfect venue for Craddock to present her unorthodox social and religious views. Under the inspiration of the freethinker Voltairine de Cleyre, this rebellious group of Philadelphia women had set up shop for themselves in 1892 apart from their gentlemanly compatriots in the Friendship Liberal League. Disdaining the limited role of a female auxiliary, the Ladies' Liberal League served as a platform for radical lecturers, especially on women's rights and the "sex question." "We know," de Cleyre enticed, "that there is forbidden fruit waiting to be gathered, the fruit of the tree of knowledge, and we propose to put up a step-ladder before every get-at-able apple and help ourselves and others to it." Craddock's knowledge of the sexual history of religion was among the most forbidden—evocative, indeed, of the original illicit apple. De Cleyre and company were not going to miss the opportunity to take a bite.[7]

De Cleyre considered the lecture programs at the Ladies' Liberal League splendid successes. Among the more compelling series was one that involved pioneering women in the fields of law, journalism, and medicine, all of whom had broken educational and professional barriers to get to where they were. Craddock's inclusion on the league's platform served a parallel purpose. "The scholarly Miss Craddock," de Cleyre explained, "has made deep researches into ancient symbolism" as part of her turn to spiritualism and sex reform. Other "thin-shelled" liberal societies in the city might have no use for her; indeed, at least one male colleague had tried to get Craddock's name scrubbed from the list of lecturers at the Ladies' Liberal League itself. Always self-possessed, de Cleyre had flicked away that intervention and stood by Craddock.[8]

The woman as lawyer, journalist, and physician—each presented a distinct professional challenge, but then there was "the scholarly Miss Craddock," a woman who, having turned her sights on the fields of folklore and comparative religions, presented herself as a "specialist" in the history of phallic worship. Craddock's claim to learned expertise was outrageous—and not only because of the immodesty of her subject. The pile of unpublished manuscripts that she produced (on everything from lunar mythology to heavenly bridegrooms to animal traits) left little doubt about the extent of her egghead dedication. But that intellectual ardor still left plenty of room to suspect Craddock was overstating her qualifications: What made her anything more than a scribbling amateur, a dabbler among real experts and professionals? Within the emergent "science" of studying religion, as in other newly imagined sciences of the era, the power of expertise was almost entirely male and distinctly credentialed. Access to the world of university chairs and specialized research remained negligible for women of Craddock's generation. Though she claimed at this point in her life that there was nothing she wanted "half so much" as "the perfection of my intellectual work," those labors always remained tenuous and inevitably amateurish. Craddock would achieve no scholarly standing to speak of, but her failure—that proved virtuosic.[9]

———·•·———

VOLTAIRINE DE CLEYRE'S very name, with its bow to the famed French philosopher, made clear that she had been christened for intellectual rebellion, but little in Craddock's own family background suggested that she had been cradled in dissent. Hers was not a lineage of religious misfits or social rebels. Born in Philadelphia on August 1, 1857, she was reared in a family of comfortable means and conventional refinement.

Only by a later, second-hand account was Ida's father, Joseph T. Craddock, taken as an augur of her intellectual discontent. A religious doubter, he had supposedly announced his opposition to his wife's plans for a firm Christian upbringing for their daughter. How much credit to give that story is impossible to determine. Her father, a purveyor of teas and patent medicines, died of consumption in his early forties when his only surviving child was still an infant. That Joseph Craddock sold cure-all tonics for the disease that killed him is apparent from his firm's advertisements, but not much else about him survives in the historical record.[10]

Joseph's death left Ida in the sole hands of his respectably devout wife, Lizzie Craddock. Widowed in her mid-twenties, Lizzie had enough of her own independent, entrepreneurial streak to run the family business after her husband's death, but she never regarded self-reliance as a good quality in her daughter. An authoritarian parent, Lizzie expected dutiful obedience from Ida and bristled at any show of willfulness. Having had no relationship with her father except through the memory of others, Ida saw her mother as being a singularly omnipotent force in her life. Once, indeed, she spoke of sensing God in the same way that "we were wont, when very, very small children, to sense our mother"—that is, "a powerful, mysterious being . . . to whom we looked with awe and to whom we clung as our protector," and yet who nevertheless remained "a vaguely understood and somewhat feared personality after all."[11]

If Ida saw her mother as a god, she was a fearsome one—and resentment of Lizzie's frightening power, more than appreciation of her mother's protectiveness, came to dominate Ida's estimate of their relationship. "While I remain with Mother," Ida subsequently observed in a tone of harsh exasperation, "I shall never do anything; my life will be a nonentity in the future as it has always been in the past. For years and years, looking back, I remember how my friends who knew my abilities, kept hoping for great things from me—but I never did them; and why? Just because I was a poodle at the end of a chain, the other end of the chain being in my Mother's hand." From a young age, Ida defined herself against her mother's authority, often with indignant defiance.[12]

Intellectual rebellion and dutiful submission were the two poles of this mother-daughter conflict. Ida saw her mother as "a woman of very little book education" who, though supportive of her daughter's schooling, did not know what to make of her child's precocity. "I was able to read at a very early age—two and a half years old," Craddock recalled, however implausibly. "As I grew into girlhood, I read with avidity all books that came into my way." Lizzie thought that the Bible was the book most worthy of her daughter's absorption, but Ida soon wandered much farther afield. In particular, she remembered how, as a ten-year-old, she had shocked her "conservative mother" by informing her that she had been reading Comte de Volney's *Ruins*, an infidel classic of the French Enlightenment, and that she had thus "found out all about the Christian religion, and that it was not what it claimed to be." Her mother cultivated fairly traditional Protestant allegiances: she played a particularly active part, for example, in the Philadelphia chapter of the Woman's Christian Temperance Union (she would bequeath $1,000 to that society in her will). As Ida moved farther and farther away from her mother's upstanding pathways, Lizzie grew ever more scornful of her daughter's intellectual captivations. "It has always been a standing joke with Mother," Ida recalled, "that I would get absorbed in reading and studying, and hear nothing outside."[13]

The first fifteen or twenty years of Craddock's life can now be seen primarily through the prism of her later ambitions and resentments, the refracted memories of a woman who had grown intensely alienated from her mother's "petty tyrannizing." One of Ida's earliest surviving letters, written at age twenty-one when on vacation with her mother, caught the glimmering outlines of her subsequent representation of her childhood and youth. A little bored with their usual "summer flight," Craddock wanted out of the trip with her mother. "I do not expect to stay here long," she wrote a friend in June 1879. "I first declared it should be only a week; but Mother has talked me into a little longer sojourn. I think I shall most likely stay over next Sunday, and come back the middle of that week. At least, that is my idea now,—unless the powers that be forbid. I expect that Mother will make a great outcry at so early a return; but I want to get back to have a jolly time all to myself among my books; and besides, I have one or two brilliant plans that I am anxious to try." The fragmentary remains of Craddock's early correspondence disclosed other snippets—her "dipping into botany" through closely examining flowers, for example, or her girlish joy over horseback riding—but none offered a better glimpse of the turbulence that she subsequently imagined as having defined her early life. Here were the joined desires of being all alone with her books and out from under her mother's thumb, the restless yearning for independence, intellectual and otherwise. "I want the universe all to myself to make my experiments in," she pronounced to her friend.[14]

The friend in this case was an old classmate, Katie Wood, who had first gotten to know Craddock at the well-regarded Quaker school, Friends' Central, which they both attended in their teen years. Katie and Ida remained close throughout their lives, but that warmth of friendship did not keep Katie from forming the retrospective judgment that young Ida's intellectual cravings had been a little too intense. Confirming the lore of Craddock having been "precocious in the extreme," Wood remembered finding her schoolmate strangely gifted, but suggested as well that her "wonderful mental ability" had generated noticeable "peculiarities of character." Katie remarked that Ida had "glorious brilliant blue eyes," almost too bright—as if Ida could not quite contain the light within her.

Among Ida's peculiarities, Katie put particular stress on her friend's overly confident bearing. Craddock's assertiveness as a student, Wood thought, had often exasperated their teachers. "Instead of confining herself to the simple answers," Katie recalled, "she always said more than asked and showed a great amount of knowledge upon each subject which was entirely unappreciated by the teachers who wished simply to rush the lessons through." The classmate marveled at her friend's gifts— her working knowledge of five languages (Greek, Latin, French, German, and Italian); her capacious memory for history and literature— but there nonetheless seemed to be "a great drawback" in Craddock's intellectual comportment. As Wood came to see it in hindsight, even as a schoolgirl Ida had manifested a self-destructive impulse "to impart knowledge without discrimination." Trying as an adult to figure out what had gone so tragically wrong for her youthful companion, how it was that Craddock had become one of Comstock's most notorious targets, Wood reached for an explanation in her friend's unregulated intelligence and the teachers who had failed to impart the lessons of self-censorship to their talented pupil.[15]

Craddock's "brilliant plans" for bookish achievement, which she had announced to Katie in 1879, were left unspecified. Certainly, Ida had been reading a lot and writing some since the completion of her schooling in 1876. In 1878, she had penned, for example, a short review of a new translation of Goethe's *Faust*, a peculiarly resonant choice for someone ever tempted by the pursuit of dangerous and forbidden knowledge. More likely than not, however, Craddock's big plans already involved laying some of the academic groundwork for her first venture into public controversy—her struggle to gain admission to the University of Pennsylvania for the fall of 1882.[16]

Craddock craved an education beyond what she had received at Friends' Central, but the path to higher learning was steep. To have even a chance of overcoming Penn's bar against admitting women, she would have to pass the entrance examinations administered to similarly aspiring young men: four days of written examinations on ancient and modern geography, mathematics, English grammar and composition, Latin grammar and hexameter verse, and Greek grammar and prose composition—all of which was followed by a fifth day for an oral examination on Cicero's orations and Horace's odes. Craddock's ambition to integrate Penn would clearly demand considerable preparation and persistence. And even if she passed the entrance exams, the likelihood was slim that she would, as a woman, actually be admitted.[17]

Through the Civil War the great majority of American colleges and universities were, without much debate, open to men only. While a handful of antebellum experiments, including Mount Holyoke and Oberlin, served as harbingers of academic opportunity for women, calls for coeducation made significant headway only in the postbellum period. Full-fledged women's colleges—Vassar (1865), Wellesley (1875), Smith (1875), and Bryn Mawr (1884)—became ever more viable options, and coeducational opportunities at state universities from Michigan to California also expanded considerably in the quarter century after the Civil War.

Many of those early battles were themselves hard-won, but the struggles at the most privileged male institutions (Harvard, Yale, Princeton, Columbia, and Penn) were still more difficult and often less successful. Columbia skirted the issue by setting up Barnard as a separate woman's college in 1889, a path that Harvard likewise followed with the founding of Radcliffe in 1894. Princeton pursued a similar course for a time by chartering Evelyn College, a short-lived experiment that only temporarily breached that male preserve. Penn, like Yale, opened some of its graduate programs to women, but held back altogether from admitting women into the undergraduate liberal arts. Even as gains for coeducation were being made elsewhere, several arch-advocates of women's rights, including the suffragist Lucy Stone, saw it as absolutely crucial to carry the battle to the gates of America's most elite institutions. Craddock joined the fight in the early 1880s, targeting Philadelphia's highest ivory tower. For two years at least, Craddock made it her cause "to force open the University of Pennsylvania for the admission of women," writing letters, studying hard, meeting with faculty and trustees, and simply refusing to be easily dismissed.[18]

The first indication of the campaign that Craddock was mounting came in a report prepared by Penn's Faculty of the Arts for the Board of Trustees in September 1882. The faculty noted that "Miss Ida C. Craddock has passed her entrance examinations very satisfactorily" and had thus qualified for admission to the freshman class. On that much the professors agreed, but they were clearly torn on how to proceed from there. Finally, on a narrow six to five vote, they recommended that the board approve Craddock's acceptance, effectively turning her application into the occasion for placing the whole question of women's admission on the trustees' agenda. When the board met the next month, Craddock's case actually came very close to carrying the day. A trustee subcommittee presented a ten-point plan, right down to the details of tuition fees and room arrangements, for the incorporation of women into the college. The proposal included the express provision that "in the case of Miss Ida C. Craddock" the faculty be "requested to afford to her all the facilities that may be practicable" for her to begin her liberal arts education right away—in advance of "the regular opening of the women's section" the next academic year. As Penn's trustees measured their own situation against parallel debates going on simultaneously at Columbia and Harvard, it looked like the door was about to crack open for Craddock particularly and women more generally.[19]

That hope soon proved illusory. At the next meeting of the trustees later in the fall, the plans for "a separate Collegiate Department for the complete education of women" foundered on an insufficiency of immediate funds. One trustee, the Episcopal bishop William Bacon Stevens, seized upon the financial uncertainty to scuttle the entire plan with a resolution in November 1882 that deemed it "inexpedient at this time to admit any women to the Department of Arts." With that declaration the door slammed shut on Craddock.

Ida would not give up so easily, but her further appeals to Penn were fruitless. Two months later she renewed her petition to join what she saw as her rightful class and to sit now for the sophomore examinations, again without success. Shortly thereafter, in February 1883, suffragist Susan B. Anthony went on record in support of Craddock's efforts to "open to young women the doors of the University of Pennsylvania" in a speech at a nearby church. That public appeal, too, was of no avail; the provost and trustees resolutely insisted that their November decision on coeducation was final. The last word on Craddock's rejection came in the minutes of a meeting of the Board of Trustees in June 1884 when the secretary duly noted receipt of another communication "from Miss Craddock requesting a reply to her application for examinations, and for the admission of women to the University." Whether the trustees paid her the courtesy of another rejection letter was by now, two years after the faculty had voted to accept her, beside the point. It would be another half century before women entered the college.[20]

Her setbacks—and ultimate failure—at Penn had to have been personally galling, if not infuriating, for Craddock. She was intellectually voracious and saw herself, quite reasonably, as a notch or two above most of her peers in her abilities. The frustration of her collegiate ambitions seems only to have deepened her self-perception as an individual brimming with underutilized brainpower. A couple of years later, for example, she reported to her friend Katie Wood that she had been reading Herbert Spencer's *Principles of Psychology* (1855) as part of an adult class. The reigning philosopher of the age, Spencer was a grand synthesizer of psychology, sociology, ethics, and evolutionary biology, and Craddock was thrilled to have found a group of intellectual peers with whom to discuss such an acclaimed thinker. "You know I have belonged to a good many clubs, and have associated with a good many thoughtful people," Ida told Katie, "but, while I have of course met individuals who were far above me, I can truly say, without the least egotism, that I have never yet been in any class or club that went quite fast enough for me; it was always easy to get to the front rank, with little or no effort." In discovering this new reading group, Craddock found herself pushed to keep up and sometimes felt like she was merely following from "afar off, picking up the crumbs that fall from this feast of reason and flow of soul." Even though she was "the youngest among those who do the talking," she was hardly cowed. "Of course, I will always have my say"; she told Katie, "you know I must put in my oar, on every occasion that interests me."[21]

Three of the group's members especially stood out in Craddock's mind as her intellectual match. The first was a doctor, "a Harvard graduate" who had "read all the leading English, German and Greek philosophers"; the second was "Miss Stevens, a quaint little old maid" who was "a thorough-going idealist and a monist"; and the third was a lawyer, "cautious, calm, cool, critical" with a strong "materialistic bias." They seemed an ideal threesome for Craddock's ongoing project of learned self-definition.

Though Craddock finally felt among intellectual equals, it was not as if this newfound salon was free of the usual presumptions about studious women. One man praised the inquisitive (and not incidentally unmarried) Miss Stevens to Craddock as having an intellect "superior to that of any woman he ever met,—being thoroughly masculine in its logical way of thinking, but manifesting itself in a sweet and gentle manner that is thoroughly feminine." Perhaps the man's praise of Miss Stevens's mien was not intended to stand as an invidious comparison with Craddock's own assertive show of female intellectualism, but it certainly suggested as much. Craddock often found herself "arrayed on opposite sides" from Miss Stevens and allied instead with the Harvard doctor, a man she admired for his "exceedingly subtle and penetrating mind." Even in the group's most spirited exchanges, the markers of collegiate achievement and female reserve remained pronounced. For all her scholarly initiative Craddock was already keenly aware of the difficulties involved in overcoming the limits placed on her education and working around the norms of proper womanly behavior. In another social setting sometime before this exchange about Miss Stevens, Craddock had overheard a gossipy remark about her demeanor. "With all her intellect, she lacks in femininity," one young woman had sniped about her to another. Craddock learned early on that her cerebral intensity was at odds with social convention and threatened to desexualize her.[22]

Despite the "wound" of having been labeled unfeminine, Craddock continued to live in a spirit of deliberate independence and self-cultivation. Sometime after her graduation from Friends' Central, she had taught herself a system of shorthand called phonography. She used that knowledge to get her first real job, a position at Girard College in Philadelphia as a teacher of stenography, a trade she pursued for several years in the 1880s and would return to again in the early 1890s. With typical initiative Craddock even produced her own textbooks on the subject, *Primary Phonography: An Introduction to Isaac Pitman's System of Phonetic Shorthand* (1882) and its sequel *Intermediate or Full Phonography* (1892).

Craddock saw shorthand as a professional skill that was eminently marketable, a technique of efficiency that was spreading rapidly from the courtroom to "the railway office, the manufactory, and the counting-room." Accordingly, she offered this instruction to her students as a self-help regimen, one that she had embraced as her own means of individual advancement. "To the ambitious young men and women who are working their way up from the foot of the business ladder," Craddock wrote in her first textbook on the subject, "the phonographer's profession holds out a helping hand; for it offers larger salaries than any other profession, for the time and money spent in acquiring it." These were tame ventures in publishing and education compared to the avenues that Craddock subsequently pursued, but standing on her own as a teacher and author, even if the subject was shorthand and not sex or religion, suggested her determination to find a social and intellectual space beyond daughterly dependence, yet short of wifely domesticity.[23]

Teaching phonography at Girard College, a richly endowed charity school in Philadelphia for orphaned boys, was far removed from the life of learning that Craddock had imagined for herself at the University of Pennsylvania. Already having begun her reading in folklore, comparative mythology, and psychical research by the late 1880s, Craddock was hardly going to find an outlet for those interests through instructing her young students in the precise dots and dashes of shorthand. In one way at least, however, her time at Girard College proved a highly fruitful experience for Craddock. During much of her tenure at the school, a vigorous debate about Christian versus secular education roiled the place, turning it into an early proving ground for freethinking arguments against the power and reach of the Protestant establishment.

Founded through a bequest of Stephen Girard, a maritime trader of immense wealth, the college had been built in the style of a stately Greek temple in the 1830s and 1840s, with an imposing neo-Gothic chapel only added in 1867. While Protestant backers saw the daily religious services required of the boys as being of "an entirely nonsectarian character," a cadre of freethinkers argued that the growing religious instruction at the college was a violation of Stephen Girard's secular intentions and the original terms of his will. Girard, who had named ships in his fleet after Montesquieu and Voltaire and who had befriended Tom Paine, stood out to later American freethinkers as an illustrious forebear, a model of the enlightened citizen and philanthropist—and a benefactor who would not appreciate any specific religion being stamped upon his students. These assumptions about Girard's intentions were not unfounded; he had, for example, explicitly barred ministers and missionaries from holding any office at the college.

Philadelphia's liberal standard-bearers, Voltairine de Cleyre included, came to see "the fight to restore Girard College to secularism" as a galvanizing cause. Inspecting the prayers and hymns of the *Manual for the Chapel of Girard College*, newly issued in 1883, liberal detractors found the services to "reek" of sectarian dogmatism, containing invocations of everything from the Trinity to the Second Coming to the Virgin Birth. Girard, they were sure, had intended to provide destitute boys with "an education free from superstition" and to have moral principles inculcated without resort to divine revelation or Christian doctrine. From the perspective of freethinking secularists, the dead benefactor's own wishes were clearly being defied: The school was being "turned into a theological seminary for the teaching of the grossest absurdities of the orthodox religion." Here was a donor-intent case beautifully designed for sustained conflict between secular liberals and Protestant institution-builders.[24]

Craddock was soon drawn into a formative alliance with the most vociferous critic of Girard College's newfangled Protestant errand, Richard Brodhead Westbrook, a clergyman turned lawyer who happily used the power of his new profession to subvert the authority of his old one. A youthful Methodist itinerant in 1840 who had moved on to Presbyterian respectability by 1852, Westbrook ended up an opponent of all sacerdotal pomp and privilege, comfortable in his success in both the legal profession and the coal industry. After 1882, when he retired from business concerns, he entered the public arena on multiple fronts— as an advocate of coeducation, a critic of Christian clout in civic affairs, and a leader of the Wagner Free Institute of Science. His animus against the "religious brigandage" that he saw being perpetrated at Girard College knew no bounds, and his anticlerical hostilities clearly helped sharpen Craddock's own rebellious edge. Equally significant, Westbrook was the spouse of the physician Henrietta Payne Westbrook, an important elder among the city's pioneering community of professional women. Together the Westbrooks became two of Craddock's principal patrons, Henrietta proving an especially dependable friend. As a trustee of the Wagner Free Institute, Richard had a hand in hiring Craddock to help curate that museum's natural history collection in the autumn of 1885, and he recruited her again in late 1889 to join him in the leadership of the American Secular Union, a national organization dedicated to fighting evangelical designs for a Christian America.[25]

Westbrook's invitation could not have come at a more opportune time for Craddock. Two years earlier in 1887, despairing over her increasingly "unbearable" relationship with her mother, Craddock had left both home and Girard College, scraping together enough money "to go West, out to California" on a fortune-seeking expedition. Initially her shorthand and typewriting skills had kept her in good stead; she reported "living a joyously Materialistic business life in San Francisco," working as a stenographer and at other jobs. By 1889, though, she found the labor market tighter, and her wages were down. As she looked in vain for meaningful employment, Craddock again felt keenly the want of "a University degree"; she found herself settling for "inferior positions" with "inferior pay" and feared being "foredoomed to a life of drudgery." She wondered indeed if she would have to become "a houseservant" and thereby accrue a social stigma that would make her "an outcast" among "people of refinement and culture." The prospect of returning to Philadelphia and admitting failure to her mother made her distraught, but she clearly faced a grim financial situation as she lived with the "wretched uncertainty of where and how I am to get my next month's victuals and shelter."[26]

The experience of economic vulnerability primed her for greater social radicalism and for association with Westbrook's league of secular reformers. She read with enthusiasm socialist Edward Bellamy's *Looking Backward* (1888), started voicing critiques of capitalist competition and looked for "deliverance" of the "toiling masses" through state-led reforms. "Now that I have stood down in the ranks of the miserable workers whom I once despised, as a race beneath me, I know how they feel when they have to daily face the prospect of starvation and misery," Craddock sympathized, hardly trying to disguise the peculiar contortions involved in her expression of cross-class solidarity.[27]

When Westbrook approached her at this very moment of desperation and informed her of a chance to help him run the American Secular Union back in Philadelphia, Craddock was elated. Westbrook, the group's incoming president, soon put her up for election as secretary of the organization, and, as his handpicked choice, she safely outpolled the three men running for the office. With a new public role as corresponding secretary of the American Secular Union, she thought her learned aspirations would finally have their appropriate outlet: "I mean to make my room a centre for the bright intellects and liberal and cultured minds of the city," she wrote Katie Wood in October 1889. "I shall have my salon yet before I die."[28]

FOR THE NEXT TWO YEARS, from November 1889 to October 1891, Craddock threw herself into her job as secretary of the American Secular Union. The society was one of the most visible, long-lasting, and controversial groups spawned by liberal organizing in the 1870s and 1880s. Dubbed the National Liberal League at its founding in 1876 and headed by the radical Unitarian Francis E. Abbot, the organization had rallied around a platform containing the "Nine Demands of Liberalism," all of which centered on protecting the state from the influence of the church. These principles included calls for the repeal of Sunday blue laws, the discontinuance of all devotional activity in the public schools, the elimination of public-funded chaplaincies, the end of state-sanctioned days of religious thanksgiving and fasting, and the taxation of church property in order to end the government's indirect subsidy of ecclesial institutions.

The American Secular Union, and the National Liberal League before it, spearheaded resistance to evangelical efforts to Christianize American public life in the late nineteenth century. Considering America's founding freedoms to be endangered by Christian groups seeking formal government endorsement of their religion, liberals mobilized under the banner of "Free Religion." Their initial foil was the National Reform Association, a Presbyterian-led group that wanted to amend the Constitution to recognize both God's sovereignty over civil government and the Lord Jesus Christ's supreme authority as ruler of all nations. The campaign to keep God and Jesus out of the Constitution

A photograph similar to this one appeared with the biographical sketch of Craddock that ran in the Freethinkers' *Magazine in 1890 and that highlighted her leadership role in the American Secular Union. Special Collections Research Center, Morris Library, Southern Illinois University, Carbondale.*

launched the National Liberal League into prominence and announced its ultimate ambition: namely, the "entire secularization" of local, state, and federal governments.[29]

Committed to thwarting the National Reform Association's plans for a Christian nation-state, many Liberal Leaguers also wanted to take on Anthony Comstock in an effort to bring down his signature anti-obscenity laws. Comstock's legal proscriptions were already being used to suppress radical writers and publishers, including D. M. Bennett, the freethinking editor of the *Truth Seeker*, and Ezra Heywood, labor

AMERICAN SECULAR UNION

WE ADVOCATE:

1. The equitable taxation of Church property in common with other property.

2. The total discontinuance of religious instruction and worship in the public schools, and especially the reading of any Bible.

3. The repeal of all laws enforcing the observance of Sunday as a *religious* institution, rather than an *economic* one, justified by physiological and other secular reasons.

4. The cessation of all appropriations of the public funds for educational and charitable institutions of a sectarian character.

5. The abolition of ecclesiastical chaplaincies paid out of the public treasury.

6. The discontinuance of the practice of the appointment by the President of the United States and the Governors of the several States of religious festivals and fasts.

7. The substitution of a solemn affirmation under the pains and penalties of perjury, in the courts, and in all other departments of the government, in place of the common forms of a judicial oath.

8. The defence through the courts of any American citizen whose equal religious and political rights are denied, or who is oppressed on account of any opinions he may have held or expressed on the subject of religion.

9. The promulgation, by all peaceable and orderly means, of the great principles of religious liberty and equal rights, devotion to truth for its own sake, and universal brotherhood on the ground of a common humanity; and the protection of the State from the encroachments of the Church.

R. B. WESTBROOK, President,
1707 Oxford Street.

F. O. MENDE, Treasurer,
IDA C. CRADDOCK, Corresponding Secretary,
S. E. Cor. Broad Street and Columbia Avenue,
Philadelphia.

The American Secular Union, the successor to the National Liberal League, served as the leading proponent of the Nine Demands of Liberalism, all of which were premised on total church-state separation. In this particular pronouncement Craddock is one of three signatories. Richard Brodhead Westbrook, A Few Plain Words Regarding Church Taxation *(Philadelphia: Lippincott, 1891), n.p.*

reformer and sex radical who, taken together, personified to Comstock the depraved "alliance of the free-lust and liberal elements" against "old-fashioned religion." The move to attack the Comstock laws soon divided the National Liberal League. Its more circumspect members, including founder Francis Abbot himself, hardly wanted to give the impression that liberals had gone soft on "dirty books and pictures," while its more combative associates thought that Comstock's crusade was a prime illustration of the political overreaching of Protestant Christianity. That deep divide made liberal mobilization difficult at best and dysfunctional at worst; indeed, disagreement over how to deal with Comstock threatened to destroy the National Liberal League entirely.[30]

By 1885, the more ardent free-speech wing of the movement had reconstituted itself as the American Secular Union. That version of the National Liberal League still primarily promoted the original Nine Demands, but with an edge that had been expressly sharpened to clip the talons of Comstock and his New York Society for the Suppression of Vice. Given her plight in San Francisco, Craddock had taken on her new job as much out of economic necessity as rousing secularism, but that hardly softened the implications of her move. Becoming a champion of the American Secular Union, successor to the National Liberal League, was enough to mark her as an enemy of Comstock's society, its political power and religious mission. To perform that new role well, tossed-off lines bashing the stock figure of the "sanctified Comstockian bigot" were de rigueur. She was no infidel, she claimed, but she was "at all times a Liberal and a Freethinker," primed to do battle with Christian theocrats. Indeed, she seemed to relish the feisty anticlericalism that the new role invited: "When I fight for Free Thought, I fight to win."[31]

From 1889 to 1891 Craddock, as much as Richard B. Westbrook, was the public voice of the American Secular Union. To be sure, many of the duties of the corresponding secretary involved bureaucratic minutiae: keeping membership lists, preparing an annual report, maintaining connections with local auxiliaries, and recurrent fundraising. The work often proved thankless. When, for example, Craddock suggested the pansy (a play on *pensée*) as an emblem of the group's commitment to freedom of thought, an Illinois jeweler named Otto Wettstein complained loudly that he had already produced a handsome gold pin featuring the torch of reason as the union's official insignia. What gall for the corresponding secretary to suggest a womanish flower when he already had for sale a manlier badge, an erect torch blazing science's triumph over superstition.

Craddock, not used to being associated with an excess of feminine delicacy, wondered what Wettstein was thinking when he laid into her over such an apparently trivial matter. For God's sake, Wettstein said, any "priest, parson, or school-girl" would be happy wearing a pansy badge, a cheap adornment available at "every 5-cent counter in every millinery and jewelry establishment." Wettstein even insinuated that he had already purchased Craddock's loyalty by giving her one of his engraved gold pins to wear and that she had now double-crossed him. That charge left her fuming that "my conscience and my personal independence" were worth more than a shiny trinket. Such were the routine snags of organizational infighting, and yet Craddock never let that silliness prevent her from taking her managerial responsibilities seriously. As she rightly observed of the demanding role she had assumed, "I supposed my duties would be those of a mere amanuensis; but I found that the secretary of a national society has practically to run the whole thing." One admirer—obviously not Wettstein—crowed that she was proving herself "worth her weight in gold to the organization."[32]

Running the whole operation also meant that Craddock was responsible for orchestrating the circulation of the society's publications—a job that put her in touch with some big names in the intellectual community. One of the major efforts of the American Secular Union in these years was staging a contest, with a $1,000 prize, for the best treatise on the principles of moral conduct that made no

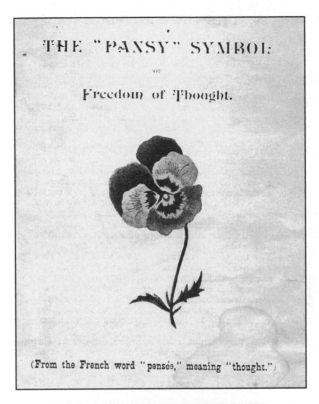

THE "PANSY" SYMBOL

OF

Freedom of Thought.

(From the French word "pensée," meaning "thought.")

Design Pat.d Feb. 24th 1885.

Otto Wettstein, a self-advertised liberal jeweler, patented the most recognized emblem of nineteenth-century secularism, the torch of reason, and marketed it as a gold badge. He flared when Craddock proposed the pansy symbol as a competitor. In the clubby male world of American freethinkers, the flaming torch held off the floral substitute. Labadie Collection, University of Michigan.

55

recourse to theological claims or revealed religion. The resulting volume, published under the title *Conduct as a Fine Art*, was presented as a way of teaching moral character in the public schools without indulging "sectarian preferences": Children did not need to be taught about God in order to be good citizens. That contest committee drew Craddock into league with Professors Felix Adler and Daniel Brinton, both of whom were prominent figures in the emergent science of religions and leading lights in wider intellectual circles. (Adler had been at Cornell before moving on to found the Ethical Culture Society; Brinton was at Penn.) Much as she had hoped, helping to lead the American Secular Union was allowing her to rub elbows with the learned and cultured.[33]

Beyond managing the American Secular Union's publications, Craddock also contributed other literary aid to the society. She served as the conduit for the distribution of Westbrook's official essays—one that endorsed church taxation and another that urged a ban on Bible reading in the public schools—but she also took her own turn, authoring a pair of pamphlets to promote membership in the society. "The army of the American Secular Union" was, by Craddock's estimate, a beleaguered force of freethinkers very much in need of new recruits to carry on the battle for "the total separation of Church and State." The language she used for recruitment was self-consciously combative—as if the fight over cultural politics in the era of Comstock and company had become its own kind of guerilla warfare. "We are shot at on all occasions," Craddock grumbled, "from behind fences of pietism, rocks of prejudice, and barriers of conventional propriety." She took it as her mission to organize the scattered ranks of liberals into a stronger, more unified body, but she soon discovered that it was nearly impossible to focus the individualistic impulses of liberalism, to keep a range of Unitarians, anarchists, agnostics, spiritualists, among others, on the same page. The American Secular Union, much like National Liberal League before it, proved an undisciplined army.[34]

Recognizing the difficulties of forging alliances across the various liberal "isms," Craddock pursued the possibility of building the movement from the ground up. With lectures in Portsmouth, Ohio, and in Newark, New Jersey, and with pieces in the *Boston Investigator* and *Freethinkers' Magazine*, she speculated with some insistence on "How to Make Freethinkers of the Young." To Craddock, then in her early thirties, it was imperative to bring some "youthful enthusiasm" to a cause peopled mostly by those "on the far side of forty" and led by those "usually on the far side of sixty." At this point, she saw her fellow secularists as being able to agree on only one cause: namely, "the protest against religious superstition, and especially against the union of Church and State." That issue, she thought, could be systematized into a curriculum for "Freethought Sunday-schools," classrooms that she imagined as open debating societies, not religious institutions. Children would be introduced to a range of philosophical views—theist versus atheist, spiritualist versus materialist—and then encouraged to enter the discussion on their own terms. "What is Liberalism worth," Craddock asked, "if it does not train our children to think for themselves, and to seize upon the truth wherever found?" The actual organization of freethought Sunday schools proved an unrealistic goal, and so Craddock spent her time working with cantankerous elders, not eager children. As corresponding secretary, she found there was no escaping the "war-dances in the Liberal papers."[35]

The hardest problem that Craddock faced was negotiating among rival versions of liberalism. She saw her task as one of widening the membership of the American Secular Union by holding secular and religious liberals together. Freethinkers relished the unmasking of pious frauds, but Craddock did not see much wisdom in making aggressive unbelief the basis of the organization. In her view the point was safeguarding religious and civil liberties, not the atheistic scolding of churchgoers. She saw liberals as defenders of a thoroughgoing religious freedom, not as hecklers whose aim was "to cripple the Church, if not to kill it off entirely." She urged freethinkers to treat church people with gentle consideration rather than dishing out all "our rude jeers at their silly superstitions." Concentrate on the positive ideal of state secularization and build alliances among religious liberals, including "Free Religionists, Quakers, Progressive Jews and Liberal Christians"—that was Craddock's program.[36]

Craddock was particularly convinced that secular liberals needed to make common cause with progressive spiritualists, those religious inquirers who embraced both spirit communication and liberal reform causes. That proposed alliance did not sit well with hard-line secularists. Liberal purists, like the lawyer Thaddeus B. Wakeman, wanted to see secularism extended over all "the domains of human hope, now occupied by supernatural religion." Spiritualists, in Wakeman's view, were beyond the pale of respect and cooperation; the American Secular Union had to keep a safe distance from such deluded spook-lovers. But Craddock well knew that spiritualists were a crucial source of support for liberal causes. She celebrated the connection she had forged with the *Progressive Thinker*, a paper of "immense circulation" that had "become our organ among the Spiritualists" and had been critical in enlisting that "large and influential body of Liberals." Tweaking the critics of such initiatives at the group's annual convention in 1891, she suggested that the financial survival of the American Secular Union had actually come to depend on "our Spiritualistic constituency." Craddock once boasted that she kept up with all the agnostic and atheistic publications of the day during her tenure as corresponding secretary, but her working relationship with spiritualists came closer to being her trademark contribution to the organization.[37]

Taking a cooperative line with spiritualists was certainly one of the reasons why Craddock's stint with the American Secular Union ended after only two years of service. Surprisingly, another issue that proved problematic for her was the relationship between secularism and sex reform. Confronted with the more radical elements of the liberal movement, Craddock seems to have decided that she was not (yet) as zealous for free sexual expression as some of her compatriots were. As she recalled the issue later,

> At the close of two years (having once been re-elected) Richard B. Westbrook, the President, and I, concluded to resign, as the Free-Lovers and other ultra members wished to force us to take up the defence of radicals who were prosecuted for sending so-called 'obscene literature' through the mails, and we would not; neither would [we] encourage Free-Love. In those days, I drew my dress very carefully aside from all such questions, and was exceedingly prim and proper in all my public expression, and careful not to give the slightest encouragement to the left wing of Radicalism.

The issue of how far to press the attack on Comstock and how much to defend his targets divided members of the American Secular Union in 1890, just as it had the National Liberal League a decade earlier. Seeing it as her job to hold a very fragile union together, Craddock tried to play, along with Westbrook, a moderating role in a conflict that would not go away.[38]

Truth be told, though, Craddock was already giving plenty of encouragement to the "ultra-radicals" on matters of women's rights and marriage reform. In February 1890 she lent the backing of the American Secular Union to the formation of the Woman's National Liberal Union, the brainchild of Elizabeth Cady Stanton's co-conspirator, Matilda Joslyn Gage. Craddock published an endorsement of the convention in all the leading freethought outlets, including the *Truth Seeker* and the *Boston Investigator*, and pushed Gage's characteristic emphasis on the church's deep complicity in women's disenfranchisement, "the doctrine of woman's inferiority by reason of her original sin." Though the National Liberal League and the American Secular Union were certainly sympathetic to the cause, neither had made women's rights one of the fundamental demands of liberalism. Craddock, for her part, suggested a joining of arms with Gage's emergent organization and thus signaled her support for a thoroughgoing political and theological critique of women's inequality within Christian institutions. Certainly in October 1891 when she stepped down, careworn and embattled, from her post as corresponding secretary, Craddock was more cautious than she would be just a couple of years later when she made headlines for her defense of belly dancing. Still, there were clear signs of the direction she was headed. Perhaps the best indicator of all was that she had already begun her learned inquiry into the history of sex worship, the peculiar vehicle for her radical emergence.[39]

WHEN CRADDOCK BEGAN promoting "Freethought Sunday-schools" as the kindergarten of the American Secular Union, the project never got off the ground, but her proposed curriculum showed how much of the skeptical study of religion she had already internalized. Her prospectus was dedicated, first of all, to combating "religious superstition"—an always-commodious notion among freethinkers that covered "pious frauds" from the ancient world to the present day. Her syllabus was also designed to inveigh against religious violence and intolerance, whether past persecutions (such as the hounding of witches or the hanging of Quakers) or contemporary dangers (such as "the would-be ecclesiastical tyranny of the God-in-the-Constitution party"). Like any freethinker worthy of the name, Craddock knew what she did not like about religion.[40]

In addition to the usual Enlightenment critiques, her approach offered a survey of "the leading mythologies of the world—Egyptian, Hindoo, Greek, Roman, Norse, Saxon." Such familiarity with a range of gods and goddesses would be of value, Craddock claimed, "in the child's literary and art education" and would also prepare him or her for appreciating how the Christian tradition itself had inspired "thousands

of works in literature, painting, sculpture, architecture, and music."
Fairness mattered: Teachers and pupils in Craddock's hypothetical
freethought schools were not only to explore the bleak history of
religion's abusive power, as evidenced in the coerced recantation of
Galileo or in Christian defenses "of chattel slavery in this country," but
also to assess religion as "a stimulus to noble work." Let the students
sort out their own sense of the balance between religion's evil and its
good, Craddock advised, through shared inquiry and discussion.

Even with that romantic nod to religion's potential for artistic
expressiveness, Craddock made clear that science was the ultimate
arbiter. Instruct the students, she insisted, "that evolution, and not special
creation, is the law under which the universe always works. The teaching
of this modern gospel of evolution should be supplemented by brief talks
on geology, astronomy, plant and animal life, etc." The faith in physical
science was to be joined to a larger faith in the physical world—not the
celestial—as the focus of human striving and hope. The all-important
theme, Craddock claimed, was "the good to be gotten out of this life,
right here and now, without waiting until we die." Christianity had for
too long cast a gloom over "the beauty, the joy of this earth-life," and
humanistic freethinkers were to lift that pall through energetic
optimism. Show the children, Craddock exhorted, that "Liberalism is,
before all, a religion of sunshine."

The emphasis on this world's joys meshed nicely with Craddock's
budding reevaluation of the human body. Already in 1891 she indicated
that freethought Sunday schools needed to be in the business of
educating children about human sexuality "from a purely impersonal
and scientific standpoint." This initiative, too, was connected in
Craddock's mind to her freethinking critique of religious superstition. "It
has been the disgrace of Christianity, that it has taught mankind to
despise the body, and especially the sexual nature, as something too
impure to be talked of. . . . Shall Liberals follow in the footsteps of the
monkish promulgators of Christian superstition?" As Craddock saw it,

the church's policy of shame and silence—that "certain organs of the body" must not be discussed "before they are put into use" within marriage—fell with particular weight upon young women. The Christian "law of modesty," in Craddock's estimation, was applied unequally, burdening women with terribly constraining forms of dress and even more cramped forms of virtue. Through the advancement of a freethinking history of religion, the church's underpinning of patriarchal tyranny—or, "sex slavery" in the radical parlance of the day— would finally be exposed and the emancipation of women would become newly realizable.

The last piece of Craddock's curriculum turned to "the proper study of the Christian Bible" itself—an inquiry more akin to an archaeological dig than to meditation on a holy text. Unlike some avowed secularists who hoped to oust the scriptures entirely from American education, Craddock saw that as a misguided impulse, inimical to literature, art, and serious learning. "The Christian Bible is a curious old book," she wryly observed, "and worthy of the most scholarly study that Liberals can put upon it." To pursue such learning required not only the historical and textual tools of the new biblical scholarship, but also the implements of comparative mythologists and folklorists. With such research methods in hand, the "persistently literal interpretation" of the Bible could then be "exploded" and the scripture's "true value" made plain to children and youth.

Craddock saw the Bible's main worth as that of "a storehouse of precious myths." Once biblical stories were placed "upon the same footing with that beautiful sun and dawn myth of Cinderella, with the solar and phallic myth of William Tell, and others," they would become valuable materials for freethinking inquiry and instruction. A blue-chip text for fathoming the evolution of religion, the Bible provided a historical record of "a primitive people" attempting "to fix the floating legends of ancient sun, moon, and star worships, of tree, phallic, serpent and fire worships, into some definite form." By analyzing the Bible as a work of the mythological imagination, scholars could form a clearer sense of humanity's archaic past and at the same time deprive the Christian scriptures of their claim to uniqueness, their aura of finality and all-sufficiency. Like other freethinking intellectuals, Craddock enveloped the biblical history of redemption under the vast canopy of comparative religion and mythology.

After her tenure with the American Secular Union ended in October 1891, Craddock's intellectual energies shifted to the program that lay behind her model curriculum for young freethinkers. For a steady income she returned to her old trade of teaching shorthand at Girard College, but she had long desired a more fulfilling life of the mind. She now started presenting herself as a student of folklore and comparative mythology, spoke of her intellectual work as her primary labor, and made her services available for the liberal lecture circuit as an inquirer into religion's evolutionary history. Having managed a side trip to Alaska during her California sojourn, she tapped into her encounter with indigenous religious carvings—totem poles and ceremonial staffs—to produce an initial article on Alaskan mythology that appeared in the *Truth Seeker Annual and Freethinkers' Almanac* in 1891. That piece made clear Craddock's resolve to pursue ethnological inquiries, even if it meant handling objects that "any comparative mythologist" would recognize as being of "phallic design." She was already more than willing to stretch the limits of decency in order to further her own theories and expertise.[41]

Craddock's scholarly efforts bubbled up within a broader confluence of women's rights activism and freethinking reflections on religion—a convergence that reached a high-water mark in the 1880s and 1890s. The outspoken lecturer Helen H. Gardener, a fearless critic of the new studies in neurology that marked women's brains as innately inferior to men's in size and complexity, led the way in 1885 with her book *Men, Women, and Gods*, a blunt attack on religion's role in female subjection. (Gardener was so committed to establishing—in physiological terms—the intellectual equality of men and women that she later willed her

During a trip to Alaska in 1889 Craddock collected photographs of totem poles that she planned to incorporate into an essay on Alaskan folklore, one of her few scholarly efforts that she actually got into print. Special Collections Research Center, Morris Library, Southern Illinois University, Carbondale.

brain to Cornell University for anatomical comparison to male specimens.) The daughter of a circuit-riding Methodist preacher, Gardener had moved by her mid-twenties to the far left of the religious and political spectrum, a protégé of agnostic Robert Ingersoll and suffragist Elizabeth Cady Stanton. Exposing sexist "fictions" wherever she found them, Gardener was an especially forthright critic of biblical revelation and Christian doctrine. "There are a great many women to-day who think that orthodoxy is as great nonsense as I do, but who are afraid to say so," she urged. "I want to help make it so that they will dare to speak."[42]

More voices were certainly heard soon. In 1892 Elizabeth E. Evans, an American inquirer who spent much of her life as an expatriate in German intellectual circles, issued *A History of Religions, Being a Condensed Statement of the Results of Scientific Research and Philosophical Criticism*. It offered a less incisive analysis of gender relations than Gardener's series of lectures, but it contained a similarly critical attitude toward Christianity. The next year suffragist Matilda Joslyn Gage followed with *Woman, Church and State*, a banner work that built its vision of women's political, legal, and economic emancipation upon a critique of Christian teachings on family, gender, and sexuality. Gage effectively turned the anticlerical posture of the Woman's National Liberal Union into a historical rumination on the power of ancient priestesses and goddesses, the ascendancy of patriarchal rule through Judaism and Christianity, the Church's enshrinement of female inferiority in canon law, and the misogyny of witchcraft accusations. That history, in turn, provided the groundwork for Gage's indictment of the contemporary clergy's resistance to women's equality and their continued insistence on women's subjugation by divine command.

Woman, Church and State provided a strong backdrop for Craddock's own inquiries, but the capstone work in this decade of intellectual ferment came in 1895 with the first of two volumes of Elizabeth Cady Stanton's *The Woman's Bible*. In its disregard for scriptural verities, that

In freethinking critiques of religion, women would gain their freedom only through breaking the chains of the male clerical establishment, an emancipation neatly embodied in this illustration by Watson Heston, the era's banner cartoonist for irreligion. Watson Heston, The Freethinkers' Pictorial Text-Book *(New York: Truth Seeker Co., 1890), facing p. 90. WHi-65505, Wisconsin Historical Society.*

project managed to raise hackles everywhere and became a serious public-relations problem for the suffrage movement. Through a series of commentaries, Stanton and allied activists sought to undercut the scriptural passages used to oppose female emancipation and confine women to domestic dependency. Verse by verse, Stanton and company offered revisionist interpretations of all the familiar passages that were used to keep women silent, disenfranchised, secondary, or cursed. Stanton intended the work as a head-on challenge to a scripture-soaked culture, and *The Woman's Bible* certainly hit the mark. "Come, come, my conservative friend," she prodded, "wipe the dew off your spectacles, and see that the world is moving. . . . We have made a fetich of the Bible long enough."[43]

Just as this group of freethinking women was forging its own identifiable tradition of religious learning and critique, the professional terrain was shifting underneath them. Amateur scholars were becoming increasingly marginalized in American and European intellectual life toward the end of the nineteenth century, after long enjoying authority in a broad range of fields. Through the 1860s and 1870s amateurs were as likely to be eminent authorities in the learned study of religion as a holder of a university chair. The sway of the amateur was evident, for example, in the towering status of John McLennan as an ethnologist, a Scottish lawyer who never held a university post, or the high standing of Lewis Henry Morgan as an ethnographer, an American lawyer who devotedly studied the Iroquois, again from outside the academy. It was all the more evident in dozens of other inquirers whose intellectual achievements were far more modest than Morgan's and McLennan's but who were of perfectly solid reputation. One more American example suffices to underline the amateur's considerable role: Alexander Wilder, a medical doctor, who dabbled in comparative religions and who spearheaded the introduction of F. Max Müller's scholarship to American audiences. The deference that Wilder accorded Müller in the early 1880s was in itself, though, a sign of shifting authority; the New Jersey physician, a dilettante, paid homage to the Oxford professor, a master of the new science of religion.[44]

In offering his pioneering *Introduction to the Science of Religion* in 1873, Müller had heralded the historical, philological, and comparative study of religions as an important venture of the emergent research university. The spread of that academic enterprise showed the familiar signs of professional consolidation. Following the lead of the Dutch universities, which established four university professorships for the scientific study of religion in 1876, American institutions gradually climbed on board: New York University in 1887, Cornell in 1891, and the University of Chicago in 1892. Lectureships were inaugurated; learned congresses convened; academic journals launched; and new professional societies organized, including the founding of an American Society of Comparative Religion in New York City in 1890. Scholarly expeditions and field sites also multiplied, giving new energy to the archaeological study of religion, and these excavations also fed museum displays of religious artifacts as well as the specialized studies of exhibition curators. By 1905 this "advancing Science" appeared so well established that the University of Chicago hosted a lecture series celebrating the discipline's international rise and flourishing over the previous quarter century. The modern study of religion had been built, the self-congratulating lecturer claimed, by experts, and for experts. The field owed its success to "the researches of Scientists of distinction and imperial outlook," well-trained masters of a new empire of knowledge that left no place for "novices."[45]

The shifting of the academic terrain toward fully accredited experts was apparent in Craddock's own backyard. Morris Jastrow, the son of an immigrant Polish rabbi, had studied in the liberal arts college at the University of Pennsylvania, graduating in 1881 just shy of his twentieth birthday. He soon headed to Europe for doctoral work in Assyrian, Arabic, and Hebrew; while there, he quickly gained access to the leading Dutch scholar of religion, C. P. Tiele, at the University of Leiden. Going on to receive his PhD from the University of Leipzig in 1884, Jastrow then returned to Philadelphia and to his alma mater as an expert on Assyrian and Babylonian religion. Highly regarded as a professor of Semitic languages, Jastrow helped pioneer the formal graduate study of religion at Penn and in the larger world of the American research university. By 1901 he had produced a standard handbook on the field, a volume he simply called *The Study of Religion*, a testimony—as he saw it—to the formation of a newly bounded discipline with carefully honed methods and with ever improving "systems of classification." As Jastrow claimed, "The study of religion has taken its place among contemporary sciences, and the importance of the study can be denied by no one who appreciates the part that religion has played in the history of mankind, and still plays at the present time." That area of inquiry, once "so frequently invaded by the dilettante," was being redefined by "properly-trained scholars," who, in order to solidify their own authority, found it necessary to drive the amateur "out of the field."[46]

The dilemma for Craddock was clear and intractable. Just as Jastrow sailed through Penn as a nineteen-year-old Jewish immigrant, Craddock at age twenty-five was still trying to figure out how to leverage her way into the college at all. By the time Jastrow was finishing his PhD at Leipzig, Craddock had despaired of ever entering her class at Penn. By the early 1890s, when Jastrow was laying plans for a formalized university curriculum in the history of religion, Craddock was stuck again at a charity school teaching shorthand to orphaned boys and finding it hard to line up lectures, even in the most liberal venues. In the European mold of C. P. Tiele and Max Müller, Jastrow's professional life as a scholar of religion flourished, while as a woman Craddock's amateur endeavors went nowhere. "Miss Craddock is a scholar of no ordinary attainments," the *Freethinkers' Magazine* had declared in puffing her talents to its readership in 1890, and yet the compliment's phrasing proved an inadvertently appropriate estimate of her academic standing. An uncertified amateur, Craddock forever lacked the "ordinary attainments" of doctorate-holding professionals like Jastrow. When credentialed specialists congratulated themselves on keeping unqualified novices out of this advancing science, "the scholarly Miss Craddock" was among the sort that got swept aside. [47]

Craddock and her freethinking companions watched this academic fence building from outside the gates, but its effects were noticed by those on the inside as well. In a caustic essay in the *Harvard Monthly* in 1903 entitled "The Ph.D. Octopus," William James blasted this rising professionalism in American universities, the "academic snobbery" and intellectual hollowness of scholarly credentialing. It had become, he warned, "a tyrannical Machine with unforeseen powers of exclusion," and yet the primary exclusion he had in mind was how stilted titles and degrees—outward badges—threatened the "bare manhood" of American intellectual life. James's desire to sever the tentacles of professionalism for the sake of manly autonomy was an insider's luxury. James offered a rebuff to the university's new academic breed, including hard-charging specialists like Jastrow, but he registered no qualms about how the PhD octopus affected amateur women like Craddock.[48]

Except for the early essay on Alaskan mythology, virtually all of Craddock's investigations into religion went unpublished. If not for the Ladies' Liberal League and a few other patrons, her learned efforts would have been little acknowledged at all. So fragile were her scholarly endeavors that the manuscript for her first book in the field, a treatise on the origin of the devil, has been lost in its entirety. Demonology, offering a grand display of religious credulity and priestly fear-mongering, was a popular topic with freethinkers, and at least two of Craddock's fellow liberals, Moncure Conway and Henry Frank, produced their own histories of the devil. She likely followed the freethinking script on Satan closely enough, including the emphasis on the long history of demonizing women as witches. Liberals often displayed a perverse love for Lucifer—not least because they saw his age-old shenanigans and hell-fire threats as a terrible embarrassment to Christian orthodoxy.

If Craddock's history of the devil is nowhere to be found, her extensive typescripts on the history of sex worship have been largely preserved. Beginning to work in earnest on this subject for her public lectures in 1893 and 1894, Craddock returned to it often over the next several years and ended up having a big book manuscript on her hands. While at least two chapters of this project have also gone missing—one on the "Pagan Rootage of Christianity" and another on the "Worship of Mother and Child"—a hefty draft, 352 legal-size pages in all, has survived. Divided into three parts—"Sun and Dawn Myths" (43 pp.), "Lunar and Sex Worship" (102 pp.), and "Sex Worship (Continued)"

(207 pp.)—Craddock's manuscript provides ample material for plumbing her unnoticed labors as a student of comparative religion and mythology.[49]

Craddock's attempt to write a history of phallic worship was no mere eccentricity; rather, it actually put her in an intellectual company both substantial and subversive. Nineteenth-century inquirers (and Craddock was no exception) looked back to Richard Payne Knight's *Discourse on the Worship of Priapus* (1786) as an especially path-breaking work. An heir of an early industrialist fortune in ironworks, Knight schooled himself as a young man through extensive travels in France and Italy in the 1770s and through the gentlemanly collecting of fine art and antiquities. A freethinking enemy of priestcraft with a typical relish for documenting Roman Catholic "superstitions," Knight began his treatise with a lengthy account of penis-shaped votive offerings. A likeminded inquirer, the British envoy William Hamilton, had recently discovered "*ex-voti* of wax, representing the male parts of generation" being used at local saints' shrines in Italy by supplicants who were seeking to promote conception or cure impotence. Those waxen phalluses and the prayers that accompanied them became the inspiration for Knight's first book, his account of the worship of Priapus, the god of male procreative power.[50]

Knight's *Discourse* quickly became infamous for its pagan infidelity and libertinism, despite the fact that the Society of Dilettanti to which Knight belonged had published the work only for private circulation among other male connoisseurs. Knight was himself unnerved by the controversy that erupted over his seminal work. A freethinker, he was deeply committed to the cause of civil liberty and to the critique of church power, but he nonetheless quickly backed away from the religious scandal that his inquiry had generated. Suppressing as many copies of the book as possible, he thereafter hid his continuing interest in phallic symbolism within safer discussions of ancient art, mythology, sculpture, and coins.

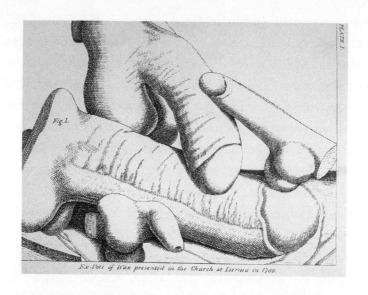

Fig. I.

Ex-Voti of Wax presented in the Church at Isernia in 1780.

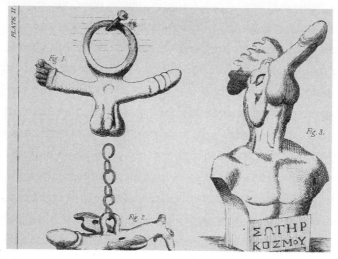

Fig. 1.

Fig. 3.

Fig. 2.

ΣΩΤΗΡ
ΚΟΣΜΟΥ

Richard Payne Knight's Discourse on the Worship of Priapus *(1786) was the gold standard among the forbidden books for studying religion and sexuality. The frontispiece to the volume pictured waxen phalluses that were used at a Roman Catholic shrine in supplications to conceive a child or cure impotence. The plate that followed showed ancient phallic amulets that Knight, a devoted collector of antiquities, saw as the archaeological font of these contemporary Christian practices. The Library Company of Philadelphia.*

However much Knight would have liked the world to forget his controversial discourse, he could not make it disappear. Possessing the frisson of forbidden learning, Knight's treatise enjoyed long-lasting powers of reproduction. Its graphic images of phallic amulets, representing "the organ of generation in that state of tension and rigidity which is necessary to the due performance of its functions," became legendary in a netherworld somewhere between sexology and erotica. Its incorporation of Christian motifs—from the cross to church spires to the kiss of peace—into the phallic cult became a routine gibe at the faithful among later freethinkers. Its insistence that "symbolical representations" of the sex organs were, from time immemorial, employed as meaningful religious emblems was also compelling to those who imagined a radical reevaluation of Victorian notions of modesty and propriety. As Knight jousted, the ancient worship of procreation no doubt appeared indecent to well-bred English Protestants—"a mockery of all piety and devotion"—but it was actually "a very natural and philosophical system of religion." Christians, it could only be concluded, did not know what they were missing.[51]

If Knight's *Discourse* remained infamous, that did not mean it was easy for subsequent researchers—including Craddock—to find the actual book. The British Library had retained a copy of the first edition, but it was carefully locked away and kept purposely inaccessible because of its graphic content. A second version, privately circulated in 1865, had only negligibly increased the availability of Knight's book. By then, the British Museum had actually created a special cabinet, known as the "Secretum," to keep their phallic antiquities and erotic books closeted from public access. As Craddock noted in her unpublished treatise, "The book is very rare but can be found in the Ridgway Library, South Broad Street, Philadelphia, and in a few other large libraries." But, since American curators followed the cagey practices of their British counterparts, knowing the book was there did not automatically make it accessible. Indeed, after passing through the Ridgway's imposing

For poking fun at Christian orthodoxy, the notion of the phallic origins of religious symbolism proved especially useful to enlightened critics. The evolutionary view of religion's long history is neatly encapsulated in another of Watson Heston's cartoons, this one on "The Uses of the Cross—Its Evolution" in which humankind rises from primitive phallicism through Christian priestcraft to scientific triumph. Watson Heston, The Freethinkers' Pictorial Text-Book *(New York: Truth Seeker Co., 1890), facing p. 288. WHi-65506, Wisconsin Historical Society.*

3^d ADOPTED BY THE SIMPLE MINDED AS AN OBJECT OF ADORATION

6th SCIENCE CONVERTS IT INTO A COMMON PROP FOR THE ELECTRIC WIRES, AND ALTHOUGH THE CROSS REMAINS, ITS ORIGINAL SIGNIFICANCE IS FORGOTTEN

Doric colonnade, Craddock had to do extra sleuthing once inside; the *Discourse* had been left out of the catalogue and "can be seen only by special request." Then the primary home of the Library Company of Philadelphia, the great subscription library inaugurated by Benjamin Franklin, the Ridgway was a quintessential cultural legacy of the American Enlightenment. Craddock had its holdings to draw upon in order to join the still shadowy enterprise of investigating the sexual history of religion, but, as Knight's carefully hidden treatise suggests, it required an almost perverse determination to explore the subject in any detail.[52]

The damage that the *Discourse* had done to Knight's reputation was enough to slow other antiquarians from taking up Priapic symbolism, but after the mid-nineteenth century more and more of them dared to broach the subject. British travelers, adventurers, and amateurs led the way: Edward Sellon, a freelance anthropologist who became notorious as a hack writer of erotica, offered *Annotations on the Sacred Writings of the Hindüs, Being an Epitome of Some of the Most Remarkable and Leading Tenets in the Faith of that People Illustrating their Priapic Rites and Phallic Principles* (1865); Thomas Wright, a prolific historian and respected folklorist, ventured to extend Knight's "great learning" with *The Worship of the Generative Powers during the Middle Ages of Western Europe* (1865); James Fergusson, a Scottish trader who spent years in India, produced *Tree and Serpent Worship: Illustrations of Mythology and Art in India* (1868); and J. G. R. Forlong, a military officer turned promoter of the science of comparative religions, tendered *Rivers of Life, Or, Sources and Streams of the Faiths of Man in All Lands* (1883).[53]

These new inquirers in the second half of the nineteenth century massively extended the reach of Knight's claims. "Phallicism" was now said to be important for understanding the whole of religion's evolutionary history. Alongside other "primitive" forms of religious observance—including fetishism and animism—the "phallic faiths" came to stand in Victorian anthropology as an elemental part of religion's origins and development. Dozens of British and European inquirers had come to see fertility broadly and human sexuality particularly as at the root of religious symbolism across vast stretches of geography and time. Phallicism provided, in short, the key to unlocking the hitherto little-known sexual history of religion.[54]

American inquirers were followers, more than leaders, in this particular excavation of religion's unseemly origins, but after the mid-nineteenth century they contributed their own share in making "phallic religion" a recognizable category in the study of the "primitive ages." The journalist and diplomat E. G. Squier had included a chapter on "Phallic Worship in the Old and New Worlds" in his extended investigation of serpent symbolism in 1851. John G. Bourke, a military officer, made use of the idea in his ethnographic observations on *The Snake-Dance of the Moquis of Arizona* (1884) as well as in his comparative examination of the *Scatologic Rites of All Nations* (1891). Before the physician Alexander Wilder introduced his countrymen to Max Müller's *India: What Can It Teach Us?* (1883), he had already edited an American edition of *Ancient Symbol Worship: Influence of the Phallic Idea in the Religions of Antiquity* (1874), a work by the British scholars Hodder M. Westropp and C. Staniland Wake. Subsequently migrating to Chicago after the Columbian Exposition, Wake conducted research at the fledgling Field Museum—a move that indicated the growing American role in the study of religion's long history.[55]

Even as the Anglo-American literature on phallic worship proliferated in the second half of the nineteenth century, one demographic column remained blank: This was not an area of learning proper for women. J. G. R. Forlong, an authority Craddock cited often, introduced his massive *Rivers of Life* with the caveat that, while he wanted "to enlighten the ordinary reading public," he needed to limit that education to "the male sex, for to our sisters, the origin of Faiths and of the various rites they continually see around them, must long remain mysterious." "This work, then, is for men," Forlong continued, "and indeed only for that class of my brothers who venture on strong food, and have permitted themselves to look beyond the swaddling bands of youth. . . . No maudlin sentiment of false delicacy must in this case keep us from calling a spade a spade." When Forlong subsequently wrote the introduction to one of Hodder Westropp's works on "the growth and spread of Phallicism," he made another telling note: Westropp had first taken up the subject in a paper read before the Anthropological Society of London in 1870, an impressive performance, Forlong reminisced, "in the days when such subjects" could still be addressed before that learned body, "as they are not now, owing to [the] admission of lady members." Simply put, women were obstructions to those ethnologists who, otherwise eager to study the subject of religion's sexual history, felt the need to shy away from it in mixed company. More than any other topic in the study of religion, phallicism was a subject deemed appropriate for "men of mature judgments" only. Not to be overly subtle, but the study of phallic worship required balls.[56]

Noticeably alone as a woman in this scholarly arena, Craddock nonetheless kept writing her book, hopeful that her fellow liberals would come around to seeing the worthiness of both the topic and her perspective on it. That expectation was not entirely naïve, given how much her work shared with the wider inquiries of the period. Like most freethinkers fascinated by this topic, she placed Christianity on the same plane with other religious mythologies and repeatedly linked Christian symbols to an underlying primeval devotion to reproduction, the elemental mystification of sexual desire and procreation. From Easter eggs to the Christmas tree to upward-thrusting church architecture, Christianity contained, so the argument went, a hodgepodge of survivals from more ancient forms of sex worship. "The eggs offered to the cross on Good Friday and eaten on our modern Easter Sunday," Craddock argued, "were types, not of the female reproductive power in nature, as is generally supposed, but of the testicles of the male phallic triad. . . . The boy who pits his Easter egg against that of another boy, trying to see whose egg is the *hardest*, unconsciously memorializes a phallic symbolism." Everywhere Craddock and her fellow freethinkers looked, they found new evidence for the sexual underpinning of Christian symbols and rites.[57]

Craddock was, though, as likely to diverge from the phallic script as she was to repeat it. That was especially true when it came to the question of what value these archaic symbols and customs possessed, the lessons to be learned from Victorian scholarship about the primitive and the civilized. Invested in the forward march of social evolution as well as the advance of the "accurate sciences," nineteenth-century ethnologists regularly dwelled on religion's primitive origins in order to discredit surviving "superstitions." Phallic worshippers, along with fetishists, were generally thought to be among the lowest of the low, and hence one of the major social payoffs of this learning was the opportunity it provided for a hearty celebration of modern civilization's ascendancy over dark savagery. As Hodder M. Westropp informed the Anthropological Society of London in 1870, among "rude and barbarous people of the present day," particularly in West Africa, phallic worship was still "uncomfortably prominent."[58]

J. G. R. Forlong was especially clear on the barbarity of primitive sex worship—just as he had been especially clear on the inappropriateness of women learning anything about it. "We know enough of African religions," he observed, "to assert that here Fetish, Tree, Phal[l]us, and Yoni worship exist in their grossest forms . . . bestial in the extreme." In alarmed tones Forlong even warned of a sprawling British empire in which "PURE PHALLIC-worshippers" vastly outnumbered Queen Victoria's Christian subjects and claimed that "far more than half the population of *the whole world*" was devoted to "phallic faiths." Ruling over an empire of Priapic ritualists—from South Asia to Africa—was a tall order. Fortunately, Forlong and other like-minded inquirers had created the intellectual diagrams to fit all those devotees of trees, serpents, pillars, and fetishes onto a neat evolutionary ladder—with

Victorian science and civilization snugly ensconced at the top. There were certainly more important resources for managing an empire, but an ethnological chart, displaying a tidy religious and cultural hierarchy, was not an inconsequential tool.[59]

Now Craddock, for her part, was hardly a progressive on race and imperial issues. As with most white liberals of the day, she expended none of her reform energies on the civil rights of black Americans, and this during a nadir in race relations, including lynching's reign of terror. Likewise, she displayed no interest in anti-imperial protests during and after the Spanish-American War as the United States extended its territories from Puerto Rico to the Philippines. Run-of-the-mill racial, ethnic, and class chauvinism blinkered her vision; she surprised herself, for example, when her daily walk to work through "the Chinese quarter" in Philadelphia aroused in her "fellow-feeling and sympathy" rather than indifference or incomprehension. Though she claimed at another point that "many a white woman" had much to learn from the "untutored" Pueblo Indians of the Southwest, she nonetheless retained an underlying clarity about the privileged importance of the "civilized white woman." Yet, for all the usual limitations, her interest in religion's elementary forms showed little of the colonial and civilizing compulsion that drove Forlong and his compatriots to their evolutionary conclusions. Craddock's concern with comparative mythology was never about lifting the Aryan over the Semitic race or the Anglo-Saxon over the African— that is, Christian over Jew or white over black.[60]

The politics of gender and sexuality, not those of race and empire, drew Craddock to the literature on phallic worship. That learning, she thought, provided her with a choice opportunity to think about the connections among religion, women's equality, and sexual expression. At first blush, phallicism seemed like a less than promising subject for Craddock's feminist purposes. The penis, after all, was the measuring rod of all religious symbolism in this line of inquiry; it stood for all the reproductive powers, subsuming the female into the male and marking the latter with transcendent supremacy. "By phallic religion in this book," one American inquirer explained in typical fashion, "is meant any cult in which the human generative organs (male or female), their use, realistic images representing them, or symbols indicating them, form an essential or important factor in the dogmas or ceremonies." A good portion of this literature, moreover, seemed no more than a transparent male fantasy about how desperate women were to procreate with men. As Hodder Westropp remarked in his paper before the (all-male) gathering of the London Anthropological Society, one of the chief sources of phallic worship was "the natural desire of women among all races, barbarous as well as civilized, to be the fruitful mother of children." Hence it was, Westropp concluded, that "the phallus became an object of reverence and especial worship among women."[61]

Despite the apparent obstacles, Craddock surmised that the studies of phallic worship worked quite well for her purposes. She knew no better place to begin in order to deflate a man's presumption of power and control—in a word, his cockiness. "As masculine deities began to gradually crowd out the ancient worship accorded to motherhood," Craddock suggested, "masculine egotism naturally hastened to erect its round towers, obelisks, steeples and other symbols of its own generative power—the higher the tower or obelisk erected, the better." Like other freethinking women of her day, including Elizabeth Cady Stanton and Matilda Joslyn Gage, Craddock embraced current archaeological speculations that powerful matriarchies and forceful goddesses had once flourished in the ancient world. Only belatedly, the conjecture went, had patriarchy and the Father-God triumphed. With those primeval struggles in mind, Craddock drew attention to the "ancient Yonic deities" and thereby challenged the reverence for male potency she found pervading prior studies of phallicism. Especially leery of the way all fertility rituals got treated as phallic worship, Craddock criticized the virile rhetoric for "having swept everything before it, and, with true masculine egoism, to have appropriated all or nearly all the sacred feminine symbols to its own typology." In challenging the scholarly projection of the phallus into the heavens as a universal symbol of power and productivity, Craddock sought to prioritize instead feminine or "yonic" symbolism in the study of religion.[62]

Craddock identified herself as a "comparative mythologist" not as a show of pedantry, but for the political implications she saw in such learning. To see the history of religion as a deep-seated battle of the sexes was to turn ancient religion into a crucible for testing Victorian Protestant assumptions about gender and sexuality. Like Helen Gardener, Craddock imagined such study as a way of exposing deep sources of women's disempowerment and subservience, the process by which women were reduced to "a thing, a slave, the mere chattel of the man." Like Elizabeth Cady Stanton, Craddock thought that ultimate success in advancing women's equality would require a hard-hitting reinterpretation of prevailing religious authorities: namely, an enfolding of scripture and church history within a larger emancipationist framework. To rediscover a form of worship that was "both a safeguard and a consolation to Woman, as well as an ever-present assertion of her equality with Man," Craddock stressed that Christianity, as the embodiment of "a male religion," had to be squarely confronted, not sidestepped.[63]

The specific politics laid bare through Craddock's study of phallic worship were those of married sexual relations. That husbands viewed their wives as "a sexual convenience," that they subjected their spouses to the "incessant demands of brutal masculinity," and that, even under decently respectful circumstances, they were selfishly hurried during intercourse—all were well-attested social facts in Craddock's view. Such concerns, commonplace among nineteenth-century marriage reformers, were initially illuminated for Craddock through her freethinking, scholarly study of phallic worship: Divine commandment was everywhere still being used to subordinate women to men; God-mandated subjection was, she observed, employed "in our own day to keep hundreds of devout and pure-minded women subject to the brutality of their husbands." Through her "extended resumé of Sex Worship and its survivals in modern Christianity," through the subject matter of the lecture she first took on tour in 1893 and 1894, Craddock began to imagine herself as a free-speaking marriage reformer.[64]

The particular sex reforms that flowed from Craddock's engagement with "Phallic antiquities" were matched by fantastic religious potentialities, and those were nothing if not soaring. Underlying the apparent "grossness" of ancient forms of sex worship, Craddock insisted, had been "a primitive wonderment, a delight, and finally a veneration of the attributes which distinguish man and woman from one another." That primeval consecration of sexuality signaled a "reverent and joyous aspiration toward a perfect life," a longing for an "ecstatic bliss" that was achieved "not by asceticism" but through the "thrills of sense." That carnal wisdom had lingered on despite "centuries of repression" aimed at crushing the "free, natural, joyous outpourings . . . of love between man and woman." The "ancient Phallicism" had enshrined, Craddock concluded, "the true religion of the heart." At one point in *Leaves of Grass*, Walt Whitman had exulted in a faith that would enclose "all worship ancient and modern"—a faith in which devotees would be "dancing yet through the streets in phallic procession." By the end of her long book on sex worship, "the scholarly Miss Craddock" looked ready to dance in her own festival of sensuous awakening and full-bodied enlightenment.[65]

Craddock, like Whitman, imagined herself to be part of an *outré* band of intellectuals and free spirits. She expressly joined her inquiries to those of "our moralists among the ultra-Liberals," "those brave ones" who were "mapping out" a new ethical, religious, and literary landscape. These daring souls were impugned, she said, as "diggers among the muck and wreckage of what is best unknown or forgot." "Bah!" she imagined their adversaries exclaiming, "we despise you—nay, more if you will not keep silence, we will imprison you, burn your literature, and set the seal of the law upon your insane lips forever!" Perhaps, with this imagined tirade, Craddock already had her own obscenity battles in view or perhaps she was calling to mind prior attempts to suppress the work of such marriage reformers as Victoria Woodhull, Ezra Heywood, and Moses Harman, to say nothing of Whitman's *Leaves of Grass*. Certainly, as she labored on her book manuscript on ancient phallic worship, she knew that her scholarly preoccupations were deeply entwined with her religious aspirations and political commitments and that a threat of enforced silence hung over the whole bundle. Her inquiries might well be kept from view as a species of obscenity, blasphemy, or madness, but, as she bravely insisted, "the digging and exploring go on just the same."[66]

The excavation of religion's sexual history did indeed continue apace. Just a few years after Craddock's defense of the Danse du Ventre and her lecture for the Ladies' Liberal League, a Michigan suffragist, Eliza Burt Gamble, entered the intellectual fray with *The God-Idea of the Ancients: Or, Sex in Religion* (1897). Like Gardener, Gage, Stanton, and Craddock, Gamble was an amateur scholar of religion with deep roots in the women's rights movement. Like them, too, she wanted to understand the history behind "our present God-idea," how it was the divine had become so entwined with male prerogatives. Not shying away from the topic of "phallic worship," Gamble was intent on exploring any religious symbols—even those involving "the organs of generation"—that cast light on the inequitable differentiation of men from women. Hers was another history in which a golden age of maternal fecundity and affection lost out to the eventual deification of male power and pleasure. In presenting women as essentially passionless nurturers and self-giving altruists, free of the brute desires and competitive drives of men, Gamble played more safely with gender norms than Craddock did. That moderation paid off: Unlike Craddock, Gamble got her manuscript on "Sex in Religion" into print. In doing so, Gamble effectively served public notice that phallicism, the favored domain of antiquarians and ethnologists from Knight to Forlong, would no longer serve the social, religious, and erotic imaginations of men only. Women, too, would have their say on the sexual history of religion.[67]

Women's archaeological digging into ancient religion soon received much more academic respect than it had managed in the hands of such amateurs as Craddock and Gamble. Jane Ellen Harrison was a scholar at Cambridge University, one so prominent that Virginia Woolf would conjure up her ghost in *A Room of One's Own*. The peer of the great classicists Francis Cornford and Gilbert Murray, Harrison herself was interested in the ritualistic, festive, and erotic dimensions of Greek religion—a set of concerns that left her open to critique and suspicion. "My interest, I am told, is unduly focused on ghosts, bogies, fetiches, pillar-cults," she observed at a meeting of the Classical Association in 1907. Her peculiar interest in "savage disorders" and "Dionysiac orgies," it was charged, had distracted her from a properly Olympian vantage point, a dispassionate recognition of the stately gods of ancient Greece. Yet, in the next moment, she was defending her self-described heresy, riffing on a visit to Chartres the previous summer during which images of "pillar-cults" and "primitive festivals" had surged "up from my archaeological subconscious" as she was gazing at the north façade. Harrison's account of the earthy fertility of ancient religion was more matriarchal than overtly sexual in inspiration; indeed, any "healthy" religion, she said, would purge itself of "elements exclusively phallic." Harrison, prim by comparison to Craddock, nonetheless discovered in religion's ancient history alternatives to male dominion and social repressiveness.[68]

For the sake of reputation and intellectual solidity, Harrison had the good fortune of winding up on the professional side of the scholarly divide—at Cambridge no less—and did not have to make her way as a local Midwestern suffragist like Gamble or a displaced sex reformer like Craddock. In that academic achievement she stood far apart from freethinking amateurs and served instead more as a British parallel to the American sociologist and folklorist Elsie Clews Parsons, likewise a woman of genteel advantage and learned accomplishment. Earning her PhD from Columbia University in 1899 under the tutelage of Franklin Giddings, a founding father of American social science, Parsons effectively moved between dual roles as feminist critic and empiricist ethnographer. In such books as *Religious Chastity: An Ethnological Study* and *Old-Fashioned Woman: Primitive Fancies about the Sex*, Parsons achieved what Craddock would have liked to accomplish: namely, she combined a scholarly mien with sharp-eyed criticism of the social conventions that hemmed in women in her own culture. All too clearly the distance that separated Craddock, whose admission had been blocked at Penn, from Harrison, whose presence at Cambridge became legendary, and from Parsons, whose fieldwork gained her national acclaim in the academy, was enormous, perhaps unbridgeable. Parsons rose to the presidency of the American Folklore Society in 1919; Craddock, a regular member of that learned society in the 1890s, never made it off the far periphery.[69]

And yet certain threads connected Craddock's amateur endeavors to later professional projects like those of Harrison and Parsons. Not least was the very notion that women should share in the masculine privilege of something "called a 'study'—a place inviolate, guarded by immemorial taboos," as Harrison phrased it in an essay in 1914. "There man thinks, and learns, and knows. . . . Well, that study stands for man's insularity; he wants to be by himself," she suggested, then jabbing: "One of the most ominous signs of the times is that woman is beginning to demand a study." An office was no mere desk and storage area; it was breathing room; it was the spatial marking of intellectual autonomy.[70]

Craddock definitely needed that room to breathe. "The slimy subject of sex," her mother once told her, was not something Ida could work on anywhere in the family's house—at least not as long as Lizzie was "above ground." When Craddock did manage to carve out study spaces for herself, they were invariably small and cramped. One of her offices in Philadelphia, for example, was no more than a converted bathroom with the fixtures removed; another in Chicago was so tiny that she had "no room to spread my papers"; in still another the talking of a chatty roommate often made for "an interruption to the work of quiet, brooding scholarship." To persist in creating intellectual space for herself under such marginal conditions was, in many ways, a feat more remarkable than persevering in the favorable climes of Cambridge or Columbia. Craddock's heap of unpublished materials—"my huge mass of Phallic Worship manuscripts," as she called her would-be book—was certainly a sign of thwarted achievement, but it was also a testimony to a persistent and perhaps even emancipating curiosity. "The scholarly Miss Craddock," always a dangerous amalgam, had remained unfazed by her own oddity—free of shame and reticence in breaching a supremely male preserve of learning. Her flagrancy would become only more conspicuous when she next claimed the mantle of pastor alongside those of freethinker and scholar.[71]

CHAPTER THREE

Pastor of the Church of Yoga

————◦•◦————

LATE NINETEENTH-CENTURY AMERICA, for all its religious diversity, still possessed a distinct Protestant power bloc—one no less commanding for being a denominational patchwork. The "Religious Announcements" section in the *Chicago Tribune* in the 1870s offered one index of that Protestant federation's prominence. An orderly catalog of church services, the announcements closely adhered to the mainstream Protestant map: Episcopal, Baptist, Presbyterian, Methodist, Congregational, and Christian (Disciples of Christ). The *Tribune*, the city's premier daily and a journalistic bastion of both the Republican Party and the Protestant elite, rarely publicized any Roman Catholic services. In a city increasingly dominated by Irish and German immigrants, the paper preferred to minimize that obvious source of competition. Even so, it would not have been particularly hard for the *Tribune* to justify its native Protestant focus without resorting to blatant xenophobia; there were at least five Methodist churches for every Catholic one in Illinois at the time. Throughout the era, the membership of the big six Protestant denominations, taken together, constituted a safe majority among religious adherents in the United States.

Loath to broadcast non-Protestant gatherings, the *Chicago Tribune* nonetheless allowed room at the tail end of its religious announcements for a mixed, yet miniscule "Miscellaneous" category of alternative services. A typical column in July 1874, for example, included a group of spiritualists who were getting together to discuss "The Social Problem" and a band of freethinkers who were congregating to hear (yet again) about "The Life of Thomas Paine." These liberal-minded dissidents, though, were more than counterbalanced in the miscellaneous category itself by a gathering of English Lutherans, another of Seventh-day Adventists, and a tabernacle meeting that featured an itinerant preacher from Kansas. Adding to the prevailing Protestant picture was the hefty and favorable coverage the *Tribune* accorded to the revival campaigns of evangelist Dwight L. Moody, the Billy Graham of his day, then at the height of his national and international fame. Judging by this snapshot from the *Tribune*, a small handful of peripheral upstarts posed little danger to the Protestant center in 1870s America.[1]

Two decades later, all hell was breaking loose. New stand-alone categories—"Jewish," "Spiritualist," and "Christian Scientist"—pushed at the seams, and the *Tribune* simply found it harder and harder to maintain the neat trim of the old Protestant order. Take as one concrete example the "Religious Announcements" for December 17, 1899. At first glance everything looked in good shape for the Christmas season: seventeen listings for Episcopal services, eleven for Methodist, ten for Congregational, nine for Baptist, and nine for Presbyterian. Still placed at the bottom, where it had always been, was the "Miscellaneous" section, but it was now the single largest category by far with forty offerings. A bewildering hodgepodge, it no longer seemed to have functioning Protestant brakes.

A quick review of some of the announced offerings makes apparent how much shakier things looked for the Protestant establishment. At the Second Eclectic Society of Spiritual Culture, a local judge was lecturing on "Infidelity, Belief, Consciousness of Truth," while the famed reformer Jane Addams was speaking on "Democracy and Social Ethics" at the Society of Ethical Culture. The First Society of Rosicrucians, a not-so-secret brotherhood of mystical adepts, was hearing a reflection on "Thought Intuition," while the Church of the Soul was attending to the medium Cora Richmond whose discourse was on "Robert G. Ingersoll in Spirit Life." At the People's Church, meeting at the grand McVicker's

Theater, the Reform rabbi Emil Hirsch and the questing Unitarian Jenkin Lloyd Jones were teaming up for an interfaith service. Swami Abhayananda, a guru from India, was speaking at a local Vedanta society to Hindu initiates and wannabes, and the Independent Church for Students of Nature was hearing from its pastor, aptly named Mrs. Summers. In all, the number of assemblies for sundry liberals and eclectics roughly equaled the combined announcements for the leading Protestant denominations. Even if that count suggested little about the totals for actual members, it certainly revealed the extent of the ferment on the cosmopolitan side of the religious spectrum.[2]

Among the better indications of Chicago's multiplying religious options was another of the small notices under "Miscellaneous" for that same day in December 1899. It read as follows:

Church of Yoga, Mrs. Ida C. Craddock, 11 a.m., Bible talk: "Man and Woman as They Were, as They Are, as They Ought to Be." 3 p.m.: "Object of the Church of Yoga." 80 Dearborn street, fourth floor.

Ida Craddock had mounted her own congregational venture—an endeavor that looked, if anything, even dicier than her labors as corresponding secretary of the American Secular Union and as a public lecturer on sex worship. That foray into religious organizing proved hazardous indeed—and short-lived. By now, six years after the Danse du Ventre blowup, Craddock had a hard time hanging on for long anywhere, but here in Chicago, for a half year or so in late 1899 and early 1900, she attempted to refashion herself as the pastor of her own Church of Yoga. With visiting swamis, prominent New Thought leaders, traveling Buddhist monks, spiritualist mediums, assorted Theosophists, and Bahá'í messengers all offering their religious wares to the city's wandering souls, Craddock dreamed up the Church of Yoga amid a whirl of spiritual variety. Evidence of that heady religious atmosphere came in her announcement of two worship services she was offering one

Sunday in late February 1900: Craddock herself would lecture in the morning on the "Symbolism of the Lamb," and in the afternoon an ostensible priest of the Zoroastrian faith, Rev. Otoman Zar-Adusht Hanish of El-Kharman Temple, Persia, would join her to lecture on "Sun Worship Philosophy."[3]

Craddock's Church of Yoga was a cipher: It never amounted to much as a congregational body, but it nonetheless symbolized a weighty religious trend in American culture. The intricacy of Craddock's spiritual trek—from Methodist holiness to Unitarian individuality right on through spiritualist séances and South Asian traditions—suggested how the evangelical ideal of a Christian America was being subverted, if not coming completely undone. To plot her passage out of Protestant respectability is to track the advance of religious miscellany against the evangelical hope for a redeemed and morally unified nation. In 1874 the prominent Presbyterian minister David Swing had been put on church trial in Chicago to sensational effect for his suspect views on such doctrines as eternal damnation, the Trinity, and justification by faith alone; a quarter century later, the sort of challenge that Swing had posed to Christian orthodoxy looked modest and restrained, if not antiquated. The doctrinal wrangling that had long absorbed Protestant America— all the disputations over what constituted sound evangelical theology— no longer came close to being an adequate measure of religious wayfaring in American culture, all the more in cosmopolitan Chicago. Mixture and medley were undermining the old benchmark of a Christian nation.

"WE FEEL QUITE AT HOME IN OCEAN GROVE," Ida Craddock wrote to her friend Katie Wood in August 1877. Ida and Lizzie had gotten "in the habit of spending a few days there every summer," and in her teenage years at least Ida loved this Methodist enclave on the Jersey Shore, the respite it provided from the stifling, noisome weather of summertime

Philadelphia: "Be it understood, Ocean Grove is a most delightful place," Craddock gushed to Katie in a rare moment of enthusiasm for a vacation taken with her mother. Ida admitted that the "chief attraction" for many attendees, likely Lizzie included, was the prolonged camp meeting, the community's signature event, but she dwelled in her letter to Katie on the appeal of boating, swimming, and fishing—and, "best of all, the grand, restless ocean."[4]

The reputation of Methodist camp meetings gradually shifted after the Civil War from all-out evangelistic fervor—with shouting, clapping, and swooning congregants—to more staid and respectable enterprises, a mix of earnest piety and pleasant recreation. Craddock emphasized the wholesome diversions, the pretty gingerbread cottages, and the sublime setting, but she and her mother nonetheless made themselves comfortable in a community designed to exemplify evangelical holiness. Here even the rolling sea was consecrated to the rhythms of Protestant renewal with evening "Surf-Meetings" that gathered thousands on the beach to sing such favored hymns as "All Hail the Power of Jesus' Name," while the crashing waves "played the accompaniment."[5]

Few places better embodied the blessed assurance of American evangelicals in the 1870s than the seaside camp meeting at Ocean Grove. Founded in 1869 as a modest six-acre encampment by a few Methodist families seeking a salubrious spot for summer worship, Ocean Grove grew over the next decade into a renowned 230-acre holiness retreat, an evangelical alternative to more fashionable and sin-indulging resorts, "a watering-place where the 'Lord God Omnipotent reigneth.'" The town was under the government of a Methodist board that imagined this little piece of the New Jersey shore as a distinct holy land, a modern Eden, a sanctified commune where the faithful could meet "with Jesus by the Sea." No liquor was permitted on the grounds, and the administration enforced strict rules on Sabbath observance.[6]

Ocean Grove's very landscape was designed to make plain the holy purposes of the place. The lake that bordered the town to the north was

SURF MEETING AT OCEAN GROVE.

Beside the sea the wondering people stood,
Or sat, or bowed, devotion's earnest throng ;
The spirit, lost in worship's attitude,
Mingled its praises with the billows' song.

O widening sea, O ever heaving flood,
Here on thy margin, where the surges roar,
Thy people rise to thee, O blessed God,
They weep, they worship, triumph and adore.

E. H. S.

Craddock's early memories of religious participation centered on Ocean Grove, a Methodist camp meeting on the Jersey Shore, which she and her mother visited most summers. E. H. Stokes, ed., Ocean Grove, Its Origin and Progress, as Shown in the Annual Reports Presented by the President *(Philadelphia: Haddock and Son, 1874), frontispiece.*

renamed in honor of John Wesley, the eighteenth-century founder of the Methodist movement, while the lake to the south was rechristened to recognize John Fletcher, one of Wesley's most prominent co-workers, famed in evangelical circles for his experiential piety and holiness. Avenues were named after the itinerant English evangelist George Whitefield and the pioneer American bishop Francis Asbury, and other landmarks reflected the biblical topography of evangelical devotion from Pilgrim Pathway to Beersheba Well to Zion Way. Its creators intended Ocean Grove as a capsule of the evangelical history of redemption, a beacon for the larger consecration of American society. A simple stroll through the grounds was a religious education unto itself.

All those summer days at Ocean Grove notwithstanding, the piety of Methodist holiness did not sink in with Ida. If she were ever attracted to the possibility of deeper evangelical engagement, as her mother would be through the Woman's Christian Temperance Union, few signs of any allure, or even ambivalence, survive: no lament of a missing conversion experience, no lingering dread of hell or Satan, no veneration of Protestant exemplars of holiness and self-denial. Craddock never suffered from wistfulness for the old-time religion; there was no melancholy in her heart for a receding sea of Christian faith. Her interior journey displayed none of the recognized signposts of the evangelical saint's progress to heaven; she walked along Pilgrim Pathway in Ocean Grove more as a summer tourist than an expectant devotee. After describing at some length a sermon she had recently heard, she confessed to her friend Katie, "I suppose these thoughts are all familiar to you,—you seem to know so very much more about the Bible than I do." Day-to-day engagement with God's holy writ was an evangelical hallmark; Craddock never managed it nor did she care much to strive after it. From early on, she had other plans for literary achievement and mastery.[7]

One feature of Methodist devotion did endure with Craddock, however: the ardent piety that focused on Jesus as "the Bridegroom of the Soul." Years later she still remembered singing the hymn, "Jesus, Lover of my Soul, Let me to thy Bosom fly!" at one of these Jersey Shore revival meetings—a gathering organized, in this case, especially for young women and presided over by an evangelist famed for reaching that target audience. "When the enthusiasm flagged," Craddock recalled, "and his hearers were slow in responding to his appeals to 'come to Christ,' [the preacher] started the above hymn, and the ardor of his fair congregation was at once kindled, girl after girl rising to publicly give herself to Christ." Unlike so many of her young companions, though,

Ida had self-consciously resisted the evangelist's invitation to walk the sawdust trail to the altar.[8]

Even as she stood apart from the religious crowd, Craddock readily admitted that the camp-meeting preacher had been onto something in teaching youthful evangelical women "to aspire to the Divine through the symbolism of earthly affection." He had shown a "keen insight into human nature," Craddock concluded; indeed, he had been "instinctively true to the teachings of the innermost truth of all religion," the deep entwining of Eros and Psyche. The gap Craddock saw between herself and evangelical Protestant devotion remained obvious in this memory of Ocean Grove—she was the observer of other girls at the revival meeting, not a yearning participant—and yet "Jesus, Lover of My Soul" stayed with her. No bride of Christ, Craddock had nonetheless gotten a taste of that kind of intimate relationship through being part of a Methodist revival. From the fervent piety of the camp meeting, she well knew the connection between bodily ecstasy and heavenly ascent.[9]

The young Craddock clearly had a hard time connecting with many of her peers at Ocean Grove—with the girls who were keen on receiving Christ as their savior, or who knew their Bible chapter and verse—but she felt much stronger affinities with her classmates at the Quaker school where she studied. Indeed, Craddock often suggested that the strongest spiritual leaven in her early life came not from the Methodists, but the Religious Society of Friends. Though there is no record of her ever being a formal member of a Quaker meeting, Craddock was involved in the Friends' Social Lyceum, a Philadelphia fellowship that pulled her into wider Quaker circles beyond those at her alma mater, Friends' Central.[10]

Quakers were a divided lot in the late nineteenth century, some looking for inspiration from the teachers of evangelical holiness, others emphasizing their orthodox commitment to the old ways of plain dress and strict community discipline. Craddock's Quaker affinities did not depend on either of those factions, but instead on a wing of denominational liberalizers, still known by the antebellum sectarian label of Hicksites. The Hicksite party controlled Friends' Central School and had gained substantial sway within the wider Quaker world in Philadelphia. This segment of the Society of Friends would prove an important inspiration for various religious vagabonds in the period: Walt Whitman, for example, had grown up admiring the preaching of Elias Hicks, the "very mystical and radical" founder of this liberalizing offshoot.[11]

Craddock saw the Hicksite educational milieu at Friends' Central as having left a deep mark on her spiritual character, but, fittingly enough, she rarely described that influence in institutional terms. Instead, her Quaker connection had bequeathed to her a love of direct and spontaneous expression. When, for example, Craddock narrated her own moments of insight in her diary, she sometimes prefaced her account with the phrase: "It was 'borne in upon me,' as the Quakers say," a religious diction of sudden prompting that worked for her far beyond any Friends' meeting. Likewise, in explaining to a freethinking audience in 1891 why she was never bashful about speaking her mind, she returned to the Quaker environment of her youth as a decisive influence:

> Those who know me best, know that I am never "ashamed" of letting any of my opinions, upon any subject whatsoever, be known. I was educated at a Quaker school, where the Quaker principle of "bearing testimony for the truth" permeated the entire moral atmosphere; and at this moment, I know no motto which I would prefer for my inspiration to those splendid words of Lucretia Mott:—"Let us have truth for authority, not authority for truth."

Lucretia Mott, the woman whose words Craddock so admired, was a Hicksite preacher, an abolitionist, an originating advocate of women's rights, and a peace activist. Taking Mott as a paragon spoke volumes about the strand of Quaker piety and politics with which Craddock identified.[12]

Mott was also a good role model for Craddock because of her extensive ties to Unitarian dissenters who talked up the importance of "Free Religion" in the spirit of the National Liberal League and the American Secular Union. Always disclaiming agnosticism and atheism, Craddock would identify, for most of her adult life, as a member of the Spring Garden Unitarian Society—likely, she boasted, the most liberal church in Philadelphia. America's quintessentially heterodox denomination, Unitarianism had initially crystallized in the 1820s and 1830s as the fashionable religion of liberal Boston. Soon it was leavened as well by the Transcendentalist yeasts of Ralph Waldo Emerson, Theodore Parker, and company. Long before the World's Parliament of Religions unfolded in Chicago in 1893, Unitarianism had already established itself as the country's leading broker of a cosmopolitan religious spirit.[13]

Exactly when Craddock joined the Unitarians is unknown, but she was certainly on board by the time she hooked up with Richard Westbrook to run the American Secular Union in 1889. "I am a Liberal Unitarian," Craddock specified in a newspaper report at the time, "with a very well defined belief." It would be easy now to deride this as an oxymoronic claim—a Unitarian with a well-defined belief system?—or a redundant one: a liberal Unitarian, what other kind is there? But Craddock's terse religious identification was nonetheless revealingly specific, for the "Liberal Unitarian" tag signaled a self-conscious withdrawal from Protestant theological conventions, including basic propositions about the divinity of Jesus, scriptural authority, and Original Sin. Unlike the Quaker moniker, this one necessarily meant that she was actively at odds with the world of evangelical devotion. Safe to say, Ocean Grove's Camp Meeting Association was not going to find much common ground with Boston's American Unitarian Association.[14]

For Craddock, the "Liberal Unitarian" affiliation was definitely not a dull, upper-crust Bostonian affair. At the heart of her adopted faith was a spiritual openness and theological elasticity, a consecration of

Frederic A. Hinckley, the pastor of Spring Garden Unitarian Church, led the congregation during much of the time of Craddock's membership. The most liberal wing of the Unitarian movement, for which Hinckley was a prominent spokesman, deeply marked her religious ideas. Unitarian Universalist Minister Files, bMS 1446, Andover-Harvard Theological Library, Harvard Divinity School, Harvard University.

individual liberty, independent thinking, and creative aspiration. Emersonian wayfarers had no need of the Westminster Confession, the Book of Common Prayer, or the sacraments, and, as for the Bible, it was simply another sheaf of literature in a world filled with inspiring poetic visions. As Craddock's own pastor, Frederic A. Hinckley, boldly claimed in a sermon in 1890, liberal Unitarians professed "a religion which says to the Bible, to Savior, to institution, to every form of belief however venerable, to every custom or ceremony however sacred, stand here to be judged by me." Under such free-spirited conditions, churches themselves could still present hearty forms of fellowship, but they had to remain permeable, ready to turn pilgrims loose as much as hold them inside. "Unbiased, unhampered, unrestrained, the mind must be free to think, the heart to feel, the soul to aspire," Hinckley exhorted.[15]

Hinckley and Craddock were obviously an excellent match. As a spiritual guide, he could hardly stop effusing about Emerson's endless seeking or about art's transcendental possibilities: "The Poet-Vision, dear friends, may it be your redeemer and mine." Politically, too, Hinckley made the Spring Garden congregation a good fit for Craddock. A devoted advocate of women's suffrage and a frank proponent of sex reform—including the emancipation of women from "the serfdom of enforced sexual relations" within marriage—Hinckley saw the church as a hub for social and political activism. In the last two decades of the nineteenth century, this Unitarian society's pulpit provided a platform for one reformer after another. Suffragists Susan B. Anthony, Rachel G. Foster, Mary Grew, Mary Livermore, and Anna Shaw all spoke there; Booker T. Washington raised scholarship money for the Tuskegee Institute and lectured on race politics; and representatives of the Knights of Labor gained a supportive hearing. Politically and spiritually, Craddock had found her church home.[16]

Craddock breathed very deeply in the free religious air of liberal Unitarianism. "As to my creed," she confessed in 1890, "I have had to make so many additions at various periods of my life, that I some time ago made up a brand-new garment, big enough to cover every portion of my then known universe, and put in an abundant supply of tucks to be let out as my knowledge of the universe grew taller and broader." No matter how many pleats Craddock later added to her novel religious garb, she continued to count herself part of the Unitarian fold. Even after her Chicago sojourn and her experiment with the Church of Yoga, Craddock kept up her ties to the Spring Garden congregation.[17]

Yet, as Craddock's image of "an abundant supply of tucks" suggested, there was always a lot of slack built into her identity as a liberal Unitarian. She did not join up with that denomination as a way to remain within a nominally Protestant household of faith; instead, it was her portal out of the religious mainstream. If the Hicksite wing of the Society of Friends had provided one potential egress for Craddock, the "Free Religion" of radical Unitarianism offered the principal exit. Craddock had discovered just the right religious community from which to launch into still more eclectic inquiries, a springboard that eventually landed her as the self-appointed pastor of the Church of Yoga.

———•◦•———

IN THE UNITED STATES in the second half of the nineteenth century, séances, mediums, and spirits appeared all over the place: from parlors to theaters to university laboratories to communitarian enclaves to Lincoln's White House. Anyone with a pulse knew about such phenomena; anyone without a pulse had a good chance of soon reappearing as a ghost. Alive or dead, credulous or skeptical, it was well-nigh impossible for Americans to avoid the spectacle of spiritualism after 1850. Sparked by a series of mysterious rappings in Hydesville, New York, in 1848 in which a murdered peddler was said to be communicating through the mediumship of two young sisters, Kate and Margaret Fox, the sensation had spread wildly during the 1850s. Quickly growing into an extensive extra-ecclesial movement, spiritualism cut across the divide of the churched and unchurched, the believing and the doubting. In post–Civil War America, psychical phenomena—from clairvoyance to telepathy to automatic writing—proved endless sources of hopeful affirmation, journalistic exposé, scientific scrutiny, and promotional hype.

It would have required a singular lapse of curiosity for someone with Craddock's inquisitiveness to ignore the cascading reports on these spectral occurrences. Hardly déclassé, such fascinations received the imprimatur of respected researchers and institutions; this was especially so in the 1880s when Craddock was coming into her own intellectually. The Society for Psychical Research at its founding in London in 1882 boasted several Fellows of the Royal Society among its membership, and, when an American branch was formed in 1885, no less a luminary than Harvard's William James played the leading role. To the end of his life James never tired of extolling the scientific importance of the organization's experiments and data collection.

An active interest in séances had also been percolating on Craddock's doorstep in Philadelphia in the early 1880s. In 1883, at the very time Craddock was agitating for her right to matriculate there, the University of Pennsylvania set up a special commission, backed by a sizeable gift from the philanthropist Henry Seybert, for the sole purpose of investigating the claims of modern spiritualism. In gathering their findings for Penn's Board of Trustees, committee members sat in on séances, waited skeptically for the spirits to communicate via table-rapping or slate-writing, watched for mediumistic sleight-of-hand, examined spirit photographs in which ghostly shades ostensibly materialized alongside the living, probed trance-states, and analyzed specimens of automatic writing. When all was said and done in May 1887, the commission issued a highly critical report emphasizing spiritualist fraud, but only after involving several faculty members and the university provost in four years of psychical research.[18]

The possibility of becoming a psychical researcher had exercised a strong pull on Craddock when she first began plotting out her plans for a post-secondary education. "I remember, when I was a schoolgirl of perhaps eighteen, I longed to investigate Spiritualism, and to demonstrate to the world its truth or its falsity, on a scientific basis," she recalled years later in 1894. "I wrote in my diary a schedule of the studies I should like to pursue—classical, scientific and medical—up to the age of thirty-five, when I felt I would be sufficiently mature to investigate and pronounce upon the phenomena with authority." That late-teen ambition, she claimed, had been an important part of why she had deemed a university education so imperative in the first place, but, with her path to Penn blocked, "the stress and turmoil of business life"—including all her shorthand teaching at Girard College—left no time for her to pursue this "youthful dream" of becoming a psychical researcher. Even so, she still paid at least intermittent attention to those kinds of inquiries throughout the 1880s, reading books on clairvoyance and perusing the publications of the Society for Psychical Research, which offered the flagship *Proceedings* in this area of inquiry.[19]

Psychical phenomena continued to pique Craddock's curiosity even as she turned toward secular activism. During her years as corresponding secretary of the American Secular Union, Craddock consistently approached spiritualist matters with the mind of a psychical researcher: curious, skeptical, theorizing, and empiricist. "I had no interest whatsoever, at that time, in the world beyond the grave," she insisted. Her concern was all about explaining paranormal occurrences without recourse to spirits, including testing out pet theories of the day like telepathy or thought-transference, a signature pursuit of the Society for Psychical Research. In one typical gesture, Craddock looked to the new technology of the phonograph as a way of possibly explaining the phenomena associated with haunted houses, another prime topic for ghost-hunting investigators. Wanting to do away with the notion of any phantom presences, Craddock speculated on the possibility that sounds could be impressed upon building materials in a way analogous to Edison's vibrational indentations on tin-foil sheets. That was not exactly a *tour de force* explanation, but it did suggest that a spiritualist victory was far from a predetermined outcome in Craddock's life—neither in this particular guesswork on haunted houses nor in her larger metaphysics.[20]

The majority of psychical researchers were, on principle, doubters as much as believers, and Craddock's phonographic reasoning was an example of that skeptical, yet open-minded posture. Much of the phenomena associated with spiritualism seemed designed, William James wrote in a final estimate of his twenty-five years of involvement in psychical research, "to prompt our curiosities and hopes and suspicions all in equal measure." It was in this intellectual space between explanation and corroboration that psychical researchers moved—and Craddock moved with them, half-hopeful, half-disbelieving, but always curious.[21]

In the heady mix of religious influences that swirled around Craddock, spiritualism and psychical research were especially pronounced. The Ouija board, a newly patented device, was the initial vehicle of her curiosity. Borderland 1 (1893–1894): 207.

The three years following her departure from the American Secular Union in the autumn of 1891 proved decisive in Craddock's religious development: In brief, she gradually moved from the avowed stance of a psychical researcher to the "desired goal" of becoming "an all-around medium." Of all things, the Ouija board was the first step in that transition. If that spirit-writing plank looks now to be little more than a clichéd parlor game—Parker Brothers, after all, holds the trademark— it was a novelty in 1891, a recently patented device poised between popular entertainment and experimental demonstration. The search for mechanical instruments that would facilitate communication with the ghostly realm was a constant among spiritualists, devotees and dabblers alike. That quest produced recurrent metaphysical reflections on the latest inventions from the telegraph to the telephone and engendered various tools (and toys) to turn such airy speculations into household practice. One of the first entries was the planchette, a small board that rolled on casters and had a pencil affixed to the end. Lightly controlled by the medium's hand, it was offered as a way for spirits to communicate messages more efficiently than through the prevailing form of table-tapping. Other spirit-writing machines—"psychographs," "pantographs," and various "talking boards"—were soon invented, and they were invariably offered up with the combined fanfare of eerie mystery, technological marvel, and scientific breakthrough.[22]

Craddock had apparently resisted the lure of spiritual-*cum*-scientific instruments hitherto, but the Ouija board managed to catch her eye as the latest experimental sensation. The teardrop pointer, quivering from one letter to the next as inquirers laid their fingertips on the board, seemed uncanny in its power to spell out messages or offer "yes" and "no" answers. As one reporter raved about this "new spiritualistic device" in 1892, "The board seems to grow electric, and questions are answered, and advice and information given with head-swimming, brain-turning dispatch. It is certainly a very wonderful performance, and one which I am totally unable to account for. Scientific experiments are now being made with Ouija in Paris, and I am informed that the results so far promise well." With that kind of journalistic coverage as advertisement, it is not hard to see why the Ouija board attracted Craddock, a psychical researcher manqué.[23]

The transformative effect of Craddock's encounter with this spiritualist instrument would have been harder to predict: "Little by little, as I experimented [with the Ouija board]," she testified, "I saw that an unseen intelligence outside of myself was moving the board." Soon she "graduated" to experiments with other spirit-writing machines and also to efforts at automatic writing as she attempted to receive impressions from these ethereal powers and to materialize fragmentary messages from these invisible realms upon a page of paper. The Ouija board had cracked open the spiritualist door for Craddock, and from there she moved from one mediumistic method to another, testing each of them as well as her own new-found capacities to commune with "these unseen intelligences." The psychical research that had long possessed Craddock's part-skeptical, part-enthralled curiosity had suddenly switched gears. It was now in the realm of the all too real.[24]

Craddock focused her sights on the mysteries of mediumship with characteristic intensity. Spiritualists had a vast repertoire for communing with unseen entities, and Craddock wanted to pursue the full range of communicative possibilities with all due diligence. Whatever visionary gifts she ended up possessing she developed through experiment, practice, and discipline, not unrehearsed inspiration. Crystal gazing worked for some, trance speaking for others, but neither did for Craddock. Likewise, automatic writing proved anything but automatic for her, so she started working next on clairaudience, on listening quietly for an inward voice that was separable from her individual subjectivity.

After considerable effort, Craddock was able to discern a voice speaking to her from beyond the margins of her own consciousness. As she reported, "This at length, to my surprise, came by what, I have since read, St. Teresa was wont to term 'the interior voice.' . . . St. Teresa says that although, at first, one's own subjective self may be mistaken for the outside intelligence which speaks through the 'interior voice,' yet, after one has had a little experience, it [becomes] easy not to confound the two. And so I have found it to be." Craddock never saw herself, of course, as a Christian mystic, but, like most other spiritualists, she took her spiritual guides from diverse corners, from a mystical "gallery of borderlanders." St. Teresa's discernment of the divine voice, along with her devotion to the heavenly bridegroom, made her a good source for amplifying the significance of the inner conversation that Craddock had started cultivating.[25]

The voices that Craddock began hearing came mostly from her own immediate past. Jesus was never among the interior presences that Craddock experienced nor did the Holy Spirit ever take over her vocal chords in a Pentecostal effusion of tongues. Rather, the voices represented a more proximate, less exalted band of spirits. Her father, vendor of teas and patent medicines, dead since Ida's infancy, spoke to her "from the world beyond the grave," and so did her sister, Nana, who had "passed over" as a baby before Ida was born. Now all grown up to "womanhood" on the other side, Nana was ready to be the sibling companion that Ida had never had. Then there was her sister's spirit husband, Iases, a wise "Brahmin" who was to become Craddock's enlightened guide and "chief trainer." Even if Iases represented an exotic new personage in her life, Craddock had managed to make him part of the family, her own close-knit clan of intermediaries.[26]

The family soon had another member as well—and the most influential of all on the course of Craddock's life. From out of this shadowy world of ghostly presences emerged the voice of a young man whom Craddock had first met "when I was little over seventeen." A callow businessman a few years older than Ida, he had made a bashful attempt at courtship. "He fell in love with me, and wanted to marry me," she recalled, "but I turned a cold shoulder to him as a lover, although I liked him immensely as a friend and companion." A few years later the young man had died, and Craddock had carried on with her own independent plans for success. But, his affections apparently left a deeper mark on her psyche than Ida's cool dismissal implied. Now about fifteen years later, he had reemerged as an angelic persona through Craddock's mediumistic experiments. Never revealing his actual given name, Ida referred to him only by his new spiritual appellation, Soph, which derived, she duly noted, from the Greek word for wisdom and shrewdness. This clairaudient reconnection would change everything about Craddock's spiritualist experience—and lastingly so. The whole tenor shifted to the renewal—and consummation—of a teenage romance that Craddock herself had nipped in the bud. Like her sister Nana, Ida too would have a spirit husband, but unlike Nana's posthumous nuptials, Ida would join her partner on this side of the grave.[27]

It was only in the wake of the Danse du Ventre episode in late 1893 that Craddock let the news slip of this revived relationship with Soph. That disclosure, she quickly realized, did her no favors, and thereafter she usually tried to keep her mystical marriage to the side—an affair of diary-keeping, not public explanation. The revelation nonetheless proved impossible to retract (or forget), and her sanity was henceforward disputed just about everywhere she went. That diagnostic entanglement eventually included, as will become evident by the end of this story, a sustained psychoanalytic reading of her fantasized love life. At this point, though, seen within the immediate context of her wider spiritualist connections—to her father, sister, and brother-in-law—her angelic romance looked like another lonesome grasping after the departed. Lost love and unfulfilled intimacy constituted Craddock's initial communion of saints. Stuck in an often-hostile real-world relationship with her mother, Craddock turned elsewhere for nurturance and support. These dear spirits, Craddock remarked, "are my real family."[28]

CRADDOCK'S SPIRITUALISM DEVELOPED rapidly after 1892, but that did not mean her mediumistic efforts took over her life. Rule number one that Craddock learned from her new spirit companions was this: "Do your daily earthly duty, undeterred by calls to mediumship, from whatever source." And she invariably heeded that advice: Even as she experimented by night with new psychical methods, she kept up her day job at Girard College, wrote another textbook on shorthand, and trained her scholarly attention on the history of phallic worship and its relation to marriage reform. The latter interests were the ones that led her back into the public eye in late 1893 and early 1894 as a lecturer on ancient sex worship. When she courted such high-profile radicals as Moses Harman, Edward Bond Foote, Voltairine de Cleyre, and Edwin C. Walker, she was doing so primarily as an up-and-coming marriage reformer and would-be scholar, not as a spiritualist mystic.[29]

The balance between Craddock's freethinking and spiritualist interests shifted in 1894 when her efforts from the previous summer to defend the Danse du Ventre caught up with her. Early that year she had received her first official warning from postal inspectors: Her *Danse du Ventre* essay was declared unmailable under the terms of Comstock's anti-obscenity laws, and she thus felt compelled to back away from an invitation for its more formal publication and dissemination. That legal notice triggered her alarm, but even more so her mother's—a combination of genuine maternal concern for her daughter's well-being along with a sizeable dose of social embarrassment over her only child having gone public as an exponent of both heathenism and female sexual expression.

All of these developments—lecturing on the history of phallic antiquities, publicizing the spiritual value of belly dancing, announcing a mission for marriage reform, cultivating mediumistic relationships with a band of spirits (including Soph), and receiving admonition from Comstock's local agents—made Craddock's mother crazy with worry, anger, and shame. "Poor Mother!" Craddock acknowledged. "It must be awfully hard [times] for her, I feel sure. She would so like to have me conventional, and I can't be, in the way she wishes." This mother-daughter impasse, already familiar from years of disagreement, was rapidly intensifying, and now Lizzie's "inborn love of domination"—as Ida saw her protectiveness—took an incarcerating turn. By early February 1894, right when Ida was lecturing in New York on sex worship, Lizzie had decided it was time to try a mental asylum as a necessary remedy for her daughter's disturbing behavior and as an antidote for her own parental distress.[30]

Knowing Ida would not assent to institutionalization of her own accord, Lizzie determined to commit her involuntarily. When Craddock discovered her mother's plot of abduction, she quickly arranged to flee the country for London. In making that escape, Craddock was introduced to a much wider world of occult inquiry. It was the beginning of the next stage of her spiritual education.

Craddock eluded capture through a stroke of good fortune and uncanny connection. Namely, she met an important benefactor in the famed British social reformer William T. Stead, editor of the *Pall Mall Gazette* and the *Review of Reviews*. Stead had come to Chicago in late 1893 just as the World's Fair was closing and had quickly seen through the city's utopian civic fantasies. Turning his sights upon the nightmarish underside of this urban dream, he had analyzed the city's poverty, vice, and corruption in painstaking detail in *If Christ Came to Chicago!* (1894), a prophetic exposé that helped energize American progressives. Reimagining the Christian church as "the Union of all who Love in the Service of all who Suffer," Stead's hot-selling critique had anticipated the popularity of Charles Sheldon's *In His Steps* (1897), a work that carried the enduring refrain of "What would Jesus do?" (should he happen to arrive in Topeka, Kansas, and confront its social ills). Stead's scathing reproof of Chicago was clearly the headline of his trip, but, on his return to New York to catch a steamer back to England in early March 1894, he stopped in Philadelphia and offered his "snap-shot" commentary on that city as well to obliging reporters.[31]

William T. Stead, the British editor of the Pall Mall Gazette *and* Borderland, *became Craddock's chief patron and protector. He offered her a job in London in 1894, provided funds to support her research, and backed her legal defense at various points in her battles with obscenity charges.* Borderland *1 (1893–1894): frontispiece.*

During this short stay in Philadelphia, Stead somehow met Craddock through a fellow editor who had once employed her as a secretary, and the two quickly fell into league with one another. Feeling the heat from both the postal inspectors and her mother's own "detectives," Craddock hoped Stead would take an interest in her case and "enable me to fight for my liberty." The ever-crusading Stead, a minister's son who relished lending his support to offbeat religious inquirers and forlorn political radicals, embraced the opportunity. A long-time champion of Annie Besant, the pastor's wife turned freethinking socialist turned leading Theosophist, Stead had just added a new journal to his editorial range, *Borderland*, a popular periodical devoted entirely to spiritualist and occult matters. Craddock was precisely the kind of religious wayfarer Stead had come to favor through his own experiments with automatic writing; in 1892, he had actually begun receiving epistolary messages from the ghost of an American journalist, Julia Ames, and happily advertised his new-found spiritual contact—along with his day-to-day telepathic connection to his coeditor at *Borderland*. Clearly, this was a fortuitous crossing of paths, and it turned out to be of lasting consequence for her and to him. Not a woman who ever caught many breaks in career development, Craddock had suddenly found a very influential new patron.[32]

Stead quickly determined that he did not want to help fight Craddock's battle on the ground in Philadelphia. He had neither the time nor the inclination for that; he already had a full plate of social causes and knew too that Craddock had backed herself into a corner on this one. He told her that she "must get out of the whole thing":

> He offered to take me over to England for a year, and give me work as his amanuensis, on a certain salary—small, but sufficient to live decently on. He said that I should have a year's breathing-time, and opportunity to study at the British Museum to see what could be said for or against my theories. But I must promise him not to say anything

about [the Danse du Ventre]. . . . And I must change my name, for I had become too well known as the writer of that essay, and he could not afford to be mixed up with me.

Taking up work for a journalistic crusader who was wary of being openly associated with her rightly raised some apprehensions, and Craddock specifically bristled at the idea of adopting an alias and becoming a clandestine operator in one of Stead's London offices. He insisted, however, and her desire to escape confinement in an insane asylum was at this moment paramount. So, Craddock sailed for England as Mrs. Irene Sophia Roberts with her books, desk, and typewriter as freight, under contract to be a free-floating researcher for Stead, a highly acclaimed editor with a mixed reputation for both radical daring and spiritualist credulity.[33]

Philadelphia was a city with a rich history of religious innovators, but the spiritual possibilities that Craddock found in London were on another order of magnitude. Settling into office work for Stead's magazine *Borderland* in April 1894, Craddock moved back and forth between her various scholarly projects and her occult training. She did not forget her plea for sex reform—her mission to preach "the gospel of the artistic and the divine in sex"—but she kept her word with Stead to maintain a low profile.[34]

Craddock redefined herself as soon as she reached the shores of England—both to appease her newfound protector and to safeguard her own identity in case her mother came looking for her. She decided, for example, "to haul down my flag of dress reform," a cause that she had long supported and upon which she had editorialized in the Philadelphia press as materially important to women's freedom. With reluctance, but for the sake of her disguise, she put aside "my beloved short dresses" and appeared only "in conventional English attire, quiet and inconspicuous." She continued to work in private on her mediumistic abilities through crystal gazing, automatic writing, and meditative visualization. She even adopted a home-based gymnastics regimen in service of her own fantasy of levitation—a feat that the celebrated British medium and one-time Anglican minister, William Stainton Moses, had reported achieving some years earlier. Craddock invoked Moses, a canonized figure in psychical-research circles, as an inspiration for her own efforts to levitate.[35]

Craddock's exile was a boon as well for her scholarly pursuits. Even as she was slinking about in hiding, she secured Stead's endorsement to apply—under the alias of Irene Sophia Roberts—for a reader's ticket at the British Museum and began studying, among other things, the history of witchcraft. Comparing the persecution of witches to her own recent brush with an insane asylum, she concluded: "The punishment of witchcraft has not yet died out, only that now, instead of burning witches at the stake, they point at them as 'mad.'" What relief the British Library's grand rotunda must have offered Craddock, the brisk air of intellectual liberty after having been almost suffocated in a mental ward in Philadelphia.[36]

Just as important as the British Library for Craddock's studies was the editorial headquarters of Stead's *Borderland*, an esoteric laboratory in its own right. Another of Stead's protégés, Ada Goodrich Freer, presided over that office, and Craddock became, for a time at least, her private secretary, once again putting her typing and shorthand skills to work for a cause in which she believed. Born in the same year as Craddock, Freer was also a highly inventive inquirer, an amateur folklorist of the Scottish Highlands and Hebrides, and a captivating seer who had been a significant contributor to the Society for Psychical Research before moving on to Stead's new journal. Craddock, not surprisingly, immediately connected with Freer, who, in a fine bit of symmetry, was also working for Stead under a pseudonym, Miss X.

Through Freer (a.k.a. Miss X), Craddock (a.k.a. Mrs. Roberts) had a good entry into London's vibrant occultist subculture. The *Borderland* workplace also sported its own extensive library with everything from the *Astrologers' Magazine* to *Zoë's Lessons on Scientific Palmistry*, and Craddock, ever the bibliophile, sunk herself into those holdings. As she summed up her first six months abroad, "I have learned more from [the] *Borderland* library . . . and from Miss X and the various books of the S.P.R. and other occult works while in London, than I could have learned in five years at home. I have dipped into Theosophy, Mysticism, Faith Cure, Christian Science, Hypnotism, Crystal Gazing, Telepathy, *et al.*, and I have learned to recognize *The Power of Thought* which is their underlying great principle. It has been a wonderful training. . . . I could not have chosen one spot in the world where I could have been so helped in my studies." All too clearly Craddock's spiritual tramping had hit its stride in London.[37]

What exactly Craddock was training for in her studies still remained unclear. She sampled London's Theosophical Society, an archetypal circle of religious eclectics and seekers, but she never had much faith in that group's founding seer, Madame Blavatsky. Finding the Theosophical Society to be too hierarchical and authoritarian—"the Roman Catholic Church of Occultism," Craddock called it—she quickly got her back up: "I don't propose to be led by the nose, even by a Mahatma." Instead, she held close to the first principle of her liberal Unitarianism, "the soul's right to individuality," and imagined life beyond the grave as wholly consonant with her idealized vision of creativity, freedom, and opportunity. In the spirit world, Craddock observed, "originality and independence of life are honored and esteemed," and "all of us eccentric folks" are spared the ostracism of "a world set in ancient grooves." In that realm women earned their own livings, wore what they wanted without being counted immodest, and did not "have to bother about cooking." In her day-to-day explorations of these spiritual borderlands, Craddock found transcendent support for her nonconformity as well as mundane reassurances about a fairer and easier world to come.[38]

Having turned aside from the Theosophical Society a few months into her London studies, Craddock also began to question her goal of becoming an all-around medium. Given her overriding desire for self-determination in matters religious as much as social, she increasingly suspected that this role was too passive for her to assume: Was not the medium little more than a mouthpiece "blindly obeying the behests of the spirits"? Prevailing notions of selflessness, whether as an ideal of Christian devotion or of Victorian womanhood, were anathema to her. The vice of degrading submission, Craddock insisted, all too frequently masqueraded as the virtue of humble self-denial: "I have always hated the very idea of unselfishness and self-sacrifice. I think they are sinful." So it was that she began to depict her training in terms of becoming a "self-controlled psychic" or "an active, willing occultist" rather than a compliant channel. Spirit possession—being the recording secretary for wiser angelic controls—continued to entice her, but self-possession— embodied through the disciplined power of her own mind—now balanced that attraction.[39]

The hinge for Craddock's swing in religious perspective was the New Thought movement, the mind-over-matter fount out of which emerged a vast array of mental healers from Mary Baker Eddy, leader of Christian Science, to Ralph Waldo Trine, best-selling author of *In Tune with the Infinite*. Whether in Boston, Chicago, or Denver, the movement was a wellspring of religious innovation, especially providing the occasion and opportunity for a host of late nineteenth-century women to create independent ministries. As such enterprises proliferated, the techniques of mental healing, calm repose, and abundant self-fulfillment became an almost fad-like vogue.

Craddock spent significant time with a New Thought teacher for the first time during her sojourn in London: Alma Gillen, an expositor of an offshoot called Divine Science and editor of *Expression: A Journal of Mind and Thought*. Like her more famous contemporary Ella Wheeler Wilcox, Gillen was a poet of the new gospel of mental affirmations and triumphant healings. Her enterprise was a British outpost of a ministry with predominantly American roots; almost all of the teachers with whom she allied herself were across the pond, including Malinda Cramer, a founder of Divine Science in San Francisco and editor of *Harmony*, and Helen Wilmans, a mental-science healer with the ambition to build a metaphysical university in Sea Breeze, Florida. Connecting with Gillen by midway in her fifteen-month stay in London, Craddock frequently met with her to discuss New Thought metaphysics. She explored the possibility of building up "my teaching of marital reform on her foundation principles" and experimented with mantra-like affirmations. "I am love, wisdom and power," Craddock dutifully intoned over and over again after one meeting. "I am spirit; the physical is under my control. I am part of God."[40]

New Thought teachers were created from New Thought students, and, not surprisingly, Gillen soon saw in Craddock the makings of a minister of Divine Science. Predictably, though, her American pupil did not stay on course for long. "You know I don't accept *all* your teachings at present," Craddock wrote Gillen in May 1895 as her time working for Stead was beginning to wind down, "but those which I do accept are opening up truth to me." If Craddock really was going to become a self-willing occultist rather than a passive medium, she could hardly turn around and become a satellite expounder of someone else's system.[41]

More interested in starting with "the world of sense" than with "the plane of the spirit," Craddock remained leery of much of "Mrs. Gillen's mysticism." On the one hand, the power of the concentrated mind to help the individual transcend everyday frustrations and rise above limiting social circumstances—that Divine Science affirmation exercised an obvious appeal to Craddock. On the other hand, recited refrains that thoroughly subordinated the body to the mind seemed perfectly designed to leave her cold. (Not that Gillen was without a sensual side—that certainly came out in her poetry. Gillen's verses positively dripped with images of soulful wooing, ardent longing, and blissful kisses. Perhaps it was there that Craddock and Gillen discovered their mutual affinity, their shared passion for passion. As Gillen put it in one of her poems, she was "in love with Love," and surely Craddock was too.) The New Thought movement was another important wayside for Craddock, but the mind-over-body core of it—the very focus on mental healing— never quite gripped her. Even after months of inquiry in London, Craddock remained a seeker on her way to somewhere else.[42]

After a little more than a year abroad, Craddock returned to the United States, well prepared, as she saw it, for "much more satisfactory occult work." Having had the opportunity to drink "unlimited draughts" from Britain's "fountains of occult wisdom," she had come to see her vocation in broadened religious terms. "It does really seem to me as tho' I *must* be intended for important work in occultism," she remarked while still in London. "I do earnestly hope and pray that the time may come when I shall be allowed to squeeze out this ingathered wisdom over the parched Materialistic life in my own country." If given that chance, what role would she choose to play—spiritualist medium, self-willing magus, minister of Divine Science, or some new part altogether? When she got back to Philadelphia in the summer of 1895, the path she would take as both sex radical and religious innovator remained unpredictable, but that the two roles would be inextricably combined had become increasingly evident. She would not be able to peddle her ideas about sexuality without promoting her ideas about religion as well.[43]

———·•·———

CRADDOCK'S YEAR-PLUS ABSENCE from the United States removed none of the problems that had driven her away in the first place. For the time being her mother had stopped trying to get her institutionalized, but Lizzie remained dead set against her daughter's marriage-reform work and stood ready to obstruct it. And as long as Craddock kept her old Danse du Ventre essay under wraps, the postal authorities would leave her alone—but then when she proceeded to produce a couple of new pamphlets offering advice to newlyweds, that truce was immediately called off. On the Monday after Thanksgiving in 1896,

Philadelphia's Post Office Inspector, General Warren P. Edgerton, put her on renewed legal notice, warning her that "no pamphlet which describes the sexual act, no matter how refined the language, nor how high the motives from which it is written, can lawfully go through the mails." In order to maintain some financial viability as she contemplated her next steps as a sex reformer, Craddock had tried hard to settle into a conventional secretarial job in the Bureau of Highways at City Hall. That position, however, fell apart in November 1897 when a coworker discovered a fragment from one of her typescripts about improving marital relations and handed the sheet over to her boss. Professing shock, anger, and disgust, he canned her after eighteen months of otherwise competent labor.[44]

Just as Craddock had hoped to serve unobtrusively as a stenographer at City Hall, she had also continued, tactfully enough, to cultivate some of her more judicious religious associations. She maintained her old ties to the Spring Garden Unitarian Society and followed up on her connection with Alma Gillen's Divine Science by joining a local group of women who had formed "a little society of 'Truth Students'" to explore New Thought teachings. She attempted as well a more respectable piece of religious writing, publishing a small book on *The Heaven of the Bible* with J. B. Lippincott in 1897. The book appeared a tame effort for a woman of Craddock's broader religious interests. It strung together scriptural passages in order to deduce what heaven was really like, the very substantiality of it—from the topography, architecture, and clothing to the industrial and municipal arrangements. In many ways *The Heaven of the Bible* looked comfortably apiece with wider Victorian efforts to domesticate heaven, to decorate the celestial parlor with lacework and flowers. For a moment at least Craddock seemed like she might be ready to curb her appetite for controversy.[45]

If her little book on heaven had a subversive streak, it was the way that Craddock used the concreteness of biblical testimony to advance her own ideas about the physicality of the spiritual world. Operating within the confines of scriptural literalism—clearly, a ploy for someone with a freethinking curriculum up her sleeve—she could then slip in her views on marriage and sexuality under the cloak of biblical allusion. She suggested, for example, that the angels of God "are by no means sexless" and are "as desirous as earthly men" to enter into marital relations. She proceeded to cite passages from the sixth chapter of Genesis and one of Paul's epistles to make her point. Perhaps Craddock thought she could housebreak her spiritual curiosities—or, at least remove some of their threat—by simply reminding Christians that the Bible's heaven was anything but purely ethereal. If the very literalism of her book was a cover, that ruse was lost on most reviewers. The book fell flat, not attracting enough notice to affect public perception of her work as a marriage reformer one way or another. Deemed a mere "curiosity" by the *Literary World* and receiving bare mention in *Outlook* as "an interesting little volume," it received full and favorable treatment only in Stead's *Borderland*. The consolation of this literary letdown: At least, *The Heaven of the Bible* did not add to Craddock's legal troubles. The book was never banned from the mails.[46]

Prudence and inconspicuousness did not suit Craddock in her spiritual life any more than in her literary endeavors. As a liberal Unitarian, a New Thought minister, or a spiritualist medium, she could have positioned herself quite to the left of center and still remained within the recognizable miscellany of American religious life. The twist that placed her among the alien and the exotic was when she started imagining herself as more in line with "Oriental psychics" than "Occidental mediums." Specifically, it was an enduring infatuation with India that called her short-lived Church of Yoga into being—a fantasy that she shared with many other occultists, mystics, and reformers of the era.[47]

Craddock's enthrallment with South Asia took many forms. She imagined that her spirit guide (and brother-in-law) Iases, a Brahmin from India, was training her "in conformity with the yogic life lived by the Oriental yogis." Less fabulously perhaps, she dreamed of becoming a student of the Buddhist monk Anagarika Dharmapala, a well-traveled guru, who had made a compelling appearance at the World's Parliament of Religions in 1893. She corresponded with him and entertained high hopes that he would "open the way for me in India"; Dharmapala's eyes, she claimed in underlining her attraction, were "good and clear," and he possessed "a spiritual face, possibly the face of a mystic." Craddock pined as well for a new technological gadget to take with her to India to enhance her "folklore work," a Kodak with which she could photograph "the ceremonies in temples." While she had to admit that her hope of actually traveling there for yogic training or folklore study felt more like "a romance" than "a possible reality," that hardly stopped her from endless daydreaming of India.[48]

Craddock's romance with India had far less to do with the religions and peoples of Britain's distant colonial domain than it did with her desire to escape the stifling strictures of her own society. While Christian missionaries often imagined the heathen as sexually depraved and dangerously libidinous, Craddock and a vanguard of fellow occultists fantasized an India of erotic wisdom and consecrated intercourse. In both cases the Orient was a screen for sexual projections, but what was Original Sin for one became primordial purity in the other. As Craddock observed, India "is a nation whose religions, for the most part, recognize the truth that sex is holy; and in this it is in strong contrast with our Western 'civilization' where the most sacred function of humanity is looked upon as vile. We occidentals have a whole life's teaching to unlearn."[49]

Craddock's elevated view of Hindu and Buddhist teachings clearly derived more from her disenchantment with American sexual politics than it did from any first-hand experience with the religious practices of India. Sometimes she came close to acknowledging as much; not long after Philadelphia's postal inspector had reissued his warning in late 1896, she felt like she was "being gradually closed in"—"stifled, gagged,

Anagarika Dharmapala, a Buddhist monk from Ceylon (now Sri Lanka) who had taken part in the World's Parliament of Religions in 1893, especially inspired Craddock. She dreamed of going abroad to study mysticism with him. John Henry Barrows, ed., The World's Parliament of Religions, *2 vols. (Chicago: Parliament Publishing, 1893), 2: 860.*

prevented from preaching"—and so again she turned in her imagination to India. "Sometimes," she confided in a diary entry that December, "I think I will try to get to India, where the sexual relation is not universally abhorred as something nasty, but is reverenced by the wisest of Brahmins as pure."[50]

Not that Craddock's vision of India and Oriental yogis arose entirely from her fertile imagination. She was well aware of Swami Vivekananda's mission to America, his triumphal visit to the World's Parliament of Religions in 1893, and his published expositions of Vedanta philosophy. Prior to announcing herself pastor of the Church of Yoga in Chicago in late 1899, she had familiarized herself with his work on *Râja-Yoga: Or, Conquering the Internal Nature* (1896), a manual of Hindu spiritual disciplines, yogic methods of purifying mind and body. Vivekananda had delivered his lectures on Râja-Yoga during his American sojourn to large classes in New York City in 1895 and 1896, but Craddock had not been able to attend any of them. "I have never had the pleasure of meeting that cultured and highly gifted man," she noted with regret. With yoga, as in most matters, books were her guru.[51]

The inspiration that *Râja-Yoga* provided Craddock was indirect more than explicit. Vivekananda's meditative techniques certainly meshed well with the New Thought forms of mental concentration that Craddock had imbibed through Gillen's Divine Science. The swami well knew that a large part of his success in reaching American audiences in the mid-1890s was the wider ascendancy of such mind-over-matter teachings: How else was he to interest Americans in sitting still for a half hour each day in an erect posture, while concentrating the mind through repeating a mantra as they methodically inhaled and exhaled?

While the swami's emphasis on focused meditation connected nicely with Craddock's New Thought leanings, his body talk was hardly conducive to her sex-reform gospel. A proponent of chastity and renunciation, Vivekananda characterized his relationship to women in desexualized, child-like terms and consistently glossed over the eroticized

Swami Vivekananda, a Hindu representative at the World's Parliament, introduced various forms of yoga to American audiences. Craddock had studied his Râja-Yoga but found her main inspiration for claiming the yogic mantle in the hand-to-hand circulation of a Tantric treatise. Eliot Bahá'í Archives, Eliot, Maine.

mysticism of his own sainted guru, Ramakrishna, in favor of a more abstractly universalistic philosophy. In many ways Vivekananda actually stood as something of a Comstockian censor of Hindu traditions, hiding the bodily concerns and anxieties of his own teacher behind a veil of pure spirituality.[52] That meditative version of yoga—no body-twisting postures, no openly erotic content—certainly helped Vivekananda make his Vedanta Society a relatively palatable offering in the American religious marketplace. More than any other figure, Vivekananda gave yoga its initial cachet among spiritual seekers and made it an identifiable idiom in the American religious vernacular. That cultural recognition clearly played an important part in Craddock's decision to label her own enterprise the Church of Yoga. Aside from that particular marker, however, she showed no sign of connecting deeply with any of Vivekananda's published lectures on the subject, whether Râja Yoga or other forms.

Craddock's disengagement from Vivekananda's bodily asceticism was starkly revealed in one steamy and impetuous episode that she reported in her diary in September 1899 around the very time she was starting up her Chicago-based congregation. Propping herself up with pillows on her bed one night to read a chapter of Vivekananda's *Râja-Yoga*, she "gradually nodded over it and drowsed off, woke, and drowsed again, and woke again, bracing myself with a determined attempt to finish that chapter before I again fell asleep, or perish in the attempt." Her self-discipline did not work—or, at least, it did not work as planned. As Craddock dutifully pushed herself to sustain attention on her reading, her mind drifted away to thoughts of Soph, her spirit husband, and marital intimacies with him. Dreamily imagining his head nestled "in the hollow of my shoulder, just above my bosom," she gave up on reading anymore of Vivekananda's book that night. Lapsing further and further into erotic fantasy, she soon lost "control of myself, or, rather of my passion." Craddock was perfectly willing to follow Vivekananda's advice—that is, to "turn the light of the mind backward and inward to explore the recesses of itself." It was just that when she went into those depths she found not "austerity," "self-surrender," "restraint of the senses," and "superconsciousness," but "a thrilling sexual struggle" of mad desires, satisfying fantasies, and phantom feelings. Like other far more famous moderns and bohemians, she was ripping away the mask of female desirelessness—and she was leaving herself dangerously exposed in the process.[53]

Safe to say, Craddock's Church of Yoga was not merely a homegrown offshoot of Swami Vivekananda's Vedanta philosophy, an idiosyncratic variant on the sundry societies that were sprouting up around the country to promote his teachings and meditative practices. She was not looking for venerable methods for subjugating the body, overcoming desire, and forgetting individuality. If the "pernicious doctrines of celibacy and asceticism" were all Vivekananda and his fellow Hindu teachers had to offer, then Craddock was not interested. Instead, she took her cues from other sources that cast India as a sanctuary for the erotic. Foremost among this reading was her old favorite: the literature on the history of sex worship and the ancient devotion to fertility. "India, beyond all other countries on the face of the earth, is preeminently the home of the worship of the Phallus," so began Hargrave Jennings's *Phallic Miscellanies* (1891) in typical fashion. "It has been so for ages and remains so still."[54]

Never mind that Craddock did not agree with Vivekananda's teachings about celibacy and asceticism—she did not believe that he agreed with them himself. She suspected the swami and his associates of keeping secrets. While Vivekananda had consistently proclaimed celibacy as a spiritual ideal to his American audiences, Craddock heard that he had offered a select few a glimpse of "the higher truth." "I have been shown a book," she noted in 1900, "which he was said to have circulated privately among his more advanced disciples in Chicago. It is a small book, but, I am informed, it costs about ten dollars in India. It is called *The Esoteric Science and Philosophy of the Tantras, Shiva Sanhita*."

India became a leading source for imagining the entanglement of religion and sexuality in both comparative scholarly projects and occultist enterprises of the nineteenth century. Richard Payne Knight had already helped point the way in his late eighteenth-century Discourse on the Worship of Priapus. *He included this plate depicting the lingam as an object of female devotion. The Library Company of Philadelphia.*

It is unclear how long Craddock had this little volume from Calcutta in her hands or by whom she was shown it—but she was certainly pleased to have beheld it.[55]

The fugitive text that Craddock glimpsed contained some teachings about yoga that she had already learned, and others that would surely have raised Anthony Comstock's eyebrows, had he seen the volume. An English translation of a classic Sanskrit treatise on yoga, it mostly focused on the very disciplines and attainments that Craddock had already shelved in reading Vivekananda's *Râja-Yoga*: the cultivation of right posture, the regulation of breath, the subjection of the senses, and the breakthrough into superconsciousness. Yet, Craddock read right past those already familiar instructions to the good part, the section entitled the Vajroli-Mudra, which contained "the most secret among all the secrets," the possibility of spiritual emancipation through proper methods of copulation.[56]

The Esoteric Science and Philosophy of the Tantras made it clear to Craddock that the religious traditions of India had much more to teach than meditative stillness and hermit-like withdrawal from the world. Amid the text's "circumlocutions," this much Craddock found clear: Would-be American yogis need not dedicate themselves to the "avoidance of sex expression," but instead could discover the "inaccessible glory" of the divine through rightly performed sexual intercourse. Reading the treatise with the selective vision of a late nineteenth-century marriage reformer, Craddock glimpsed in Tantrism a specific validation of her own body-spirit connections. Out of multilayered Hindu and Buddhist traditions, crossing more than a millennium of South Asian history, Craddock's glancing recognition of Tantra made it singularly about spiritualized sex.[57]

Unlike so many American appropriators in recent decades, though, Craddock was not turning to Tantrism for its supposed blessing of orgiastic expression and countercultural license. She had no more interest in Tantric practice as a toolkit for ritualized transgression than she did in yoga as a regimen for ascetic renunciation. Craddock had a very limited—and quite negative—sense of "the left-hand path," an element of Tantric traditions that employed the intentional violation of food, sex, and caste taboos as a means of spiritual initiation and awakening. Some Western occultists eagerly exploited that notion (Aleister Crowley most infamously), but Craddock maintained only a dim view of those "profligate" Tantric practitioners who thought themselves incapable of being "polluted by sin," so that they could drink wine, steal, or violate the marriage bed and not be held accountable "for any of these transgressions." She wanted nothing to do with powers gained through taboo-breaking excess; she concerned herself only with the "self-controlled voluptuousness" of wedded bliss. Heterosexual monogamy, not bohemian experimentation or transgressive magic, remained her singular reference point.[58]

Within the monogamous bounds she had set for herself, Craddock gladly found inspiration for her sex radicalism in *The Esoteric Science and Philosophy of the Tantras*. In its pages, however narrowly perused, Craddock saw a joining of sexual union with divine realization and doubtless took that as another opportunity to visualize "the Masculinity" and "the Femininity of the Universe" in concretely physical terms. In the same months that the Sunday meetings of her Church of Yoga unfolded in Chicago in late 1899 and early 1900, she was uttering nighttime prayers to the "Penis of God" and the "Vagina and Uterus of God" and expressly imagining "God's infinite love" in terms of sexual intercourse. Clearly, Craddock was trying to practice what she preached: she had made an erotic spirituality, Tantric and otherwise, part and parcel of her own devotional experiments.[59]

Adapting her Tantric discoveries for private meditation was one thing; broadcasting them, however, quite another. The text that had fallen into her hands was intended only for a small circle of initiates, who were forbidden from revealing the book's secrets to those outside their own closely guarded sphere of knowledge. "It is the most secret of all secrets that ever were or shall be;" the Vajroli-Mudra warned, "therefore let the prudent Yogi keep it with the greatest secrecy possible." Concealment, silence, and inscrutability—those were essential elements of an esoteric tradition like Tantra.[60]

The mysterious veiling commanded in *The Esoteric Science and Philosophy of the Tantras* was lost on Craddock. If these teachings were "hidden and kept secret in all the TANTRAS," that was not a confidence she was at all interested in preserving. Such tight-lipped rules were utterly contrary to the frankness of speech and freedom of expression for which

American marriage reformers were fighting. Craddock, after all, had already experienced more than enough of the hush-hush operations of Comstock and company, so she fully intended to share her discoveries with anyone who sought marital advice from her or who happened to visit her Sunday gatherings. She saw herself, after all, as a religious teacher and public educator, not a privileged initiate. Esoteric secrecy did not sit well with either her testifying spirit or her freethinking temper. Craddock was not one to hide her light under a bushel.[61]

Getting her hands on this scarce book on the esoteric philosophy of the Tantras was a brief, yet dramatic episode for Craddock. It marked her as a rather startling innovator within the broader American religious scene. Her congregational experiment with the Church of Yoga came several years before Pierre Arnold Bernard, a notorious self-made guru from San Francisco, set up the Tantrik Order of America in 1906 and then established his "Oriental Sanctum" in New York City in 1910. Bernard, known in the media as the Omnipotent Oom, was a more accomplished huckster and showman than Craddock—and hence far more successful at sustaining his fellowship and making it work for him financially. A scandalous figure in his own right, Bernard nonetheless found ways to weather Anthony Comstock's vigilance as well as police harassment; by the 1920s and 1930s, the authorities mostly winked at his manly transgressions as the leader of a "love cult." Craddock was not so lucky and paid a heavier price for her eccentricity. The Omnipotent Oom eventually became a successful businessman in Nyack, New York, with something of a sporting reputation for his special abilities at pleasuring women. Scoffed at in newspapers across the country as the High Priestess of the Church of Yoga, Craddock never escaped Comstock's charge of obscenity and blasphemy. Secrets like those contained in the Tantras were obviously still safer for a man to possess than for a woman to proclaim.[62]

Far more important than who appropriated what first was the exuberant religious experimentation that made Craddock's endeavor (as much as Bernard's) possible. Craddock was not an American Tantrika, but a composite of the religious inquiries, yearnings, and serendipitous encounters that unsettled the nation's Protestant establishment over the course of the 1890s. In declaring herself pastor of the Church of Yoga, she remained just as much a Divine Science teacher, a spiritualist medium, a liberal Unitarian, a Quaker reformer, a dabbling Theosophist, and a freethinking sex radical, as she was the exponent of recognizable yogic practices.

By 1900 Craddock had moved a long way from the evangelical revivalism of Ocean Grove, but that drift, however much an expression of her own individuality, was an epitome of a wider religious and cultural transformation. Putting a single occultist label on her religious trek would create a safe pigeonhole, but it would miss the larger challenge Craddock embodied, the very blurring of identities that was straining the culture's Protestant focus. The teeming variety of liberal religious dissent—all those "Miscellaneous" options that the *Chicago Tribune* was publicizing in its "Religious Announcements" by the 1890s—had not yet dimmed the evangelical vision of a Christian America, but the proliferation of choices had certainly begun to befuddle that proposition. No single drifter captured the fullness of that dynamic unrest, but a few came close, and Craddock was without a doubt one of them.[63]

Perhaps the *pièce de résistance* of Craddock's spiritual eclecticism was her association with Otoman Zar-Adusht Hanish, the self-proclaimed Zoroastrian priest who briefly joined forces with Craddock in Chicago in her Church of Yoga meetings. To naysayers, Hanish was simply one more con man and imposter. The muckraker Upton Sinclair found him easy to dismiss as the ne'er-do-well son of an immigrant German family in Milwaukee who had put together "a farrago" of Persian, Hindu, Christian, and New Thought sources and had thus become part of the "plague of Eastern cults" afflicting the country. The founder of the Mazdaznan Temple in Chicago, Hanish presented himself as the genuine article, an Oriental mystic of Persian background, a princely bearer of "the Sun-Worship Philosophy." Like Craddock's yoga, however, Hanish's Zoroastrian wisdom was an American pastiche. It entailed a mélange of breathing rituals, bodily exercises, concentration techniques, fasting guidelines, and dietary recommendations. Among his more distinctive teachings was the importance he accorded sunbathing, preferably nude, as a vitalizing and healing practice: "You will soon learn to appreciate these sun-baths," Hanish counseled. "Follow them as a foremost religious duty that you owe to your own self, your own well-being."[64]

If nude sunbaths and other physical-culture fads were all that this faux Persian magus had to offer, Craddock would probably not have teamed up with him. What made them a likelier pair was that most of Hanish's inspiration had actually come from the same yogic and occultist materials that Craddock had been reading, not from any particular Zoroastrian sources. Mazdaznan sun worship was an angle that Hanish played with dramatic flair to draw attention to his lectures and to set his lessons apart from other self-made magi and gurus. Inside his *Inner Studies* (1902) were the same religious curiosities that had characterized Craddock's inquiries, including the point that behind yogic professions of celibacy and asceticism lay secrets of sexual knowledge and satisfaction.

Hanish very much mirrored Craddock on the topic of sexuality; on that subject, she seems indeed to have been his guru. He followed her on a number of points, including the need for greater anatomical knowledge in preparation for the wedding night and the importance of the husband being able to prolong sexual intercourse in order for his wife to reach orgasm. "What is there in the ordinary method," Hanish asked, "which usually takes less than five minutes and consists only of premature orgasm, as compared with the continuous enjoyment for one or more hours?" For Hanish, like Craddock, "Oriental mysticism" was a vehicle—or, even a front—for broaching the supercharged subject of "the marital embrace." As Craddock readily acknowledged, the Church of Yoga's name was in part tactical; it made the "religious aspect" of her mission "the prominent feature," so that the "sexual teaching" could be brought in "edgeways."[65]

Craddock's association with Hanish did not last long, but the difficulties facing their religious projects continued to echo one another. The Mazdaznan Temple was itself soon the site of ongoing legal battles: In 1904, Hanish was arrested for practicing medicine without a license and was also blamed for driving one of his followers mad through his fasting regimen. The accusations of cultic fanaticism cascaded from there, and sensationalized press accounts of sexual depravity followed him from Chicago to Denver to Los Angeles. The line between legal finding and journalistic fiction was rarely drawn clearly: "HANISH IN JAIL; U.S. RANSACKS TEMPLE OF SUN," screamed one headline; "JURORS THRILLED BY HANISH BOOK . . . HEAR OF NUDE SUN BATHS," bellowed another. The media had gotten hold of Hanish, and it did not intend to let him go.

By 1913, Hanish had learned the same painful lesson that Craddock had more than a decade earlier. Claiming a religious mantle was no protection from Comstock's obscenity laws. Lured by decoy letters into sending his *Inner Studies* to "Julia B. Gardner," a stand-in for Chicago's snooping postal inspector, Hanish was arrested for circulating obscene literature. During the trial the prosecuting attorney blasted *Inner Studies* as a "mess of unspeakable filth"—one made worse because it had been diabolically packaged as a "book of faith." Hanish's tome was "so full of immorality as to be a menace" to public decency, the prosecutor continued, before closing with a psychological flourish. "It was conceived and written by a sex neurotic." To no one's surprise, Hanish was convicted, fined, and sentenced to six months in prison. The Mazdaznan Temple survived this legal blow in 1913, but its founder never lived down the charges of obscenity and immorality.[66]

Craddock's Church of Yoga was, by the time of Hanish's imprisonment, a distant memory. Having hoped "to settle down to Church of Yoga work" in Chicago for the long haul, she nonetheless felt compelled to migrate to Denver by the summer of 1900. There she had planned to set up an office for marital advising and to hold a new round of Church of Yoga meetings, but, with fresh financial support coming in from her old patron William T. Stead in London, she decided to turn her attention to "writing a big book" on marriage and sexuality. (She was not kidding about its size—it ran to 437 double-spaced, type-written, legal-sized pages and was intended to be her definitive statement on marriage reform, though by then there was little reason for her to think that she could actually get it published under the current obscenity regulations.) After holing up in Denver to work on her latest unprintable book, Craddock returned to the East Coast the next year and landed in New York City. There she dreamed of launching a quarterly publication called the *Church of Yoga Messenger* and starting up a new congregation for regular Sunday meetings. Neither hope materialized. Caught up ever more tightly in the legal system's grip, she was unable to produce her planned journal or to resurrect her Church of Yoga in Manhattan. Her congregational experiment had died aborning in Chicago.[67]

Craddock was never able to separate her work as a marriage reformer from her religious labors. The two roles were inextricably entwined, often to her own detriment. The hyped epithet, High Priestess of the Church of Yoga, followed her through her legal showdown with Anthony Comstock in the state and federal courts. In those proceedings and the news reports upon them, that title would be attached to her only with contempt. "The Pastor of the Holy Church of Yoga," Comstock scoffed to reporters after her arrest in February 1902. "I believe she herself is pastor, congregation, Yoga, and everything else."[68]

Given how much energy Craddock had poured into remaking her religious identity, it was perhaps only fitting that she had to defend her sex reform work under yoga's spiritual banner. "I feel pretty much as Moses did when the Lord told him to go and deliver the Israelites from

Pharaoh; I'd rather beg off," she wrote William T. Stead from New York in the fall of 1901:

> I should a whole lot rather not stand sponsor for a new religion. I am kind of afraid of the thing; I don't know whether to shoot it off or not; the recoil may kick in a mortifying and wholly unexpected way. On the other hand, I know that my private pupils are touched by me religiously and emotionally . . . I know—if ever I knew anything— that the proper way to teach what I have to give, is to put it forth as a religion. There *is* absolutely no other way which is so rounded, so satisfying to my sense of the intellectual fitness of things as just this.

The spiritualist Stead may have understood Craddock's prophetic urge to "stand sponsor for a new religion," but, for most people, her view of the sex educator as sibyl was hard to fathom. That mystical proposition could make her liberal allies cringe—almost as much as it did Comstock, and yet Craddock was hardly in a position to relinquish her visionary status. That sensibility was, after all, essential to her bravest and most self-endangering claim: namely, that she had the authority to speak as a sexologist and to serve as a knowledgeable guide for married couples.[69]

CHAPTER FOUR

An Expert in Sexology

———◦•◦———

Eunice Parsons, a young nurse newly engaged in the summer of 1902, was worried about her fiancé, a piano tuner. The couple had recently had "some frank talks," and it turned out Eunice's betrothed, "a very pure-minded man," was of the opinion that "people should have intercourse only for childbearing." Parsons, taken aback, objected, "Suppose I don't want *any* children; what then? Are we *never* to have intercourse?" As their discussion turned into a quarrel, her fiancé reproached her for being too passionate, and now she wondered if their apparent sexual incompatibility made it necessary for them to call off the wedding. "I have made up my mind never to marry any man until he can look at the sex relation as a pure act and a sacred act," Eunice vowed. Her would-be husband, however prudish he sounded, held the stronger hand in this dispute: Most marital advice literature of the period, religious or not, refused to disjoin the pleasure of sex from the purpose of procreation and would have seen this particular stand-off as a worrying reversal of the usual relation of male desire and female modesty.

Parsons had no effective recourse against her fiancé's convictions— until she discovered the counseling services of Ida C. Craddock. With her Church of Yoga abandoned, Craddock was now operating out of an apartment in New York City on West 23rd Street. There, in a very snug office space, she pursued a lively, face-to-face program of instruction: advising clients who were struggling with bodily, spiritual, and relational issues. Parsons learned of Craddock's lessons on married sexual relations through a physician to whom she had complained of her troubles and soon, fortified by Craddock's teachings, she pressed her fiancé to reconsider his views. Improbably, Eunice even convinced him to go in for a lesson himself.

Meeting with Craddock could not have been comfortable for a resolute virgin like Eunice's fiancé. For her pedagogy to be effective, Craddock thought it essential to explore the sexual history of her clients with a battery of diagnostic questions, including blunt inquiries about masturbation (yes, he had done that "to some extent when a boy") and erotic dreams (yes, he had experienced a few). The piano tuner, no doubt uncomfortable with the frankness of Craddock's inquiry, tried to shift the tenor of the exchange through religious argument and scriptural citation: "Quoted the Bible very earnestly," Craddock wrote in her case notes, "about there being a war between the spirit and the flesh, to prove his contention that coition should take place only for child-bearing; say once every few years." The young man argued that sex within marriage was divinely sanctioned only for the procreative end of replenishing the earth.

Unfortunately for the Bible-quoting piano tuner, Craddock wanted nothing more than to have their sex talk turn spiritual. Soon she was explaining how in her understanding of the divine, "God was feminine as well as masculine"—a concept that in itself would have sounded foreign to anyone used to intoning the most routine Christian prayer: "Our Father, who art in heaven." But Craddock's theories about God were not nearly as radical—or as shocking—as her philosophy about the female body. "I told him to think of his wife's yoni as containing a chapel, into which he was to enter to worship—not worship the woman, but worship God," Craddock instructed. That lesson left Eunice's fiancé red-faced; he kept sputtering "his one idea of no coition except for child-bearing" and even insisted that his fiancée's physical affections were supposed to be purely maternal in expression. Eunice need only dote on their prospective children, not satisfy (let alone incite) his sexual desires.

"Well, well," Craddock concluded, "if he doesn't manage to rid himself of his *idée fixe*, he'll find himself minus his sweetheart before long."

Only at the insistence of his betrothed did the piano tuner return for three more lessons. He bristled at his fiancée's newly acquired "independence of thought and action" in pushing him into this highly disagreeable situation, but criticizing a woman for "thinking for herself" was a non-starter with Craddock, who greeted this male presumption only with barbs. Forced quickly into retreat on that point, the piano tuner found himself losing ground on the main argument as well, finally acknowledging that sex for non-procreative purposes could be "pure and holy and perhaps 'normal' after all." By the close of the fourth session Craddock had gone a long way toward saving the engagement—not just by normalizing the idea of regular intercourse between spouses, but also by explaining to the would-be husband that he needed to embrace his wife's passion and be considerate of her pleasure. If the piano tuner remained wary of Eunice's alliance with Ida, he at least had begun displaying a new appreciation for his lover's sexual appetites and was ready to reconsider his own asceticism. The physician who had made the initial referral was so impressed with the change Craddock's instruction had wrought that she immediately sought to sign up her own son and daughter for guidance in their respective relationships.[1]

In Craddock's ever-troubled role as a sex educator, this couple's case was a success story. Even in this moment of victory, however, it is impossible to gauge whether her intervention proved lasting: Did her advice get the pair through their wedding night, and, even if it did, would Eunice come to regret her decision to go through with the marriage? Or, would her husband prove a lasting convert to Craddock's way of thinking? After learning how important it was for his spouse to achieve orgasm and how devoted he had to be to her unhurried arousal, would he succeed at mastering the requisite techniques or end up feeling inept in the bedroom? And what if the couple did indeed decide to have children? Would the husband then lose interest in his wife, and prefer to exalt her as a mother rather than attend to her as a lover? Even with the best of sources—and the case records that Craddock left from her pioneering efforts are unusually vivid—so many relational intimacies and struggles slip entirely from view. Sex and marriage were too muddled with failure and frustration, too laced with manipulation and resentment, for anyone to serve simply as a heroic liberator. Craddock, however bold, could not free herself or her students from recurrent fears of impurity, perversion, abnormality, and lost self-control.

No matter the challenges she faced, Craddock remained alertly focused on developing this new therapeutic role for herself. In her other incarnations of specialized expertise—as scholar and pastor—she was playing off well-established professions, but the craft of sexual consultant was, quite obviously, less recognized than those. In describing that new vocation, she variously presented herself as an "instructor and counselor upon the right way to live as husband and wife"; "an expert in sexology"; or, in a particularly evocative moment of self-description, "a physician of the emotions." No title, it seemed, was too specific—or too opaque—for Craddock's purposes.[2]

A fancy calling card was not enough to make Craddock a credible professional. She was not a trained physician, even though the sort of physiological knowledge she pursued was widely seen as the particular domain of medical doctors. She relied instead on alliances with supportive physicians, such as Henrietta Westbrook and Edward Bond Foote, to provide some cover for her own therapeutic venture. Having a handful of sympathetic doctors in her camp was always crucial; they gave her a tincture of medical trustworthiness—as well as referrals. Likewise, Craddock did not possess the professional bona fides of a psychologist or a sexologist, new scientific roles that had gained identifiable authority by the end of the nineteenth century and that would become increasingly entwined in the early twentieth century in the figure of the psychoanalyst. While she lacked the standing of physicians and scientists, Craddock also shared little with the fortuneteller, potion peddler, or amulet-producing conjurer—canny figures who had long boasted uncanny powers in the ways of love and fertility. Neither a medical doctor nor a folk healer, Craddock was something in between the two. A self-educated anatomical guide and metaphysical teacher, she was a makeshift therapist who sought to improve marriages through helping couples understand both their sexual functions and their spiritual needs. As she wrote of the new path she was on, "I have had to carve out my own road without any predecessors to guide me."[3]

Craddock's need to improvise the role of sex educator as she went along did not mean her labors were entirely a product of creative isolation and idiosyncrasy. Her marriage reforms were a patchwork of cultural scraps drawn from multiple sources—medical, religious, legal, and freethinking. She stitched these materials together in an enterprise that combined a perilous publishing agenda with a program of personal instruction. While it was Craddock's pamphleteering that would land her in court, her face-to-face tutoring carried its own risks. Prime among these were male clients who repeatedly pestered her to demonstrate her teachings in the flesh; they saw her less as an educator than as a showgirl or prostitute and treated her accordingly. Hassled by both her male customers and Anthony Comstock's vice-fighting agents, Craddock was stuck between the booming market for sexual commodities and the Protestant effort to suppress those very obscenities. In her frankness about sexuality Craddock could sound almost bohemian, yet she was hardly carefree. She inevitably remained tethered to various social conventions and moral fears, including the dangers of masturbation and same-sex love. Exalting married heterosexual intercourse to the heavens, as Craddock did, necessarily served to reemphasize a host of taboos. She often wound up the mouthpiece for familiar prohibitions rather than the visionary of new freedoms.

Even if her teachings repeated common admonitions, Craddock's recasting of married sex as a mystical act proved a consequential shift well beyond the bedroom. The spiritual blessing she bestowed upon sexual satisfaction lined up surprisingly well with the demands of secular liberals for a singularly private version of religion. If the state was to denude itself of all church entanglements and sectarian expressions—as secularists hoped—where better to divert religion's surplus passions than to the marriage bed? That boudoir piety was effectively designed to channel religion away from the public realm to the innermost sanctum of the domestic sphere. Comstock's Christian America, with all its snooping into public morals, would be replaced with hearty secular notions of free expression, individual liberty, and protected privacy. Making religion and sex private affairs—in effect, putting the two together behind closed doors—Craddock attempted to liberalize sexuality through redrawing religion's bounds. Privacy would be a shelter for both religious liberty and sexual enlightenment.[4]

———— ·•·• ————

CRADDOCK'S INITIAL DEDICATION to the cause of sex education flowed through the notorious editor Moses Harman, a firebrand of social reform who had begun his career in Missouri in the 1850s as a hobbled schoolteacher turned circuit-riding Methodist preacher. Leaving the evangelical ministry to pursue freethinking anticlericalism, Harman boasted an intellectual and religious pilgrimage almost as jagged as Craddock's own. By 1879, he had settled in Valley Falls, Kansas; then a widower with two children and little means, Harman was intent on becoming a local agitator for the National Liberal League against Protestant efforts to make the United States an avowedly Christian nation.

As was the case for other defenders of secularism, Harman was spurred to action by the perceived threat that evangelical initiatives posed to the country's liberties. Comstock's anti-obscenity crusade, along with the National Reform Association's proposal to put God and Jesus in the Constitution, galvanized Harman to build up midwestern connections for the Liberal Leaguers. Looking to safeguard the land from further Protestant encroachments, Harman started the *Valley Falls Liberal* in 1880, which evolved the next year into the *Kansas Liberal* and in August 1883 into *Lucifer the Light-Bearer*. That sardonic title—a rebellious blast at the biblical God who had, Harman claimed, doomed humanity to "perpetual ignorance" through his unfortunate response to Adam and Eve when they ate from the tree of knowledge—was enough to indicate where the journal was headed. *Lucifer the Light-Bearer* quickly emerged as one of the great mastheads of radical dissent and would remain an influential force for the next two decades. A diehard proponent of the liberal demands of the American Secular Union, Harman expanded that church-state agenda to include populist economic reforms and women's rights. Above all, he extended the liberal cause to include the transformation of love, marriage, and sexuality.[5]

Its critics always caricatured Free Love as a free-lust movement, but its bedrock was marriage reform, not pleasure-seeking. It wished marital relations to be free of all coercion, and for no husband to have the power to impose his sexual demands upon his wife. Pure love, not legal restraint or social convention, was to be the basis of any genuine union between husband and wife. Harman took those durable Free-Love propositions and gave them startlingly forthright expression. Plainspoken and blunt by principle, Harman acquired an especially sleazy reputation when he published correspondence from a Tennessee radical, W. G. Markland, in 1886. "If a man stabs his wife to death with a knife," the Markland letter asked, "does not the law hold him for murder? If he murders her with his penis, what does the law do? . . . Can a Czar have more absolute power over a subject than a man has over the genitals of his wife?" That "awful" communication got Harman indicted on obscenity charges in early 1887, the subsequent trial and conviction for which helped transform him into a freedom-of-the-press icon. Doing jail time was no lightweight burden, but being taken down by Comstock definitely made for a certain celebrity in liberal circles.

Moses Harman, an especially daring publisher among nineteenth-century marriage reformers, provided Craddock with recurrent backing and publicity in his journal Lucifer the Light-Bearer. *Harman, already a graybeard among sex radicals by the time Craddock came on the scene, is pictured here with one of his grandchildren. WHi-65507, Wisconsin Historical Society.*

Harman was notorious for more than his publishing ventures. Coincident with the Markland episode, Harman had also created outrage for solemnizing the Free-Love union of his daughter Lillian and fellow agitator Edwin C. Walker, a voluntary coupling that disregarded both civil and ecclesial norms and looked to its critics like nothing more than "illicit cohabitation." After that notorious ceremony and his initial arrest, Harman was perpetually enmeshed in interconnected legal battles for free speech and marriage reform. The editor of *Lucifer* clearly had a knack for scandal, but most of the commotion he generated came from tenaciously asserting the fundamental question: "Has freedom gender?" Or, as he answered the question in his own attempt at a liberal credo, "Freedom that is not equal is not freedom."[6]

Craddock was much indebted to Harman's rabblerousing journalism for initial notice and ongoing support. Presenting Craddock's unusual defense of belly dancing to his readers in late 1893, Harman hailed the piece as her coming out "among the radical thinkers and agitators of the social revolution," those "fearless investigators" of women's chronic inequalities within "our so-called civilized society." Craddock's essay offered just the kind of iconoclastic thinking that appealed to Harman, but what made it even better was that it flew in the face of his own arch-nemesis, Anthony Comstock. In a head-note Harman first introduced Craddock to his readers as the former secretary of the American Secular Union, effectively highlighting her alliance with him as a fellow Liberal Leaguer, but then he immediately pivoted to point out how much the performance in the Cairo Street Theatre had upset Comstock, "the American censor of morals." From there he let Craddock speak for herself on "those old uplifting days of Phallic or Sex Worship" and on belly dancing as an unexpected means of grace.

Precisely because Craddock's theories could seem so outlandish, Harman delighted in lending them public support and visibility. Her arguments on behalf of belly dancing might "shock or repel the average reader," the editor of *Lucifer* admitted, but he clearly did not give a damn about that. Despite his having already served time in the state penitentiary for his paper's obscenities, Harman happily presented Craddock's essay as a model of reasonableness and purity. A few years later he would admit that he found her rather "superstitious" about the "sacredness" of marriage and too given to "speculative theology" for his rationalist frame of mind, but he always remained enamored with her "lofty courage." Indeed, after the journal and its editorial cadre moved to Chicago in the late 1890s, Harman invited Craddock to lecture twice in his own home, and his daughter Lillian (the infamous cohabitator) even showed up to support Craddock's Church of Yoga meetings.[7]

Craddock's debut in *Lucifer the Light-Bearer* aligned her with Harman's Free-Love rebellion against "sex slavery," but the essay itself actually pointed more directly to her debt to utopian John Humphrey Noyes, founder of the Oneida Community. Noyes, a Vermont preacher whose Yale theological education had been cut short after he made a wild-eyed claim to sinless purity, was an imposing visionary in search of social and religious perfection. Like so many other Americans of his era—Bronson Alcott at Fruitlands and George Ripley at Brook Farm were only two of the more famous—Noyes turned to a communitarian experiment for the fulfillment of his quest. Organized in 1848, his Bible-based commune endured until 1879 and proved one of the most influential of the era, particularly in its role as a crucible for sexual and marital innovations. In an industrializing economy that seemed to drive an ever-sharper distinction between work and home as well as between the roles of men and women, new religious communities became especially important places to test alternative social adjustments of family life. The Shakers tried celibacy and orphan adoptions; the Mormons embraced "plural marriage" and a restored patriarchal order; and the Oneida Community, under Noyes's autocratic direction, experimented with a distinct version of perfectionist sex.[8]

Craddock herself had no personal connection to Oneida, but she nonetheless looked to Noyes for inspiration on how to improve American marriages. She explicitly embraced his emphasis on *coitus reservatus* or "male continence," a practice that was seen as both a means of contraception and a way to prolong the sexual encounter to the woman's advantage. While Craddock had no interest in the side of Noyes's experimental regimen that included a variety of sexual partners, she very much followed him on disjoining the "amative" joys of sex from their "propagative" consequences. With birth-control devices relatively unreliable and shadowed by legal strictures, many nineteenth-century reformers adopted the disciplined retention of semen as a more satisfying preventive than abstinence. "Male continence," in the parlance Craddock borrowed from Noyes, was offered as a good method by which married couples could have many of the delights of physical intimacy, while minimizing the possibility of unwanted pregnancy. Noyes, like Craddock after him, took sex to be "an act of communion," and that sacramental blessing was separable from sex as "an act of propagation." Noyes had included only those in his small and carefully regulated community in his quest to tap into the spirituality of sexual intercourse, but Craddock stood ready to invite all married couples to join in this new communion.[9]

Craddock was far from alone in the 1890s in promoting Noyes's teachings under new banners. The nephew of Oneida's founder, George Noyes Miller, who was raised in the community and who helped launch its famed line of silver-plated tableware, promoted his uncle's birth-control technique in the novelistic *After the Sex Struck; Or, Zugassent's Discovery* (1895). Miller's fictitious character Immanuel Zugassent, like Craddock, offered a relatively tame, monogamous version of male continence through which married couples were able "to subject human propagation to the control of reason." "Zugassent's wonderful Discovery," Miller effused, would release women from the "treadmill" of reproduction and would serve "as a splendid stimulus to [the] spirituality" of both partners. Likewise, another Oneida-inspired disciple, Albert Chavannes, encouraged this form of sexual self-control under the heading "the philosophy of Magnetation." A Knoxville businessman, he spent much of his time pondering his favored subjects of theology, socialism, and sex—and publishing upon them in his own journal the *Modern Philosopher.*[10]

Craddock drew on the work of Noyes, Miller, and Chavannes as evidence for the contraceptive effectiveness and religious desirability of male continence. While she initially favored John Humphrey Noyes's nomenclature, she shifted smoothly between the period's varied designations for *coitus reservatus.* When Craddock eventually placed the practice of male continence under a yogic banner, she was not conceiving a Tantric novelty, but instead performing her own fanciful re-labeling of these homegrown American teachings on sexual control and spiritual communion.

The advocate of male continence with whom Craddock most clearly aligned herself was Alice B. Stockham, author of *Tokology: A Book for Every Woman* (1886) and *Karezza: Ethics of Marriage* (1896). A Midwestern physician whose medical advice on pregnancy and childbirth earned her a national and even international readership, Stockham was a supportive elder for Craddock. A quarter century her senior, Stockham shared Craddock's enthusiasm for metaphysics and promoted a version of Divine Science through her successful publishing company. Eventually, in June 1905, Comstock's Society for the Suppression of Vice caught up with Stockham as well; the censors, marking a small subset of her medical writings on married sexuality obscene, significantly damaged her business through hefty fines. Stockham's association with Craddock certainly did not help with the postal inspectors. Her protégé, whom the aged physician had publicly defended against Comstock, fondly served as a promoter of both *Tokology* and *Karezza,* and declared the latter "the best book I know of

Physician Alice B. Stockham, a marital advisor and metaphysical speculator, exercised a strong influence on Craddock through her Karezza: Ethics of Marriage *(1896). Alice B. Stockham,* Tokology: A Book for Every Woman *(Chicago: Stockham Publishing, 1891), frontispiece.*

on this sacred and delicate subject of the right sexual relation of husband and wife." In that volume Stockham directly replaced the concept of "Male Continence" with that of "Karezza," a term that she saw as more appropriately inclusive of male and female sexual experience and more evocative of the spiritual exaltation of "love's appointed consummation." On mystical religion, marital relations, and sexual expression, Stockham and Craddock very much spoke in the same dialect.[11]

The spiritual-sexual idiom that Stockham and Craddock shared between them had much more to it than a rehashing of male continence. Stockham, like most other sex reformers of the day, placed a strong emphasis on improving the human stock through carefully planned pregnancies, limited propagation, and better parenting. That women should have full jurisdiction over their reproductive capacity and that all babies should be "desired and welcome offspring" were twin propositions in the literature aimed at combating "sex slavery." Without more attention to "pre-natal culture," without reliable techniques for limiting family size, various social ills—including poverty, delinquency, child abuse, and domestic division—had little chance of being ameliorated. New technologies, from electricity to the telephone, were enlarging "nearly every department of life," Stockham explained in *Karezza*, and that same spirit of "revolutionizing discovery" needed to be applied to sexual matters. Whether it was the control of orgasms or pregnancies, Stockham and Craddock saw their teachings as part of the forward march of scientific mastery. The sex instinct, including the Darwinian biology of sexual attraction and selection, was an evolutionary force not to disdain, but to harness for civilization's advance. The reality that various agents of this sexual enlightenment would eventually endorse quite unenlightened public policies for eugenicist purposes—including forced sterilization of the unfit—had yet to dampen progressive enthusiasms. Aligning sex with science was still seen as all gain.[12]

Beyond the scientific ambitions for reproductive planning, Stockham and Craddock drew as well on the resources of the "Social Purity" movement. With many reformers of record in its ranks, the Social Purity crusade was a force to reckon with in late nineteenth-century America. Its leaders targeted, among other ills, prostitution, polygamy, venereal disease, and drunkenness; they cast an especially critical eye on the double standard for men and women when it came to premarital and extramarital sexual relations. Men were now to be held to the same benchmarks of purity and piety as women had long been; "a single code of ethics," Stockham insisted, should govern husband and wife. Suggestive of the overlapping worlds of reform—the ways in which temperance advocates, suffragists, vice crusaders, and sex radicals could all be in bed together on marital ethics—Craddock initially identified herself in her public work as a "Lecturer and Correspondent on Social Purity." As she saw it, earnest reformers among evangelical "Church-women" and "thinking women among the Liberals" were equally ready to embrace the sanitized sexual ethics embodied in *Karezza*. Both groups, after all, would be quite happy to see a decline in prostitution, male philandering, and venereal disease. The *lingua franca* of marriage reform and moral hygiene spanned a broad spectrum: Frances Willard, leader of the Woman's Christian Temperance Union, and Alice

Stockham, metaphysical obstetrician, could speak it fluently—and so could Craddock, yogic spiritualist.[13]

If Stockham and Craddock both took serious heed of the Social Purity movement, that emphasis nonetheless paled before their religious vision for love and marriage. "Work your passion up into poetry," Stockham quoted Emerson fondly, using that snippet to present intense sexual expression as a manifestation of the inspired soul. "When the signs of this creative power come throbbing and pulsating into every fibre," Stockham averred, "it only shows that one has greater ability to create than ever before." The poetry of "sex energy" reached its peak only when it entered the realm of the spirit; transcendental aspirations, in Stockham's view, necessarily led the way in improving married sexual relations. "Religion and philosophy are required in consecrating passion," Stockham insisted. For its most exalted expression, coitus had to produce "true soul union," "a union of the sexes on the spiritual plane."

The romantic spirituality embodied in Stockham's *Karezza* provided an absolutely crucial shift of perspective for those thinking about marital relations at the end of the nineteenth century. Sexual experience was no longer a metaphor for mystical union; it was in itself a form of exquisite religious communion; it created "spiritual exaltation" and opened "visions of a transcendent life." Married sex was fundamentally a devotional exercise, a sacred relation to be expressed, not a shameful act to be repressed. When fellow radical Lois Waisbrooker spoke of a "sex revolution" in the 1890s, she was hardly imagining a secular strike for women's rights that jettisoned religion. Indeed, she could not imagine a revolution of this kind without giving it a sacred aura. In these circles, "spiritualized sex" was the sexual revolution. That religious transformation was, without doubt, the *sine qua non* of Craddock's own therapeutic efforts; her sexual insurgency depended on this broader transcendental uprising.[14]

By the turn of the twentieth century, Stockham's publishing ventures extended well beyond Chicago's medical and mind-cure circles into a transatlantic company of radicals, poets, and seekers. Nothing suggested those broader currents so much as the alliance that Stockham struck with Edward Carpenter, a British socialist, an ardent admirer of Walt Whitman, a leading critic of modern civilization's stifling repressiveness, a sandal-wearing vegetarian, and a defender of same-sex love. In 1900 Stockham published the first American edition of Carpenter's *Love's Coming-of-Age: A Series of Papers on the Relations of the Sexes*. It was, all at once, a blast at conventional marriage, a brief for women's equality, and a blessing of sexual passion.

Carpenter's work was among the final pieces to fall into place for Craddock's marital reform message. Whether she obtained a copy of Stockham's edition or a prior English version (the Labour Press in Manchester had originally published the book in 1896), Craddock heartily embraced *Love's Coming of Age*. She lifted out a long passage on the importance of educating young people in sexual matters, typing it up as confirmation of her own teaching mission: "That we should leave our children to pick up their information about the most sacred, the most profound and vital, of all human functions, from the mere gutter, and learn to know it from the lips of ignorance and vice, seems almost incredible." Carpenter, poet and progressive, joined his call for honest talk about sexuality to feminist exhortation, and that only made him more appealing: "Let every woman . . . hasten to declare herself and constitute herself, as far as she possibly can, a free woman. Let her . . . insist on her right to speak, dress, think, act, and above all to use her sex, as she deems best." Carpenter's avant-garde perspective was hardly a perfect fit for Stockham and Craddock—neither followed his lead on same-sex or "homogenic" love, for example—but their affinities with England's Whitman remained pronounced.[15]

Carpenter's attractiveness to Stockham and Craddock also derived from his offbeat religious sensibilities. Stockham, like Craddock, had become increasingly interested in appropriating spiritual strands from India for her own purposes, especially after she traveled there as a wide-eyed tourist in 1891. Making her sympathies explicit in a glowing introduction, Stockham published Carpenter's memoir of pilgrimage through India and Ceylon, *A Visit to a Gñani* (1900), a four-chapter excerpt on religion from his more diffuse travelogue, *From Adam's Peak to Elephanta* (1892). That extract described Carpenter's extensive encounter with a white-robed guru, the portrait of whom he came to value right alongside a cherished photograph of the gray-bearded Whitman. However impressed Carpenter was with his aged Hindu teacher, he made a move that very much jibed with how Stockham and Craddock viewed yogic disciplines: Namely, he concluded that new levels of consciousness would not be entered through the willed suppression of desire or such ascetic disciplines as fasting and sensory denial, but instead through the path of outpoured love. Carpenter, like Whitman, represented a literary, religious, and sexual avant-garde— bold, iconoclastic, and subversive. Stockham and Craddock were hardly artsy bohemians themselves, but they certainly knew what it was like to be part of a literary underground of feared writers. They were both primed to recognize in Carpenter a fellow prophet of a free society.[16]

Craddock's sexology, however quirky, emerged out of a dense forest of intellectual precedents and influences. Free-Love radicals, women's rights activists, amorous communitarians, eclectic physicians, Social-Purity reformers, Divine Science speculators, and avant-garde literati— Craddock riffed on ideas borrowed from all of them. No matter how much her spiritualist eccentricity made it look to skeptics as if she floated about in airy castles of mystic isolation and mad delusion, Craddock stood very much within the religious, medical, and erotic landscape of her day. Perhaps she was an American original, but, if so, her improvisation nonetheless bespoke everyday preoccupations—with damaged relationships and bedroom anxieties, with patched-up miscommunications and confusing desires. She was out there on a limb—and yet she had plenty of company.

IN HER EFFORTS TO CREATE a niche for herself as a sexologist, Craddock started with a literary program: the production of small-scale advice manuals for married couples. That publishing program had gotten off to a shaky start in 1893 when she publicly defended the Danse du Ventre as "a most valuable object lesson" for the better performance of "marital duties." That plea contained a modicum of explicit sexual advice, particularly on her concomitant goals of strict male self-control over ejaculation and released female passion through protracted foreplay. Preoccupied with her grand scholarly projects as well as her spiritualist training, Craddock largely held back on her sex-radical agenda for the next three years. She also already had the inglorious distinction of being on the postal inspector's watch-list, which necessarily made it dangerous for her to pursue her publishing efforts at all.[17]

Craddock laid low, first in one of William Stead's editorial offices in London in 1894 and 1895, and then in the Bureau of Highways in Philadelphia—but she was unable to keep quiet much longer. In 1896 she again entered the fray with a sixteen-page tract entitled *Helps to Happy Wedlock: No. 1 for Husbands*, mainly a recommendation of male continence compiled from the work of John Humphrey Noyes and Albert Chavannes. She followed the next year with a pair of her own little guides called *Letter to a Prospective Bride* and *Advice to a Bridegroom*, both of which were designed to prepare the betrothed for the "psycho-physiology of marriage." Two years later in September 1899 she produced a slightly more substantial work on *Right Marital Living*, a piece that she had previewed a few months earlier in the safer confines of a medical journal, the *Chicago Clinic*. Lastly, in 1900, she issued *The Wedding Night*, another truncated version of her teachings, the bulk of which remained tucked away in typescripts and lecture notes, including her 437-page book manuscript on "The Marriage Relation," a ten-chapter summation of her whole enterprise.[18]

If most of her teachings remained unpublished, Craddock still managed to get her ideas into at least limited circulation through her sundry booklets and circulars. A ledger she kept, titled "Address Book of Customers for Books and of Pupils in Divine Science," contained 867 names (just for 1899 and 1900), many of whom ordered more than one of her pamphlets. A hypnotist in Riverside, California, for example, purchased a copy of the *Danse du Ventre*, *Letter to a Prospective Bride*, and *Right Marital Living*, while a Congregational minister in Chicago bought a copy of four of her pamphlets, plus an edition of Stockham's *Karezza*, which Craddock continued to promote as an important companion volume. Most customers were less voracious, and, like the professor at Trinity College (later Duke University) in Durham, simply ordered one pamphlet; his choice, *Right Marital Living*, was the favored one on this client list. Getting the word out through advertising in newspapers, medical journals, and freethinking periodicals, Craddock managed to develop a decent customer base for her writings. Her patrons especially came from the big cities in which she had already labored in person, but dozens were scattered in small towns across the country: East Prairie, Missouri; Waterville, Maine; Abbeville, South Carolina; Aztec, New Mexico; Gardener, North Dakota, and the like.[19]

Craddock's program began with the notion that those on the verge of marriage needed to be better prepared for sexual relations on the wedding night and thereafter. "The usual custom," Craddock remarked in her *Letter to a Prospective Bride*, "is to keep a woman as ignorant as possible in regard to this matter previous to her wedding night." This lack of awareness resulted in "all sorts of awkward embarrassments" as well as more momentous disharmonies, Craddock explained. It often made the groom's sexual passion shocking to the bride; jarring, rushed, and perhaps even brutal, the consummation of the marriage could deteriorate into "a night of rape and torture to the woman, violating all instincts of her purity." The marriage rite shifted the man from suitor to possessor; he all too frequently presumed an ownership of the woman's body, a conjugal right to her sexual favors; she felt reduced to a convenience or even "a slop-pail."

The wedding night should be a mutually joyous experience, swore Craddock—not a traumatizing experience for the bride. It should be, she said, "a night of poetry and tender passion, of serene self-control, and exaltation of mystic rapture for both parties." Craddock joined these romantic abstractions to very concrete advice to the husband. He should be patient and gentle at first entry, should consider "anointing" the vagina with "some harmless unguent, such as vaseline," and attend to the very deliberate process of bringing his bride to "final ecstasy." Endurance and focus were crucial: If either party was exhausted from the wedding day, then it was best to wait until the next morning for "the first marital endearments." Sexual union demanded physical vigor and mental alertness, not to mention "artistic skill and spiritual insight." The wedding night, given both its erotic and mystical possibilities, was not a time for thoughtless impetuosity or heedless gratification.[20]

To ensure a successful marriage, Craddock instructed, couples needed to carry forward what they had learned in preparation for the wedding night. She held out the hope that, with proper coaching, married couples could enjoy "a perpetual honeymoon," but she knew that the demand for her advice came from the fact that husbands and wives regularly experienced "growing disappointment or estrangement" in their sex lives. To make marital relations healthier and happier, to reduce frustration and division, Craddock offered several ground-rules for couples to follow:

1. **Practice good grooming.** Pay close attention to "*la toilette intime*," to bodily hygiene and physical appearance. "Cleanliness is next to godliness at the genitals, as elsewhere," Craddock advised, as she exuberantly combined the hygienic recommendations of medical works like Edward Bliss Foote's *Plain Home Talk and Medical Common Sense* with detailed fashion tips for happy domesticity. Husbands, sadly lacking in "color expression" in their standard wardrobe, needed to cultivate their

"aesthetic sensibilities," and wives should give careful attention to, among other things, the luxuriance of their hair and the frilliness of their lingerie, which could be "made beautiful with laces and ribbons."

2. **Slow down.** Small gestures of physical affection were important to display throughout the day and, once in bed together, the couple should lavish kisses and caresses upon one another. They should savor lying naked in each other's arms— or, in marriage-reform parlance, take delight in "the nude embrace" as "a pure and beautiful approach to that sacred moment" of actual intercourse. "Do not be in a hurry," Craddock counseled. "'Patience and a little oil will do wonders,' is a saying which applies here."

3. **Be naked and not ashamed.** Women especially had been enjoined to sexual passivity, indifference, and modesty, all of which stifled the appropriate passions of lovemaking. "They clinch their hands," Craddock wrote of severe cases, "as they force themselves to lie still, resolutely trying to resist any answering throb of passion during sexual union." That miseducation of women had to be undone—right down to the acceptability and desirability of vigorous "pelvic movements" during sex. In wrongly taking passionlessness as a sign of "womanly purity," all too many wives, Craddock feared, were choking back the very "sexual responsiveness" for which their partners longed. Indeed, Craddock suggested that faking orgasm ("to pretend rapture") was actually preferable to lying there "like a log, without response."

4. **Try different positions.** While she acknowledged that the "natural position" was for the man to be on top, she noted that "it is sometimes better for the woman to mount the man." Not to be forgotten were "various side positions, which different couples can find out for themselves, by experimentation."

Ideally, the resourceful couple would find just the right position for maximizing their mutual satisfaction—one that lifted them to new heights as "sexual comrades."

5. **Keep the mind focused, engaged, and free of distracting worries.** Ever-cerebral, Craddock saw physical intimacy as a vehicle of "intellectual blending": "Think and talk during the nude embrace, and also at intervals during the sexual embrace, of good books, pictures, statuary, music, sermons, plans for benefiting other people, noble deeds, spiritual aspirations." A couple achieved "perfect oneness" only when their minds as well as their bodies merged during their leisurely-paced sexual encounters.

Even as Craddock wanted to keep couples on the high road of spiritual and cultural uplift, she was offering manuals of sexual advice that were unmatched at the time for their candor and directness. Indeed, if she had been able to get her big book on "The Marriage Relation" into print, it would have left Stockham's *Karezza* looking spare and prim in comparison. As it was, Craddock presented an original voice in a body of advice literature filled with euphemisms, unintelligible whispers, and full-throated rants against self-abuse. Her very prose seemed designed to destroy the canard of the passionless woman.[21]

However emancipating, Craddock's guidelines for sexual expression came with severe regulations, as many "don'ts" as "dos." This was especially the case for men. The release of female ardor would happen only through the restraint of male excitement. From the couple's very first night together, the husband's "selfish passion" was the particular object of Craddock's scorn and disciplinary guidelines. The man, to be an accomplished and considerate lover, had to develop control over his own orgasm. To be sure, many of the men Craddock dealt with needed her admonition. Asked how long he lasted, one of her clients, whose wife was not enjoying sex that much, "answered carelessly, 'the average time for a man.'" To which Craddock rejoined, "And what may that be in your case?'" "Oh, about forty seconds," the man replied. "He was much astonished," she deadpanned, "when I told him that he ought not to terminate the act short of a half hour or hour after entrance, so as to give time for his wife to come to climax." Ejaculation, Craddock insisted, was always to be delayed and almost always suppressed. (The only obvious exception to the latter was in those cases in which the woman considered it a "fitting time" for her to become pregnant.) In that light, premature ejaculation was seen as a triple violation of the rules: It failed on the grounds of leisurely satisfaction, mind-over-body discipline, and birth control. Lasting only forty seconds made a man a derisory failure.[22]

Craddock knew that many physicians, including Edward Bond Foote, as well as many of her male clients thought her prescriptions for manly self-control unrealistic, if not harmful. Ejaculation was a necessary relief, not a dangerous expenditure; the very purpose of coitus, not a sign of failed discipline. But Craddock kept invoking her own male authorities, including Noyes and Chavannes, in defense of both the rigor and the practicality of such continence. As Craddock saw it, a husband who subjected himself to this training, stopping repeatedly on the verge of emission, would eventually gain the ability to have a "controlled orgasm": that is, he would be able to experience the full thrill of sexual climax, while strictly retaining his semen.

Not all of Craddock's ostensible supporters shared her enthusiasm for these theories about restricted ejaculation. Foote, open-minded about male continence, had nonetheless lost regard for it through "personal experiments" as well as the frustrations of his own patients. Putting his trust in improved birth-control devices, he tried valiantly to convince Craddock that she should not be emphasizing a *controlled* orgasm but a *complete* one. She remained unconvinced, holding fast to the protracted discipline of semen retention. While she did not present this directive— at least not overtly—as a female avenging of male haste, she certainly wanted to turn the husband into a tireless self-monitor of his own performance: "In all things, let him seek, not to get the most pleasure possible out of the relation for himself, but to give his wife the most pleasure," she instructed. "Let him study his own movements, in their possibilities of conferring pleasure." Long an act that prioritized the male experience, as Craddock saw it, sex was to be shifted to recognize female needs and desires.[23]

Some of Craddock's other proscriptions made the strenuous demand for female satisfaction even more challenging for the husband. While she encouraged ample foreplay, including the husband's gentle stroking of his wife's breasts and face, she still drew strict lines on the body. "Upon no account use the hand to arouse excitement at the woman's genitals," she specified. "There is but one lawful finger of love with which to approach her sexual organs for purposes of excitation—the erectile organ of the male. Many men, in order to arouse passion quickly in the woman, are accustomed to titillate the clitoris with the finger—a proceeding distinctly masturbative." To be counted a successful lover, the husband had to bring his wife to orgasm—but this was to occur only during vaginal intercourse, not through any substitutive techniques. The clitoris, Craddock claimed, should be "saluted, at most, in passing, and afterwards ignored as far as possible."[24]

Clitoral orgasm appeared to Craddock a dangerous sensual indulgence—one that rightly enlightened couples would avoid. Clitoral stimulation, she warned, created "a fury for satisfaction," and it encouraged masturbatory habits, which were likely to leave the wife haggard and coarsened. Though Craddock thought that the morbid effects of masturbation—insanity, epilepsy, acne, asthma, eye troubles, and sundry other calamities—had been "greatly exaggerated," she still condemned it as an asocial behavior and moral ill. She had digested the more dispassionate treatment of autoeroticism in the *au courant* sexology of Havelock Ellis, whose writings debunked the more sensational claims about masturbation's ill effects—but Craddock was not prepared to follow him down the path toward normalizing it. Masturbation, that "colossal bogy," retained much of its horror in her outlook.[25]

Craddock's antipathy towards clitoral stimulation was representative of a deeper strain of anxiety within her sexual mores. Even worse than its masturbatory quality, clitoral stimulation partook of "sexual perversion"— a category that Craddock invoked most often when the "unnatural relations" of same-sex love lurched into view. And it quickly became apparent that this was her underlying problem with the clitoris as well. By Craddock's anatomical account (which she shared with Freud, among others), the clitoris was "not a female organ at all, but a rudimentary male organ." Hence the man who stimulated it was actually entering a danger zone of same-sex genital contact and the woman who wanted it was showing herself to be "semi-masculine." Husband and wife were both straying from expected norms, but the man especially seemed to be edging into the perilously unacceptable. "What a man needs, in order to establish a perfectly wholesome channel for the outlet of his sex magnetism at the genitals," Craddock claimed, "is to have genital contact, not with a grown man, nor with an immature boy, nor with the rudiment of a male procreative organ in a woman; what he needs is genital contact with the female organs of a thoroughly well sexed woman." She readily admitted that many women liked "the excitement produced there" and were wont to insist on it from their husbands, but, given the specter of same-sex love, clitoral stimulation was indelibly marked as abnormal, "an out and out act of sexual perversion." Clearly, Craddock's regimen was anything but a free-for-all.[26]

Craddock's long list of taboos was regularly at cross-purposes with facilitating one of her most fetishized goals: female orgasm. Needless to say, her multiple anxieties about the clitoris made cunnilingus off limits as well, erecting another hurdle for the ardent husband gamely pursuing his wife's sexual satisfaction. So fearful indeed were such oral-genital acts that Craddock avoided them as unmentionables in her shorter published manuals and took them up only briefly in her big manuscript on "The Marriage Relation." There the topic arose primarily as fellatio—"that widespread sex perversion which in modern times is termed the French method." As Craddock saw it, all too many men had been exposed to that method through frequenting prostitutes, leaving virtuous wives at a severe disadvantage to compete with such "abominable allurements." Cunnilingus, she thought, was a comparably rarer but equally perverse practice. A woman's desire for it was mainly a result of a husband's failure to satisfy her in the proper way. Marital relations had to be improved, in this case to defend against the immoral enticements of prostitution and the perversion of approved forms of sexual expression. Simply put, Craddock saw oral sex as off limits; it needed to be resisted, not indulged.[27]

Craddock' sexual advice carried one more requirement for good behavior: Amid all the mind-body melding in the bedroom, lovers could not talk dirty. Spiritual sex was much too exalted for the bawdy vernacular, especially pronounced in the male sporting culture, that celebrated "good square fucks" or the rough-and-tumble of "fucking matches." Before and during sex, "do not tell indelicate stories," Craddock warned. "Shut out the world, with all its baseness, all its impurity," and rise into a realm of "lofty religious sentiment." Sexual pleasure was licensed as religious rapture, not as vulgar physicality; as mystical exaltation, not sweaty passion. If all went as Craddock hoped and dreamed, nobody would be *fucking* at all. Married couples would be devoutly preparing instead for a sacrament, for sharing in "God's attributes of purity, tenderness, [and] unselfishness." They would be refined and uplifted, not coarsened and degraded. Theirs would be a mystical marriage—one that preserved them from impurity, perversion, and vulgarity while bringing blissful satisfaction to body and soul.[28]

Craddock's teachings on sexuality—both the dos and the don'ts—always came back, in the end, to religion. For all her scientific posturing—the repeated nods to sexology and evolutionary science—

Craddock's instructions, like Stockham's, were designed to hold the ground for metaphysical ideals against the determinism of base physical drives. As Craddock succinctly concluded, "The sexual act is . . . in its last analysis, a religious act." God was to be sought in the very midst of that activity—in effect, through a hallowed *ménage a trois* in which the divine filled out the threesome. "Not until you make God the third partner, so to say, in your unions," Craddock claimed, "will you . . . understand the serene and lofty enjoyment of the truly wedded, whose marital embrace is blessed physically, mentally and spiritually by the Power which upholds the universe." God cared deeply about marriage, about its intimacies and alienations, its satisfactions and inequities; God wanted couples to have no sex of a coercive kind, but much sex of a spiritual kind; and God wanted that in order to share in the grace and ecstasy of the greatest sacrament of all, a married couple's sexual union. To say that Craddock had a theology of embodiment is not strong enough: She had no theology apart from fleshly incarnation. "It is through the body," she related, "that the Spirit of God is ever seeking to express itself to the world. And through sex-life most of all."[29]

———•·•———

IT WAS ONE THING FOR Craddock to preach a theology of sexual embodiment, and quite another thing to help people live it out day-to-day or night-to-night. The practical dilemmas she faced in her counseling sessions were sundry, as was evident in an exchange she had with one of her clients. Voicing bafflement at his failure to get in the right frame of mind during intercourse, she pressed him: "You did not fix your thoughts, then, as I told you to do, on the highest power you recognize in the universe, God?" "No," he replied, "it seems sort of odd, don't you know, to think of God at that time." Craddock's advisees— whether earnest, quizzical, or just curious—pushed back with their own experiences. In moving out of her one-size-fits-all manuals into face-to-face meetings, she navigated a terrain tangled with distinct personal problems, intense relational crises, conflicting religious identities, and erratic sexual impulses. Craddock had turned to personal counseling in part as a way to sidestep Comstock's control over obscene publications— but there turned out to be nothing secure or predictable about this approach to marriage reform either. Even for a teacher who was quite ready to celebrate creative individuality, Craddock often found the sex lives of her pupils disturbing and filled with intractable challenges.[30]

Craddock was convinced that the majority of divorces began in the bedroom. Certainly her "Records of Cases in Marital Reform Work" and her "Record of Cases in Oral Instruction" offered ample substantiation of that proposition. She wanted to help save as many troubled marriages as she could, but the alienations between husband and wife often ran deep. There was the middle-aged lawyer who wanted "to do all he can, quietly, to win his wife all over again," even though she no longer wanted to have sex with him, "disliked it intensely," and had of late begun to scream at him whenever he attempted to approach her sexually. The rifts and the betrayals were many. A young factory worker came to her brokenhearted. To help make ends meet, his wife had taken a job as a waitress and had inexplicably decided "to pass as a single woman" at the restaurant. Soon she started carrying on with another man and had now threatened to move out. The desperate husband had turned to Craddock for help.[31]

In some disputes Craddock ended up privy to both sides of disagreement. One young man, raised a devout Christian, told her that he had prayed to find "his proper marital partner" and had thought at the time that his prayer had been well answered with his chosen bride. Now he felt utterly disillusioned. His wife had turned out to be quite "excessive in her demands upon him, requiring union about every other night" and had in the process become downright dissatisfied with his performance. Deciding to sample a variety of "illicit relations," she had cheerily told her husband (or so he reported): "I guess I am a regular whore by nature, and want more than one man." Since they had two

Craddock had various business cards and flyers to advertise her services as an adviser on how to improve marital relations. This is the front and back of one of them that she used in Chicago and Denver. WHi 65508–65509, Wisconsin Historical Society.

small children, he told Craddock that he did not want a divorce. Instead, he had now determined to give up his scruples about extramarital affairs and embark on his own adventures. Craddock offered some of her standard religious advice and sexual tips, but mostly all she could do was to despair over this hellish descent: "Are not such things sufficient to make one sick at heart for the future of the race!"

When the man's slender, dark-haired wife showed up for her own session, however, she hardly seemed the harlot her husband had claimed her to be. Indeed, Craddock's heart went out to her as the young woman explained that she would be "perfectly content" in her marriage if only her husband would be more affectionate and less given to "business worries when they were embracing in bed." "Poor woman!" Craddock exclaimed, "I just longed to *make* him take her in his arms and caress her and love her, love her, love her, in the way a woman wants to be loved." Craddock's poignant yearning for the couple's healing faced long odds against fulfillment. The husband, after all, had resolved to match the wife's infidelities with his own, a tit-for-tat arrangement that was sure to heighten, not mitigate, their divisions. Further estrangement seemed all but inevitable.[32]

Craddock met with many other clients whose marital problems looked much easier to repair than those of the couple whose alienation had turned into unfaithfulness. Take, for example, the youthful pair, married three years, each of whom visited her separately: The wife dreaded the thought of getting pregnant, wanted to avoid sex as much as possible, and could not enjoy it at all; the husband felt ashamed of himself for wanting to have sex with her when he knew that she took no pleasure in it. While he had never visited a prostitute, he often felt that it would actually be the more considerate thing to do given his wife's anxieties about having sex. Craddock bristled at the suggestion of his resorting to a "harlot": "I promptly tabooed anything of the sort." The husband and wife each talked to her, got a copy of *Right Marital Living*, and went away feeling like Craddock had offered them "a possible solution": Lots of nude embraces, "night after night, without genital contact," as a way of building up the affection between them and as a way of alleviating the wife's fears of getting pregnant. In this instance, both counselor and counselees were hopeful about finding a way out of this marital impasse and were happy with the progress being made.[33]

Craddock had other cases that made her feel optimistic about success, but the ones that really weighed on were those involving irresolvable anguish. No one exemplified that more clearly than "Mrs. G," a middle-aged married woman, with a "sweet face, refined by suffering," whom Craddock stood ready to help without taking her usual fee. Unfaithful and mean, Mrs. G's husband had contracted gonorrhea in one of his trysts and passed the disease along to his wife. He had, moreover, committed incest with their daughter from the time she was nine years old, all the while treating his wife with callous indifference. Mrs. G had found out about his sexual violation of their daughter only years later, when the daughter, terminally ill with consumption, "unburdened her soul to her mother." Never confronting her husband with his guilt, Mrs. G feared that, if he found out that she knew about it, he would kill himself. Craddock noted, as an aside in her case notes, that this would have been "good riddance of bad rubbish," but she held back from telling that to Mrs. G. Craddock recognized Mrs. G's case as absolutely critical, a defining moment in her counseling—one that revealed just how necessary and difficult her labors were. "If I helped only this one woman," Craddock said, then her ministry would all "have been worth while."

Despite Craddock's personal investment in Mrs. G's case, it would be hard to count this face-to-face instruction a success. Mrs. G had decided that she wanted to try to "save" her husband and told Craddock that she had silently forgiven him for his betrayals. That prayerful decision looked ill-advised, if not masochistic, and yet Craddock consented to Mrs. G's quiet resolve. Previous to their face-to-face meeting, Mrs. G had heard Craddock give one of her lectures on marital relations and had already decided, based on that talk, to seek "God's blessing" for the renewal of her marriage, including the spiritualization of her sex life with her husband. Craddock seemed all too pleased to hear that Mrs. G was on this path, even advising her "to put my books" in her husband's hands. In this harshly abusive case Craddock was, by her own standards, culpably acquiescent. She firmly supported the liberalization of divorce laws and often advised divorce in cases of extramarital affairs, but with Mrs. G she held her tongue: Here was rubbish that needed to be dumped, and yet Craddock declined to recommend that course of action. Perhaps trying to justify her silence— her own failure at truth-telling—Craddock noted that Mrs. G had found some tiny measure of peace in the "grace" of reclaiming her husband. Tribulations like Mrs. G's, Craddock had decided, could be assuaged only "in the world beyond the grave." That compensatory gesture was necessarily a tragic deferral, and Craddock, despite her own faith in a spiritualist afterlife, surely knew that.[34]

Craddock found herself in similarly treacherous and heartrending territory when cases of same-sex love arose. With one young man, for example, she could tell that she was failing "to touch the deepest chord in his nature" in their session. "I kept feeling around for it, but, apparently, in vain," Craddock noted. At the close of their exchange, though, he began asking about Richard von Krafft-Ebing's *Psychopathia Sexualis*, a formidable European work of sexology known for its detailed categorization of sexual perversions and abnormalities. The young man wanted to know what Craddock thought about Krafft-Ebing's proposed cures, including the use of hypnotism, and it was at that point Craddock knew she was dealing with "a sexual pervert." He told her that he wanted to get married, even though he knew that he was not at all attracted to women and was very much in love with another young man. Obsessed with thoughts of "his beloved boy-friend," he was heartsick that his would-be lover remained infatuated with a girl. He had sought out one treatment after another and appeared to Craddock to be suffering as "would-be ascetics do." Despite her knee-jerk response to label him a pervert, she could not help but feel for him.

The emotional intensity of these face-to-face meetings often pushed Craddock to temper her initial, reactive judgments. Seeing how much her pupil was suffering, she kept the conversation going—within herself as well as with him. Craddock urged him to bypass sketchy hypnotists and to go talk to a radical Unitarian minister whom she trusted, Jenkin Lloyd Jones, whose church was a bastion for Emersonian wayfaring and self-exploration. As for her client's same-sex attraction, she suggested he try to transmute it into a spiritual love and leave off any "bodily caresses." By thus allowing for the spiritualization of same-sex love, Craddock wanted to remove the "stigma on his desire to feel lovingly toward the boy." "I told him that he might love him inwardly all he wished," Craddock noted. But, even as she tried to connect with this young man's "deepest chord," she foundered on the limits of what she counted "natural." When he asked her, "almost pleadingly," whether he could not just give his beloved "a little hug," Craddock sternly replied, "No!" Same-sex love might be spiritualized, but it should not be physically expressed.[35]

The one other case of same-sex love that Craddock dealt with in detail in her counseling records did not have the same face-to-face intensity, but it still pushed her off her familiar script. A friend of one of her other pupils very much wanted her advice but was too embarrassed to visit on his own and wished to rely on indirect instruction. "With the body of a man, he yet has no liking for women sexually," Craddock summarized; "all his yearnings are for men." Tormented and suicidal, he had consorted with prostitutes to try to find arousal with a woman but to no avail. Physicians, likewise, were of no help to him. He had plotted respectability through marriage but broke off the engagement, realizing that he could be happy only with men and that "Nature had evidently made him so." By the time this man sought advice from Craddock through a friend, he was clearly nearing an option of last resort. Craddock discussed various alternatives out there—an "electric cure" prescribed by one doctor, for example—but mostly she recommended a month of meditation and sexual abstinence. That experiment could serve as a means for the young man to discover for himself the truth about his sexuality. Displaying in this moment a notable elasticity in her approach, Craddock accorded the anonymous inquirer the liberty of self-discernment: "Personally, I believed his friend's condition to be a perversion," she concluded; "nevertheless, it might happen that I was wrong, and his friend right, in thinking himself a woman in a man's body." Craddock's solution was not more medical quackery, but a path of intuitive enlightenment.[36]

Craddock's flexibility as a counselor was especially evident in her knack for working across religious lines. She was unfazed by denominational differences, by the escalating diversity of American religious (and irreligious) life. "Young married woman; Roman Catholic; Polish," so read Craddock's terse opening to Case 5 in her records. "Was very grateful for my instruction, and especially pleased to find that I treated her religion with respect, and said she would tell her friends about this way that I respected her religion." Four cases later Craddock was talking easily with a young Baptist woman; she was "deeply impressed by what I said of consecrating the *entire* life (sexual desires included) to God, and making God the third partner; her eyes glistened as I talked to her." People from a wide variety of religious backgrounds showed up at her office, and Craddock was usually able to step far enough back from her own metaphysical inclinations to offer help.[37]

Just as she was happy to work with pupils from different denominations, Craddock was also quite capable of adjusting herself to agnostics and unbelievers. When, for example, an irreligious barber told her, "with a cheery toss of his head," that his shop was "the highest thing in his thoughts at present" and "pooh-poohed any reference to 'God' or the 'Divine,'" Craddock deftly shifted her approach. Instead of becoming peremptory with him over his joking irreverence, she replaced her usual spiritual language with a discussion of "thought-force" and "the impulsive power of primordial matter." She would have preferred to talk about "Yoga as Applied to Married Life" or to expound on New Thought metaphysics, which she did, of course, when the opportunity presented itself. What made her especially adept in these sessions, though, was her willingness to wander "to all points of the compass" with her students.[38]

Not surprisingly, Craddock ambled with particular ease into discussions of spiritualism, especially moving into those byways as a counselor to the bereaved. That strategy was exemplified in the case of a widower, who, still in grief, spoke to her about his loneliness. Craddock took that as an occasion to edge the conversation toward the subject of possible "communion with the blessed dead," but at the mere suggestion of spirit communication the man had laughed at her. When he returned for another visit, she grudgingly broached the subject again, and this time he "seemed exceedingly interested." Craddock did not switch roles from counselor to medium, but she did assure her patient of her own spiritualist convictions: "I told him I was not at all sure as to the way in which she would communicate with him; it might be by touch, by sight, by hearing, by the interior voice, by writing, by planchette or the Ouija board, by raps, by table-tipping, by a dream," Craddock enumerated, "but I felt sure that in *some* way he could become at least dimly conscious of her presence."[39]

The widower's initial laughter at Craddock's spiritualism was revealing of the kind of resistance she often met. In this case, the man had first decided to visit Craddock mostly as a diversion; he considered her "one of the interesting sights of Chicago," not much more than that. Time and again, Craddock found a gap in the way that men and women responded to her: Women usually looked favorably on the religious side of her instruction—they "take to it, for the most part, as a duck takes to water," she said—while men had a much harder time getting a fix on her and her ideas. As Craddock observed of one of her middle-aged male clients, "He did not appear to have paid sufficient attention to the metaphysical side of the teaching, and I told him so. (So few men do!)." That parenthetic aside applied as a general rule, and not just to the men who came out of "idle, lascivious curiosity" to see what Craddock had to offer.[40]

Craddock often found that her male patients were far more interested in her carnal teachings than her spiritual instruction. Another widower, an Episcopalian of aristocratic bearing—"age, 59; slender, fastidious and selfish"—came to her for help, feeling ashamed of "leading an irregular life" and certain "the Lord didn't approve of him." He wished to regularize his life by finding a new mate, but most definitely did not want "some clever college girl" or a career woman. Instead, he specified that he desired "a blonde, with a beautiful, voluptuous form, which he could take pleasure in gazing at." He wanted, in other words, a trophy wife. He told Craddock that he was ruling out one prospect, despite her bright and lively disposition, simply because she did not have large enough breasts. "As usual," Craddock moaned, "the metaphysical part of my teaching fell on dull ears. I supposed, as he was Episcopalian, that he could take his medicine as religious pills; but he gagged at it. Said he was materialistically inclined. . . . And it is these sensual swine before whom I am doomed to cast my pearls."[41]

Swine, that was a strong word, but it did not necessarily overstate the piggish behavior that Craddock encountered in several of her male clients. Her face-to-face sessions often turned out to be every bit as risky as her publishing efforts as she came to occupy, at least in the eyes of men about town, a niche in the economy of commercialized sex. In that flourishing marketplace of bawdy houses, concert halls, stripteases, masked balls, and sex districts that characterized urban nightlife by the 1880s and 1890s, Craddock's offerings could look like one more peep show. "I observe that most of these men who come to me for lessons," she remarked after meeting with a deceptively charming gentleman, "evidently cherish hopes of being eventually admitted to intimacy with me. . . . Oh, what lying, sensual beasts men are!"[42]

In her role as counselor, Craddock had to fend off one advance after another. An unhappily married man, who had previously attended the Church of Yoga, came in for a one-on-one lesson. Since he had never heard of the clitoris, Craddock started with basic physiology, pulling out two anatomical charts, and the man was instantly entranced by "the chart of the woman's genitals." He soon returned for another visit, wanting to hear the very same lecture again, mostly in order to see "that chart." Reluctantly Craddock opened it up again and tried to be as "cool and scientific" as possible, when the man suddenly blurted out that the diagram had given him an erection. "To say I felt outraged, but feebly expresses it. I closed the chart, and froze to a white heat," she seethed. Her client quickly apologized for offending her, but the situation only got worse. "A little later, he said he would give five dollars—he would give ten dollars—just for the sight of a woman's genitals," Craddock noted as her loathing for him deepened. The implication, of course, was that the man wanted her to be the specimen. Craddock scornfully pointed him to harlots, but he kept his attentions awhile longer on her. Finally, after a last plea to see the chart yet again, he gave up, wished her well as "a brave little woman," and went away.[43]

Craddock's self-image as a virtuous woman was repeatedly called into question by those who saw her as a sex worker of one kind or another. A stout German man, sent to her by a local physician, quickly made it evident that he was uninterested in her usual counseling. Smiling and laughing, he told her that he found her spiritual lessons to be "a fake" and that she "ought to give objective teaching." Craddock quickly assured him that "I wasn't here for that sort of thing." Well then, he suggested, she "ought to have some beautiful young girls here for purposes of objective teaching." In other words, she should stop the silliness of marital advising and instead pursue a real sex trade. "There are times when I think maleness in men is something diabolical and loathsome," she swore. One elderly man especially occasioned her bitterness and anger. Taking a little too much pleasure in hearing her talk about the history of sex worship, he had put his hand on her waist as she was opening the door for him to leave. Utterly exasperated, she wondered why he could not keep his hands to himself, why he looked at her with such lust in his eyes. "Oh God, I just loathe the memory of him!" she railed. "I think I could at times grind that man to powder; I could tear his eyes out." [44]

If Craddock were a physician of the emotions, that expertise proved of little help to her in dealing with her own feelings of disgust over these wayward male clients. Her anger simply flamed from the pages of her case notes. Was it the exposure of spiritualized sex as an impossibility, as a phony mystification of unredeemable sexual drives, that made her rage so violently against such men? Was it the massive commercialization of sex as urban entertainment, a net vast enough to catch her up in it as one more commodity, that made her want to pluck out that one man's eyes? "I didn't care to be looked at as though I were a monkey in a show, or an actress in a vaudeville," she fumed. Was it all the privileges and prerogatives that the culture accorded male over female, or, was it finally a primal disorder—the brutish nature of men—that was laid bare when her male clients hassled her? Burdened by all those things, Craddock sometimes despaired of ever communicating her gospel to men, her spiritual idealism utterly deflated. [45]

One thing Craddock's rage did not stem from was naiveté; hers was not the shock of prudish innocence. The heaviness of sexual aggression repeatedly weighed down the lightness of her banter about ecstatically good sex. Craddock discerned a blood lust in "the male human animal," a "passion of destructiveness," that instinctively rejoices in everything from cockfights to boxing to sexual conquest. Slipping into "medical parlance," she detailed the prevalence of sadism in men, those who found satisfaction in inflicting pain or humiliation on their sexual partners. "Sadism, too, is back of the habit in which men of a certain stripe indulge—that of beating and kicking their wives or mistresses," she observed. The male presumption of having "purchased the privilege of coition" through marriage reinforced both sexual aggression and domestic abuse, Craddock averred in urgent tones familiar among marriage reformers of the day.[46]

Beyond the coercion women faced within marriage, Craddock confronted the broader incidence of violence against women in American society. The prevalence of "sexual crimes"—assault, rape, and even murder—made Craddock despair of ever adequately educating "our male population along the lines of right sexual living." At best, reform would be "a slow matter," and hence she found it necessary to offer explicit guidance to girls and women on the necessity of self-defense. However indelicate it seemed to discuss such matters, mothers needed to instruct their daughters about how to protect themselves if they ever encountered a "would-be raper." If assaulted, Craddock detailed, a woman "should watch her opportunity, and seize both his testicles in her hands with a firm grip, squeezing them tightly," which will make him "drop like a stone." A hard kick in the groin might also prove sufficient to disable the assailant.[47]

For all her mystical flights, Craddock kept her advice to women gritty and down-to-earth—and not only on sexual matters. She called out child-custody laws that left mothers empty-handed just as she criticized unequal property rights that kept women economically dependent. Craddock saw a role model for women in Carrie Burnham Kilgore, a pioneering Philadelphia lawyer: Before getting married, Kilgore had been "wise enough" to get her fiancé to sign an "ante-nuptial agreement" by which the couple agreed to equal property and child-custody rights. In her educational program, too, Craddock invariably insisted that she was a marriage reformer and not simply a sex enhancer. "Just as long as wives remain, by reason of their wifehood, economically dependent upon their husbands," she exhorted, "just as long as they are willing to fill, at one and the same time, the various positions of cook, chambermaid, seamstress, laundress, housekeeper, child's nurse, governess and concubine, with no salary for their exhausting labors and no remuneration beyond their board and clothing—and often not that: Just so long will marriage mean for the average wife sexual slavery and thankless household drudgery." Couples were not going to have the good sex both partners desired until they reconstructed their domestic world in cooperative terms. Inhabiting "neither matriarchate nor patriarchate," they needed to be "comrades" and "equals" before they could become contented lovers.[48]

———•◦•———

A CARD-CARRYING LIBERAL, Craddock saw religion and sex as intensely "private affairs," things that priests and magistrates should not presumptuously legislate for free and equal individuals. "Are we free, can we be free as long as our sex life is under the control of church and state?" queried one of Craddock's fellow radicals. "I advocate complete freedom for sexuality the same as for religion," insisted another fellow traveler. If these reformers had their way, sex would join religion in the sheltered domain of individual liberty, private judgment, and personal choice. Sexual emancipation would then be able to move forward, arm-in-arm, with religious freedom. As Craddock would have it, the bedroom was a "little temple," a private sanctuary for the joined expression of religious aspirations and sexual ecstasies. Comstock and company had no business invading that safe haven. [49]

In the view of Craddock and her allies, making religion and sex private matters was important for the effectiveness of liberal statecraft. Marriage reformers offered the government a cuddly domesticated version of religion—one that would focus on blissful personal experiences rather than zealous church-state entanglements. The "foaming rapids" of these religious passions swept through the bedroom, not the public square. Extending liberal ideals of freedom and individuality from religion to sexuality would cut the taproot of Comstock's evangelical politics. "The Holy Fathers of the American Inquisition" would have no right to impose their notions of public decency on such private, intimate affairs.[50]

Apologists for liberal secularism were unable to advance their vision of privacy, free expression, and strict church-state separation very far during Craddock's lifetime. Instead, Comstock's vice society, very much maintaining its legal force and political power, kept an ever-vigilant eye on sex reformers, Craddock included. As she bitterly noted, "the sanctities of my private life"—by which she meant the "peculiarities" of both her religion and her sexuality—went unprotected from the "prying questions" of inspectors, lawyers, and judges. Comstock and his allies sometimes even managed to intrude upon the personal confidences of her face-to-face sessions, disrupting that zone of privacy too. As she typed up her notes on one of her clients, an "earnest Christian" who had benefited from reading *Right Marital Living,* she confessed that she could not remember the details of his case. The postal inspectors had arrived unannounced right after she finished her lesson with him, and that confrontation had caused her so much "worriment" that it "drove his affairs out of my mind."[51]

If Craddock felt anxious or even paranoid, she had every right to be; Comstock and his agents seemed to be everywhere. During another counseling session, this one in New York in August 1902, Craddock had become extremely apprehensive—even "sort of dazed"—when she started thinking that the client looked disquietingly familiar. He reminded her so much of a detective who had once accused her of distributing obscene literature. Had he shaved his moustache, she wondered? No, it was a false alarm. The man turned out not to be a postal inspector or a police officer—just one more "insolent sensualist" who could not help hitting on her. "I am not here to be touched; I am here to teach; that is all, sir," she admonished him, as she had so many others before him.[52]

"America and Americans are ripe for [my] teaching," Craddock continued to hope, despite all the signs to the contrary. To teach Americans in candid and heartfelt ways about sex, to be an expert in sexology, to be a physician of the emotions—these were not easy tasks at the turn of the twentieth century, especially for a single woman with queer religious and political views. Harassment was a constant in Craddock's work—and not only because of Anthony Comstock, but also because sex was now so unavoidably commercialized in American society. Obscenity laws and strip-shows, vice suppression and merchandized sex—these were Craddock's Scylla and Charybdis. She often wondered if any sanctuary of liberty, privacy, and legal protection remained for her as she navigated the tough straits of the country's sexual politics. American freedoms of speech, press, and religion—surely these would buoy her up as she continued her perilous struggle.[53]

CHAPTER FIVE

Every Inch a Martyr

IDA CRADDOCK MADE HER FIRST APPEARANCE in Anthony Comstock's massive logbook, "Names and Record of Persons Arrested under the Auspices of the New York Society for the Suppression of Vice" on May 27, 1898. Comstock squeezed her name in among booksellers, peddlers, and saloonkeepers, but at this point he had no occupation to list for Craddock, only an offense: sending obscene literature by mail. By the time he registered her arrest in New York City in February 1902, Comstock had become more precise; he pegged Craddock's profession as "Pastor of Church of Yoga" and "Lecturer of filth." Right before this latest notation on Craddock, Comstock recorded the case of a German Jewish youth, the son of a rabbi, who had been arrested for mailing a lewd postcard; right after his entry on her, Comstock made note of a "Dealer in ob[scene] books & pictures," who had fled to Canada after Comstock confiscated his inventory.[1]

In Comstock's long-running war on vice, Craddock was only one offender among thousands. A lot of the crimes were miniscule infractions like that of the unfortunate Jewish teenager who, otherwise a well-behaved student in school, had been picked up for indulging in a little erotic juvenilia. Some of those arrested were big-time gambling operators and sex traffickers, but many more were minor leaguers—a bartender, an actress, a housekeeper, a newspaper reporter, a nostrum-selling quack—caught in Comstock's vast imagining of obscenity. If the eventual public visibility of Craddock's case was unusual, it was at the outset quite typical in its ordinariness: The New York Society for the

In the Protestant hagiography, Comstock was pictured as a savior of innocent children. The caption on this photograph read: "These are the citizens for whom 'Uncle Tony' has lived and 'died daily' for more than forty years, and to whom his heart goes out." Charles Gallaudet Trumbull, Anthony Comstock, Fighter: Some Impressions of a Lifetime of Adventure in Conflict with the Powers of Evil *(New York: Fleming, 1913), facing p. 153.*

Suppression of Vice pursued a woman of modest means—a secretary and teacher of stenography—as a threat to public safety and moral decency, a purveyor of obscene literature. For every Walt Whitman or George Bernard Shaw he went after, Comstock snared innumerable obscure offenders.

Comstock's vice squad would not have been half so controversial—or significant—if it had simply been one more Protestant voluntary society trying to effect moral reform through pious persuasion and hellfire denunciation. Not content with being an evangelist or a scold, Comstock wanted the power of the state behind his anti-obscenity campaign; in a word, he wanted a badge. To that end, he successfully lobbied the New

York state legislature to strengthen its anti-obscenity laws and then scored his big coup in 1873 when the U.S. Congress passed "An Act for the Suppression of Trade in, and Circulation of, Obscene Literature and Articles of Immoral Use." Parlaying his legislative successes into a federal appointment as a special agent of the U.S. Post Office, Comstock thereafter had the means to take his fight against obscenity all across the country. He proudly made these new powers of enforcement the basis for the vice society's logo: On one side, a police officer pushes a cuffed prisoner into a jail cell; in the other half of the seal, a gentlemanly reformer throws confiscated books into the flames. For more than four decades, Comstock relished his combined role of evangelical crusader and federal agent.[2]

In spearheading the national campaign against obscenity, Comstock was hardly a Protestant rarity. Working within the precedents of English common law and its American corollaries, Comstock viewed the government as the strict guardian of public morals. Federal, state, and

The emblem of Comstock's New York Society for the Suppression of Vice featured a reformer tossing bad books into a bonfire and an officer pushing a wrongdoer into a prison cell. Nineteenth Annual Report of the New York Society for the Suppression of Vice *(New York: n.p., 1893), cover.*

local statutes should create a seamless legal fabric for the protection of commonly recognized standards of decency. The nation's judicial and police powers were to be deployed against anything that threatened to corrupt public morality, whether a poem, novel, painting, photograph, dance, phonograph recording, or contraceptive device. A particular alertness needed to be shown in regulating those materials that had a marked tendency to corrupt inexperienced youth or harm innocent children. Obscenity was not so much defined in this legal tradition, but imagined as a sinister force that depraved people's imaginations and damaged the public welfare.

Late nineteenth-century American jurisprudence on obscenity was particularly beholden to a specific British precedent of 1868 known as the *Hicklin* standard. That benchmark made no bones about placing the control of indecent printed matter above the freedom of the press. Lascivious acts were not even at issue: For a published work to be suppressed in its entirety, all it had to contain was a single passage deemed a stimulant of lewd thoughts. The bar for conviction could thereby be set very low: If an item was considered capable of making an impure impression on the most innocent member of a community, that was enough to label the piece obscene and prosecute its vendors. Comstock often displayed a cocksure attitude about the cases he sent to trial—and no wonder given the way obscenity standards were being interpreted in American courts in the late nineteenth century. Comstock had put Ezra Heywood, the founder of the New England Free-Love League, behind bars and had snared the freethinker D. M. Bennett as well for distributing one of Heywood's publications. Doing battle with obscenity laws by asserting a right to free expression proved, time and again, a losing proposition well into the twentieth century.[3]

On the other liberty that Craddock wanted to claim—the freedom of religion—the legal messages were slightly more mixed. At first glance, it looked like the minders of Christian orthodoxy were losing their ability to treat blasphemy as a prosecutable offense. Abner Kneeland, a Massachusetts freethinker, had been famously convicted of the crime in 1838, but thereafter, American courts had shown greater wariness in taking up cases involving blasphemy charges, especially in comparison to their English counterparts. Though the laws remained on the books in most states, only the rare infidel actually got hauled in for blasphemy after the Civil War. Charles B. Reynolds in Morristown, New Jersey, in 1887 and Charles C. Moore in Lexington, Kentucky, in 1894, were two examples, but the results were hardly what the prosecutors were seeking. In the New Jersey case, the judge handed down a token fine, and the agnostic orator Robert Ingersoll scored big publicity points with his theatrical closing argument for the defense. In the Kentucky case, the judge expressly found the notion of blasphemy irreconcilable with American formulations of religious freedom and church-state separation. "There is no place for the common law crime of blasphemy," the judge concluded, in a constitutional system of government that prized religious liberty above erstwhile legal offenses such as heresy, apostasy, and profane scoffing.[4]

Despite the difficulties involved in prosecuting blasphemy, it was not simply given a pass in the late nineteenth century. A reputation for outrageous infidelity made it a lot easier for the prosecution to press the obscenity charge. The Kentucky agitator Charles Moore, a few years after the judge had dismissed the blasphemy indictment against him, faced an obscenity trial in Ohio for distributing an issue of his paper, the *Blue-grass Blade*, that had ventured near the dangerous terrain of Free Love. Marriage reform was hardly his leading cause, but Moore, the grandson of the famed revivalist Barton W. Stone, had grown weary of the "holy hush" surrounding the "sex question." That Free-Love flirtation was enough to attract the attention of the postal inspectors: The Comstock law against mailing obscene literature prevailed where the blasphemy charge had failed; Moore received a two-year sentence in the state penitentiary in Columbus. Not too long after his release Moore, as recalcitrant as ever, would turn the pages of the *Blue-grass Blade* over to the fiery defense of Craddock. [5]

Indecency, as Moore's fate indicates, had come to represent a greater legal vulnerability for freethinkers than irreverence. Expressing contrary views about God, Jesus, the Virgin Birth, or the Bible won them few public friends, but, as long as those anticlerical notions were not laced with bawdy vulgarities, infidels were generally at liberty to vent them. So when Comstock proclaimed that Craddock was guilty of blasphemy, that allegation was socially damning more than it was legally hazardous; it provided a rhetorical flourish to the much weightier legal charges he brought of lewdness and indecency. In short, the growing heft accorded obscenity provided a way for censors to keep harassing cheeky freethinkers and Free-Love liberals, while sidestepping the church-state issues that the blasphemy statutes raised.

That the charge of obscenity could be used to attack freethinking dissidents certainly muddied the waters of religious liberty, but what made American religious freedom even murkier was the way Protestant Christianity remained the standard by which church-state relations were refereed in the nineteenth century. When in 1892 the Supreme Court pronounced a clear consensus on the fact that the United States was a Christian nation, the justices meant, above all, a Protestant Christian nation. Craddock hoped that her case would allow a hearing for a more expansive view of church-state separation and the free exercise of religion. Her legal struggles, she thought, "differed from those of previous sex reformers, in that my religious rights had been invaded." As she explained her stand, "Now, the First Amendment to the Constitution of the United States says, expressly; 'Congress shall make no law respecting an establishment of religion, or prohibiting the free exercise thereof.' But the postal law passed by Congress against the use of the mails for obscene literature, has been twisted so as to . . . exclude my religious teachings." She considered that infringement unconstitutional and very much wanted her lawyers to turn this into a religious freedom case: "I am taking my stand in the last ditch," she wrote to her patron William Stead, "in this appeal for my religious liberty." [6]

Craddock deeply hoped that the free-exercise clause of the First Amendment would trump the regulation of obscenity, but that plan remained a risky leap of faith. Free-exercise cases were primarily a matter of later twentieth-century jurisprudence, not nineteenth-century precedent, so her legal foundation for this last-ditch stand was shaky at best. The maintenance of public morality, safety, and decency through the suppression of obscenity would almost certainly eclipse claims about individual religious liberty. The bedrock for church-state relations remained a virtuous Protestant republic, and that foundation still had a determinative effect on how the edges of religious freedom were defined. The courts were to preserve the generalized moral standards of a Christian nation, not to protect the religious liberty of dangerous eccentrics who openly subverted those values. Craddock was, in sum, proposing an unlikely free-exercise gambit—that her avowed spiritualism provided a constitutional protection for her frank sexology. [7]

"Comstock vs. Craddock," as the face-off came to be known, put all the chips on the table: obscenity and First Amendment liberties, Protestant orthodoxy and freethinking blasphemy, vice suppression and sexual enlightenment. Anteing up more than he had initially imagined necessary, Comstock wagered his reputation and that of his sponsoring society in his efforts to silence Craddock. With not much respectability left to gamble away, Craddock at least had her personal liberty, but she was now quite ready to risk that as well. If Comstock liked a good ruse in the service of evangelical morality—the use of decoy letters with assumed identities was a staple for him—he was hardly bluffing about fines, prisons, and insane asylums. He once reminisced that as a boy he had enjoyed building stone-traps in the woods; when the rabbit or squirrel nibbled on the bait, it would be crushed to death by a large falling stone. Just as Satan devised snares to catch his victims—Free Lovers, fine-art aficionados, and liberals were among the devil's fiendish lures—Comstock had to counter with his own godly contrivances to flatten his smut-mongering quarry. Craddock looked like easy enough prey, but the showdown she triggered would prove anything but trouble-free for Comstock.[8]

ALTHOUGH CRADDOCK ONLY appeared in Comstock's logbook in 1898, he was surely aware of her well before that arrest. Perhaps her tenure as corresponding secretary for the Comstock-bashing American Secular Union had first drawn the great vice reformer's attention. He was certainly on constant guard against liberal organizers with their inflated sense of free expression. "Liberals and infidels are the only class who have undertaken by a systematic and organized effort, to defend the dealers in obscene literature," he claimed, "or repeal the laws of Congress prohibiting the transmission through the mails of this infamous matter." Comstock had five chapters on "so-called liberals" in his sensational *Frauds Exposed* (1880) and two more on them in his equally lurid *Traps for the Young* (1883), manifestos in which he pictured pornographers and freethinking liberals as yoked at the hip in a diabolical alliance against him.

Comstock pointed to the National Liberal League, the direct precursor of the American Secular Union, as the brain trust for the unholy coalition opposing his reform efforts. He clearly kept an eye on that organization's leadership, "their blasphemous speeches and publications." "The National Liberal League through its officers has become the champion of obscenity," he remarked. Craddock was small fry compared to some of the more vocal and visible Liberal Leaguers—infidel Robert Ingersoll always topped the list; Free-Lover Moses Harman was not far behind—but the president and corresponding secretary remained obvious personifications of the group's efforts to roll back Comstock's trademark laws. The hybrid image of "the Liberal obscenity peddler" was a well-established character type in Comstock's mind, and it would be easy for him to see Craddock as the latest player of that abominable part.[9]

If her role in the American Secular Union had not already sealed Craddock's reputation with Comstock as one of the devil's sharp-shooters, then certainly her part in the small-scale culture war over the Danse du Ventre did so. Comstock's local agents in Philadelphia had immediately put Craddock on legal notice that her essay on belly dancing was considered obscene and could not be sent through the mails. Toward the end of November in 1896, as she was preparing a handful of pamphlets for the cause (including a revised version of the *Danse du Ventre* essay), she received a harsh warning from Philadelphia's Post Office Inspector, Warren P. Edgerton. He reminded her in no uncertain terms of the illegality of sending such indecent materials through the mails. That encounter left her, to say the least, "quite down in the mouth"; she "cried and cried" that late autumn afternoon.[10]

The extent of the ban, as Edgerton presented it to her, felt utterly stifling, and she began to despair of her "beautiful gospel" getting any hearing at all. Edgerton's lecture had been so severe that it left her doubting whether she could safely keep up a private correspondence with her pupils. "If a printed pamphlet cannot thus go through the mails, is a written letter any more exempt?" she asked bleakly in her diary. "Can I give advice by mail, as a correspondent on social purity, to people seeking to live aright? . . . Apparently not." She feared, moreover, that the postal inspector was even warning her against conferring with friends on personal matters through the mail. "No matter how I may yearn for the wise counsel of some earthly friend, I am forbidden by law to write to that friend to ask for counsel, if the advice sought has anything to do with right living in the sexual relation," she despaired. "Is it not terrible?" One legal adviser she consulted at the time reassured her that her private letters were safe from interference, but Craddock did a lot of frank marital advising through correspondence and so she remained justifiably anxious. Certainly, the authorities were going to do nothing to relieve those worries. It served the government's correctional purposes to have Craddock "fretting my heart out."[11]

With the written word looking like a risky medium across the board, Craddock turned to spoken communication as a refuge for her teachings. Now there was only "one thing to do—teach orally," Craddock resolved in her diary. By the spring of 1897 she had started running advertisements in local newspapers, which were aimed initially at women as her chosen audience: "INSTRUCTION GIVEN TO WOMEN UPON SCIENTIFIC MOTHERHOOD AND RIGHT LIVING IN THE MARITAL RELATION." While she ended up working just as much with men as with women, she always saw women as more promising and fitting customers—on religious, social, and sexual grounds. Twisting the usual association of hysteria with women, Craddock explained her preference for female clients in her diary: "Women are less hysterical over sexual matters than are men, so that there is some chance of having women study up right sexual living in seriousness and from a high plane; whereas a majority of men are liable to have sexual hysterics while discussing the physiology and hygiene of sex." Given how many of her male students wound up occupying anything but a spiritual plane in their behavior toward her as a teacher, Craddock no doubt often wished that she had stuck with this initial mission of instructing women only.[12]

Despite the damper that Inspector Edgerton had placed upon her labors, Craddock held at least a frail hope for success through the shift to oral instruction. "I *may* succeed in this. But Heaven knows what infernal laws may be brought into requisition to choke me off even here," she acknowledged. Scraping together seven dollars in rent for a modest space on Arch Street not far from her secretarial job at City Hall, she set up shop. Even though this little office had "once been a small bathroom," she was thrilled with it, the skylight, the pale blue wallpaper, the refinished wood floor. It was hers, "a dear little box of a room." Being able to conduct face-to-face instruction had become, in Craddock's reckoning, the last citadel for "my soul's freedom of speech." She was ready, she now started telling her friends, to fight hard for this liberty, come what may: "I cannot and will not be silenced!"[13]

The satisfaction Craddock took in having her own office for counseling and study soon collided with grimmer realities. However much Edgerton's warning had rattled her in late 1896, the effects of it gradually wore off over the next several months. Perhaps she needed the mail-order income; perhaps she had gathered renewed courage to speak her mind; perhaps she was courting persecution—"The blood of the martyrs is the seed of the Church," she reminded herself in her diary. Whatever the combination of reasons, she started sending out her new pamphlets and actively promoting them little more than six months after Edgerton had spooked her. That move did not go unnoticed for long: A formal postal complaint was filed against her on November 13, 1897, this one for depositing *Helps to Happy Wedlock* and *Letter to a Prospective Bride* in the mails. Except for another grave warning from Edgerton not to mail her pamphlets—and now he added Alice Stockham's *Karezza* to the list of books that Craddock was forbidden to distribute—no immediate federal action was taken.[14]

For a brief moment it looked like Craddock was going to get off with another slap on the wrist. Two days later, however, her renewed involvement in sex reform received a more severe smack when she was abruptly fired from her municipal job at the Bureau of Highways. Her extracurricular activities on behalf of sex reform had caught the notice of a coworker and raised the ire of her boss. The close timing of her firing and Edgerton's latest warning might have been mere coincidence, but that seems unlikely. Craddock was moving up on the postal inspector's watch-list, and that added attention was starting to catch up with her. In any case, Craddock's job loss doubled the financial squeeze that was being put on her: It cut off a reliable source of income at the same time the post office was trying to close down her mail-order business. Cruelly, Craddock now felt keen pressure simply to return remittances rather than risk fulfilling orders by sending her pamphlets through the mail. Her livelihood had been all but extinguished.[15]

Just how far and fast Craddock was sinking into a legal quagmire became evident the spring after her dismissal from the Bureau of Highways. On May 13, 1898, a second postal offense was registered against her, this time for mailing her other two pamphlets, *Advice to a Bridegroom* and *The Danse du Ventre*. There was no room left now for more warnings: Craddock was summarily arrested for depositing obscene literature in the mail.

The chain of events following Craddock's arrest moved swiftly. She was arraigned in federal court by the end of the month, her case sent to the grand jury for likely indictment. It was now at the end of May 1898 that Craddock entered Comstock's record keeping for the first time. The gravity of her predicament was not lost on Craddock. "I have come to grief at last," she wrote her long-time ally Edward Bond Foote in early June. After her initial hearing, but before any actual trial, the "Post Office authorities" had made it clear to her that all four of her pamphlets were now considered contraband. "This prohibition covers the entire United States," she reported to Foote. "As I have been dependent, somewhat, on my mail business, I shall now give up my office, and betake myself to Chicago—that Mecca of Freethought." There, while awaiting the grand jury's decision, she hoped to start up her practice of oral instruction again and somehow steer clear of any further legal entanglements.[16]

Her legal mess, however, proved to be only half of Craddock's worries. She had told Foote that she planned to leave for Chicago the next week where her admired mentor Alice Stockham offered connections and temporary shelter. Craddock had aimed to depart on June 13 or 14, but that turned out not to be soon enough. Her mother, again ashamed of her daughter for getting her "name dragged through the papers," turned for help to an assistant district attorney, Thomas Barlow, who was one of Comstock's most dependable allies in Philadelphia. Together Barlow and Lizzie obtained from two physicians the requisite certification that

Ida was "an insane person" and thereby managed to get her locked up in the Friends Asylum, located in the Philadelphia suburb of Frankford, on June 10th. Six days later the State Committee on Lunacy transferred her from that sanitarium to the Pennsylvania Hospital for the Insane where the doctor in charge was apparently surer about her pathology than was the head physician at Friends. To Craddock's mother, a plea of insanity had become both necessary and accurate—for mitigating the damage to the family's good name and for saving Ida from herself. Lizzie now had the district attorney's office as well as the medical establishment to back up her motherly assessment.[17]

Craddock's abduction had been terrifying. Lizzie had shown up with two accompanying officers ready to detain her daughter; screaming out for help, Ida had tried to escape but was held by force. The two doctors were called in to verify the medical case against her, and her mother and two of the four men then took her away to the asylum in a carriage. Over the next several days, Craddock made repeated requests to be allowed to contact her friends as well as her lawyer, but these pleas were refused: She tried to get word to Henrietta Westbrook no less than fourteen times; she was similarly determined in her efforts to notify William Stead by cable; and she had begged to telephone her attorney.

Craddock was eventually allowed to contact the outside world, but the initial experience of being robbed of her freedom had been unforgettably chilling. "The agony of those first few days, before I got into communication with my friends," she wrote a couple of months afterward, "was something frightful. Had I had the slightest tendency to insanity, I should have gone stark, staring mad, with the shock and horror of it." Craddock felt, indeed, as if her whereabouts might remain a mystery indefinitely. Since she had told all her friends that she was leaving for Chicago, she figured they would have little reason to suspect that she had been confined and thus no occasion to make a search for her. She feared that her mother had finally found a way to put an end to "my sex reform teaching" and "to get me completely and forever into her power."[18]

After the first few days of fear, Craddock regained her balance and was soon fighting for her release. Word somehow made its way to Henrietta Westbrook who, in turn, spread the news about what had happened; soon Stead was weighing in as well on Craddock's behalf. The crucial aid in this instance, though, came from Craddock's attorney Carrie Burnham Kilgore, the first—and for a long time only—woman admitted to the bar in Philadelphia. Unlike Craddock's failed efforts to crack open Penn's undergraduate program for women, Kilgore had successfully broken down the men-only barrier at the Law School, though it took her ten years of repeated petitions to do so. Going on in 1886 to win the right to practice law in the state, she was one of a small cadre of professional women who never deserted Craddock. Kilgore had informally advised Ida the first time her mother had tried to institutionalize her in 1894 and quickly came to her defense in this much more urgent instance as well. Though the details of her legal strategy have not survived, Kilgore somehow managed to bring enough heat to bear on the reigning authorities that, within three months, Ida was out of the asylum.[19]

Kilgore was working at the same time on the federal charges against Craddock. The grand jury handed down an indictment on August 16, 1898, but Kilgore managed to get it dropped two weeks later, apparently by cutting a deal with the district attorney's office: All four of Craddock's pamphlets would remain barred from circulation through the mails, but, in promising to abide by that judgment, Craddock would not have to stand trial and hence would avoid the possibility of jail time as well as ongoing confinement in the asylum. The joined ambitions of her mother and the assistant district attorney had been to shut down all facets of Craddock's sex-education program, including the oral instruction and the distribution of her pamphlets by hand. With Kilgore's help, the prosecution settled for the narrower censure much to the regret of Lizzie, who had reached the sorrowful conclusion that her daughter needed to be permanently confined to a hospital for the insane, lest she continue her downward spiral to an even more humiliating end.

Upon her release from the Pennsylvania Hospital—and even with the federal indictment resolved—Craddock knew that she had to stay far away from her mother. Kilgore had "unhesitatingly advised me to get out of the State as quickly as possible" and under no circumstances to return to her mother's house. Ever fearful of the asylum, Craddock headed to Newcastle, Delaware, to stay with a friend, her flight complicated by the fact that Lizzie had possession of most of her clothes and furnishings (though Ida, ever the self-recorder, had somehow escaped with her typewriter in hand). A particular frustration nagged Craddock—her mother had her books. "There is a valuable Latin dictionary; a Greek Testament, dictionaries and text-books in Greek, German, French, Italian, Spanish; works on psychology, on travels, on folklore, etc.," she enumerated, feeling very much the want of them. Her books were "like good old friends," and she had often taken "great comfort" from just looking at the shelves and seeing her favorite volumes lined up near her. Lizzie would not relinquish any of the books or other personal articles, holding onto them for whatever leverage they offered over her "poor, misguided, insane daughter."[20]

From Newcastle, Delaware, Craddock made her way back to London with an invitation to work for Stead again, this time in the *Review of Reviews* office. Stead had launched that publication in London in 1890 and soon had versions of it coming out in New York and Melbourne as well. It focused on literary updates and world news, not the spiritualist frontiers represented by *Borderland*, the editorial office in which Craddock had worked during her first stay in London in 1894 and 1895. That latter journal, after four years of occultist reportage, had recently folded, so Stead needed to place Craddock elsewhere in his sprawling publishing enterprise.

Craddock had been back in England all of two weeks when Stead's plan to have her work at the *Review of Reviews* blew up. The office manager had gotten hold of some of Craddock's personal correspondence with Stead and was put off by her discussions of spiritualism. (Few of his colleagues found Stead's appetite for religious eccentrics to be his most impressive side, and certainly the occult interests that he and Craddock shared could look to skeptics like the tassels on the cultural fringe.) Also, one of the letters that the office manager discovered was actually from Ida's mother to Stead, and that only made matters worse: Lizzie, after all, was never her daughter's best character witness. The letter called Ida a liar for trying to pass as "Mrs. Craddock" rather than Miss Craddock. As Ida saw it, since she had been forced to masquerade as Mrs. Roberts the last time she was in London, she could not show up this time as a "Miss." Once a Mrs., Miss was not an option. Mr. Roberts had passed on, so the story went, and Ida had returned to her maiden name. More than a cover-up of a previous disguise, though, Craddock also thought being a "Mrs." was a useful cloak for her work as a marriage reformer. Lizzie, of course, would have none of it and no doubt provided Stead with an earful in her letter to him.

The revelations the office manager found in this stack of correspondence proved disastrous for Craddock. Word soon passed from the snooping office administrator to Stead's son and then on to Stead's wife. No one suggested that the letters implied an illicit sexual relationship between Stead and Craddock; Stead's concern for Ida's welfare appeared "fatherly." Nonetheless, Stead's wife and son had come to see her as a shady and disreputable character—a lying, spiritualist crank—and that disfavor, combined with the opposition of the office manager, made Craddock's employment at the *Review of Reviews* untenable. After finishing up some research at the British Museum, she packed her bags and headed back across the Atlantic. So it was that in January 1899 Craddock made her way belatedly to Chicago—the onetime stage of the Danse du Ventre, now the "Mecca of Freethought"—where she hoped for a fresh start.[21]

In America's second city Craddock established a new office for marital instruction and within the next several months had obtained a large enough space to begin holding regular Sunday meetings of her new Church of Yoga fellowship. At this point she was living more by the letter of her agreement with the Philadelphia prosecutors than by the spirit of it. Although, as required, she had stopped circulating her previous four pamphlets through the mails, she was still happily selling them by hand. Also, she insisted that there was nothing stopping her from publishing a new pamphlet and circulating that one through the mails. Hence *Right Marital Living*, a modestly expanded version of her teachings, was out by summer. It did not take long for Chicago's postal inspectors to react.

On August 16, 1899, a Boston editor turned Craddock in for sending him the new pamphlet for review, and two months later she was again under federal indictment for depositing obscene literature in the mails. The irony this time was that the initial complaint to the postal inspectors came from someone whom Craddock had reason to believe was on her side: the eminent reformer Henry B. Blackwell, widower of suffragist Lucy Stone and publisher of the *Woman's Journal*. Blackwell, a lionized activist for women's rights, objected to Craddock's separation of the physical pleasure of intercourse from its procreative function. The obscenities of a radical like Craddock threatened the good name of the suffrage movement, and Blackwell had thus taken it upon himself to become one of Comstock's informers. That Craddock then dismissed Blackwell, with his halo of white whiskers and receding hairline, as a sexually frustrated old geezer only added to the impasse between them.[22]

Craddock was saved again by a good lawyer. Clarence Darrow, the celebrated attorney for the damned, posted the $500 bail-bond for her release on October 31 and took on her case *pro bono*. Darrow, the very same age as Craddock at forty-one, had come to particular prominence in Chicago as the defender of the railway union leader, Eugene Debs, in 1894. Known for his snide distance from Christian orthodoxy, Darrow became infamous a quarter century later for taking on evangelical standard-bearer and populist Democrat William Jennings Bryan at the Scopes Monkey Trial in Dayton, Tennessee. For his tenacious defense of teaching evolutionary biology in the public schools and for his storied cross-examination of Bryan, Darrow would be immortalized as one of America's great freethinkers, the shrewd advocate of scientific rationality in the face of the country's Fundamentalist bumpkins.

If a cantankerous agnostic much of the time, Darrow nonetheless had a soft spot for spiritualism, nearly akin to William James's attractions to psychical research. Darrow reported having visited mediums and séances in "most American cities of any importance, and many in Europe." "I really wanted to believe it all," he observed in his autobiography, "and therefore tried to, but in vain." Even if his fascination with spiritualism failed to overcome his skepticism, Darrow had other facets of his religious background that very much mirrored his new client's circumstances. He was the son of Methodist-turned-Unitarian parents who, as he described their trek, had left Christianity behind and sailed "out on the open sea without a rudder or compass, and with no port in sight." Perhaps Craddock and Darrow were, after all, then something of a match: He liked lost progressive causes more than routine legal work, freethinkers and spiritualists more than well-anchored Christians. Craddock fit that bill perfectly.[23]

Darrow entered a plea of not guilty on Craddock's behalf on November 11th. In short order, Henry Blackwell and Anthony Comstock were both subpoenaed to testify. If Darrow was entertaining fantasies of a courtroom drama with Comstock—on the order of his later showdown with William Jennings Bryan—he did not get his chance. He quickly decided instead that Craddock's best hope was for him to work out a plea deal. "If I wished to fight, he would make the best fight possible," she reported. "But he warned me in advance that I was certain to be pronounced guilty and sent to the penitentiary." Faced with that prediction, Craddock reluctantly agreed to change her plea to guilty and, in doing so, allowed Darrow to pursue a "compromise": namely, a three-month suspended sentence rather than imprisonment. Clemency came this time at a premium—upon the condition that Craddock turn over all copies of her sex-reform pamphlets "to be burned." As she noted, "The prosecution had me in a hole, and could practically dictate their own terms." The entire stock of her latest manual, *Right Marital Living*—along with the remaining stash of her old pamphlets—went up in flames. When Comstock put the image of a book-burning reformer on his society's seal, he very much meant the emblem to be taken literally.[24]

Looking again for a more hospitable place to carry on her work, Craddock traveled west to Denver where she offered lectures, worked diligently on her big book on marriage reform, and pursued her Divine Science interests over the next year. She also published a carefully expurgated version of her teachings that she hoped would prove acceptable to the censors. Her edits included turning the word *semen* into *generative fluid*, dropping every mention of the word *testicles*, and eliminating her advice on different positions and lubricants. Those efforts apparently worked, at least for the time being; Craddock experienced no legal trouble in Colorado.

In the spring of 1901, she returned east to Washington, D.C., where she would cause a far greater stir than she had out West. Ever the brainworker, she wanted to conduct research at the Library of Congress, but she also had a new publication to distribute, *The Wedding Night*—one that was as frank (and obscene) as ever. It seemed designed to outrage Comstock and his agents, whom she was now affectionately referring to in print and correspondence as "the Holy Fathers of the American Inquisition." Later Comstock would specify three passages from this latest work as unspeakably nasty—one of which praised anew the "wifely duty to perform pelvic movements during the embrace, riding your husband's organ gently, and, at times, passionately, with various movements, up and down, sideways, and with a semi-rotary movement." *The Danse du Ventre* lived on in *The Wedding Night*, and the latter provoked the same horror of female ardor that Craddock's original defense of belly dancing had. Indeed, her latest musings on pelvic movements seemed to condense all the furor and offense, the passage from motionless modesty to undulating passion.[25]

In April 1901, the same month that Craddock had first opened an office in the nation's capital, she once again found herself under arrest for circulating "obscene, lewd, [and] lascivious pamphlets." A statute in the District prohibited circulation of indecent publications by hand, in addition to the usual ban protecting the mails. Craddock spent the night of April 23 in jail and was arraigned in police court the next day. The morning newspapers had picked up the story of her arrest, so the courtroom was crowded with "curiosity-seekers" hoping "to hear something spicy," along with a smattering of "radical women" wanting to show their support. The voyeurs got what they wanted: At the hearing the prosecution read objectionable passages from *The Wedding Night* to make the case for charging Craddock.

Allowed by the judge a moment to respond to the charges against her, Craddock laid claim to her First Amendment rights. The judge, unconvinced of that point's relevance to the charge at hand, instead "took occasion to rebuke me for my supposed violation of good taste and propriety," a scolding that she had "to swallow in silence." With the judge having found clear grounds for proceeding to trial, the prosecutor suggested a way to put an end to the matter, jauntily remarking that Craddock "might possibly find the climate of another city better for my health." The judge agreed, urging Craddock to leave the city rather than face trial and conviction. She accepted the offer and left the nation's capital two days later.[26]

Weary and dispirited, Craddock now migrated to New York City and set up a little office for oral instruction at 134 West 23rd Street. "Thus have I thrice escaped the penitentiary," Craddock remarked of her legal battles in Philadelphia, Chicago, and Washington, "but each time at the cost of a harder battle and greater publicity. I do not deem it prudent to risk [the] danger of a fourth time. I am now reckoned an old offender." She knew that each brush with the law increased the likelihood that the full weight of the Comstock act would be brought down upon her—five years in prison and a $5,000 fine. She told herself and her patrons that she was withdrawing from the world of print entirely, at least until she could secure some legal protection for her writings and get them lifted out of the category of obscene literature. She would mail none of her books; she would sell none of them by hand; she would not even show them to her pupils during their office visits. Her teaching existed now "only by word of mouth," only as a form of speech. "I am withdrawing my books from the public," she notified readers of *Lucifer the Light-Bearer* in August 1901, "and confining myself to oral instruction, which, so lawyers inform me, is perfectly safe for me legally." Surely, with that limited mission, she would be beyond Comstock's reach, even on his home turf.[27]

After her scrape in Washington, D.C., Craddock swore that discretion was the better part of valor, but she faced several obstacles in upholding that dictum for any length of time. Primarily, of course, she did not believe it: Tact was not a particularly good measure of courage and conviction in matters of sexual enlightenment. Financially, too, she was quite strapped, so economic worry readily kicked in as an incentive to restart her mail-order business. She had been reduced, at least initially, to sleeping on the floor of her New York office with a wad of blankets for a mattress. At the beginning of August 1901 she counted up her savings and found that she "had exactly $6.96 in all the world." When an order for two of her books arrived later that day, it promised to add one dollar to the sum, should she have the wherewithal to fulfill the request.[28]

Even with her newly avowed cautiousness, Craddock faced the added problem that her opponents seemed intent on drawing her right back into the fray. With the New York Society for the Suppression of Vice on red alert against her, she began to receive decoy letters designed to entrap her in one violation or another of the Comstock law. The group also relied on concerned citizens to act as informants, and unfortunately for Craddock her Manhattan landlord, a builder active in Baptist missionary work, was greatly concerned about her activities. He feared for his "Christian reputation" after learning of her teachings and had consulted Comstock directly about the matter. That Craddock had given a lesson to the landlord's son and two of his "college chums" could not have helped the situation. All things considered, it did not take long for Craddock's latest profession of prudence to be thoroughly undone.[29]

Made aware of Craddock's labors in Manhattan, Comstock sent her a letter of warning in late January 1902 informing her that she appeared to be in violation of both state and federal laws. It was illegal, he told her, "to debauch the minds of the young or place in their hands, matters which suggest lewd and lascivious thoughts," and he stretched that prohibition in his cautionary notice to include her oral instruction as well as her printed matter. He would not give her long to heed his advice.[30]

Comstock and three of his deputies arrived at Craddock's room on West 23rd Street on February 4. They were there to arrest her for continuing to defy the law, to search for additional incriminating evidence, and to seize her contraband publications. The immediate warrant accused her of depositing "a sealed envelope . . . containing obscene, lewd and lascivious matter of an indecent character" at a Manhattan post office on January 30. Craddock had been working on the fly to issue new editions of *The Wedding Night* and *Right Marital Living* (all she could afford to print was 500 copies of each). She had sent both of those pamphlets, along with a circular and a diagnostic questionnaire, to a supposed customer in a New Jersey suburb. Whether or not the recipient, Frank Lea, was one of Comstock's plants, the result was the same: He immediately turned Craddock's mailed materials over to the postal inspectors. Indeed, "Frank Lea" may have been a cover for Comstock himself. As the vice crusader informed Henrietta Westbrook in late February when she once again rushed to her friend's defense, "I personally secured from Ida C. Craddock, the foul stuff which she was sending through the mails in violation of the Law."[31]

Craddock was now in Comstock's hands, and he appeared, as she remarked shortly after he came to arrest her, "as hungry as a Jersey mosquito . . . for my blood." And, indeed, Comstock felt good about finally nabbing Craddock; he openly celebrated her detainment as a triumph for moral decency. Amid the self-congratulation he made the sinister claim that Craddock had been preying on pubescent girls with her teachings and was personally preparing them for seduction at the hands of young toughs. These were dubious allegations, given Craddock's commitments to marriage and monogamy, but in Comstock's view the science of sexology was little more than the science of seduction. That Craddock might be some kind of debased procurer of virgins for randy young men was an over-the-top accusation—and yet Comstock even hinted at something more ominous about her than that.[32]

In running down the list of Craddock's offenses, Comstock momentarily paused to conjure up the specter of witchcraft. Craddock's spiritualism, he said, had left her the captive of "a familiar spirit"; in other words, a supernatural force might indeed have hold of her, but it was of the devil, not heaven. Though no doubt rumors of her having a "spirit husband" had prompted Comstock's accusation, Craddock responded like an old freethinker, not an insulted spiritualist. She simply scoffed at Comstock's implication that she had "an imp or a little black devil tagging around after me" and finished with a pair of caustic rhetorical questions: "Does Mr. Anthony Comstock propose, I wonder, to enlarge his present field of operations by combining the medieval business of witch-finder with that of official taster of obscene literature? Is he rolling under his tongue as a sweet morsel, the possibilities of burning me at the stake?" If Comstock's imagination was now "running amuck" in fantasizing about Craddock's crimes, that was hardly surprising: He always believed that he faced a demonic congress of adversaries who were hell-bent on corrupting America's youth.[33]

Given the scandal and danger he saw in Craddock, it was no surprise that Comstock pursued the case against her as aggressively as possible.

At the state level, he brought criminal charges against Craddock on March 5, 1902 in New York's Court of Special Sessions for selling *The Wedding Night* to one of the vice society's undercover detectives. At the same time in the U.S. District Court he pursued federal charges against her for having knowingly deposited obscene literature in the mails. A week later on March 12, the grand jury delivered an indictment in the federal case, thus putting her in double jeopardy.

Craddock was very much ready for a fight. She pushed her latest lawyer, Hugh Pentecost, to prepare for a serious battle for the freedoms of speech, press, and religion. There would be no plea bargains, no insanity defenses, no skipping town; rather, Craddock would take a final stand for her principles, and suffer the full wrath of the law if she lost. If she really wanted a damn-the-torpedoes approach, Craddock would have been better off with a different lawyer, Darrow perhaps rather than Pentecost. A prominent New York editor and agitator, a thoroughgoing rationalist, and an active debunker of Christian and occult superstitions, Pentecost was "one of the best known attorneys in New York City," an account in the *Boston Investigator* assured. That Craddock again had a lawyer of such high repute suggested the draw of her case for social radicals, but Pentecost nonetheless proved a rather poor fit with her.[34]

An open critic of Comstock and his evangelical crusade, Pentecost also took a dim view of his new client's mystical sexology. Craddock needed a lawyer with at least a modicum of sympathy for the way she combined spirituality and sexual candor, but Pentecost was prone to expressing regret over Craddock's excesses in both areas. Her religious views he found especially inane; her gospel, he said plainly, was of "very little importance." She was "different from most other people," Pentecost later remarked, and, when she talked about religion and sex, he thought he saw a strange glitter in her eyes, a sign of craziness more than intelligence. Perhaps Comstock had Craddock dead to rights, but Pentecost's low estimation of his client's ideas was not going to help matters. Craddock sensed Pentecost's tepidness and tried to light a fire:

"We Liberals have never had a fair chance at our sex literature cases because our lawyers have always been so apologetic for us." It was not the first, or the last time that a secular-minded liberal would fail to connect with a religiously motivated one. Craddock had experienced that dilemma at several points in her career, yet it had never threatened her more than it did now.[35]

It was the physician Edward Bond Foote, not Pentecost, who stepped forward to press Craddock's case as an important free-speech battle. Within a couple of weeks of her arrest, Foote had produced a circular, entitled "Comstock versus Craddock," to rally liberal supporters to her cause and to initiate a legal-defense fund for her. Foote, whose own father had run afoul of Comstock for publishing a pamphlet on contraception, was unwavering in his support for Craddock. "Sexual education, scientifically studied and plainly presented, must come eventually, but 'woe to them' who have not wisdom to keep but little in advance of public opinion," he wrote. Craddock was, in Foote's estimation, another brave reformer turned into a martyr by those who were the enemies of progress, freedom, and enlightenment. "The world is not yet entirely reconciled to hear women talk religion from pulpits or politics from platforms," he lamented, "and the prejudice against her entering the field of remodeling the marital manners of men is simply insuperable." Anyone who cared about a "free press" and "fair play," anyone committed to marriage reform and women's rights, should match those sympathies with a donation to his newly established Craddock Fund.[36]

The criminal case in New York's Court of Special Sessions went to trial on Friday, March 14, well ahead of the federal obscenity case that was pending in the U.S. District Court. Pentecost called three physicians as expert witnesses, including R. W. Shufeldt, an army surgeon and a member of the Medico-Legal Society, who testified both to the value of Craddock's writings on sexology and to her sanity. Pentecost also entered two notes of support from Rev. William Rainsford, a prominent Episcopal priest in New York City, who found Comstock's prosecution of Craddock far more troubling than anything she had published. Pentecost presented as well a strong character witness in the form of a letter from William Stead, still serving as editor of the *Review of Reviews*. Stead, who had sent money for her legal defense, testified to Craddock's "lofty religious motives." "As one who was for two years your employer when you were in England seven years ago, and who has ever since regarded it as a privilege and an honor to call you his friend," Stead averred, "I have no hesitation in bearing the strongest possible testimony to your high moral character." Granting that some of her phrases "may have been ill chosen" and that her zeal often ran roughshod over social convention, Stead still found the war against Craddock's writings to be "an outrage abhorrent to the principles of religious liberty and of the freedom of the press which are guaranteed in the American Constitution." Just as he had during his visit to Chicago in 1893, Stead again prodded Americans to remember their own principles of justice.[37]

For her part, Craddock made a direct and unadorned plea in her own defense: "I have only tried to put forth plain facts, which every person ought to know," she said. "I am not ashamed myself to speak plain truths plainly." There was an elegant simplicity to that piece of testimony; it breathed a little bit of the old spirit of Lucretia Mott, the Quaker activist Craddock had long ago invoked as a role model. Craddock was on the stand for the country's sexual enlightenment, and she brought to that effort a cherished idiom of American reform: plain truths, plainly spoken.[38]

The defense that Pentecost presented left the three-judge panel unmoved, especially once they had heard the indelicate passages from *The Wedding Night*. "This is the most awful case that ever came into this court," the senior justice, Elizur Brace Hinsdale, pronounced. The judge liked the moralizing part of his job a little too much, perhaps a residue of his own strict Presbyterian upbringing during which, as Hinsdale reported in his memoir, he had "received constant admonition in the principles of religion and morality." A few months earlier Hinsdale had made headlines for so vehemently rebuking convicted anarchist Johann Most that the notorious incendiary had reportedly been reduced to a dead faint right there in the courtroom. Hinsdale, who in blasting Most had conjured up Emma Goldman and other offenders of "public decency," was clearly warming to the task of "scathing denunciation" in Craddock's case as well.

With a strong sense of the country's Christian character, the seventy-year-old Hinsdale was not a good judge for Craddock to face. His impassioned tirade against her made it clear that he had very little doubt about the trial's rightful outcome. "I have never before known of such indescribable filth," he railed. "I cannot believe that this woman is in her right mind." (Hinsdale had some personal grounds for comparison on both points: He had committed his first wife to the Bloomingdale Lunatic Asylum and had been engulfed in an ugly public scandal in the early 1880s in which he had been accused of having an affair with his brother's wife.) "No woman in her right mind, gentle born and well educated, as the literary style of this book shows, could conceive such filthy phrases," he continued. "She has caused just such trouble as this in Chicago, Washington and Philadelphia before she came to this city. We consider her a danger to the public morals." Hinsdale was clearly very much on the same page with Comstock.[39]

Hinsdale did most of the scolding, but the second judge, Irish Catholic John Bell McKean, was every bit as incensed and hyperbolic. In reprimanding Craddock he condemned her pamphlet as "obscene, criminal, and outrageously blasphemous"—indeed, "the most blasphemous book I ever saw." The allegation of blasphemy particularly sent tremors through Craddock's liberal camp, suggesting to them that the justice was continuing the tradition of loading an obscenity charge with religious ballast. Although the legal proceedings clearly rested on obscenity, not blasphemy, it remained all too apparent how much the latter continued to color the former: Hinsdale and McKean, Edward

Bond Foote argued, had actually arraigned Craddock for "blasphemous obscenity"—that is, for having the gall to inaugurate a Church of Yoga as much as for daring to preach sexology. Indeed, by one newspaper's account, the prosecution had openly referred during the trial to Craddock's pamphlet on the *Wedding Night* as "the book of the Church of Yoga." This ready-at-hand conflation of blasphemy and obscenity was hardly new, but it was one that civil-liberties watchmen like Foote very much wanted to disentangle. McKean's visceral censure of Craddock's blasphemy, along with the prosecution's insinuations, underscored the difficulty of rescuing unorthodox religious ideas from their routine association with indecency.[40]

The third judge, Julius Marshuetz Mayer, was more cool-headed and kept his cards close to his chest. He would go on to a distinguished career as New York's attorney general, but, at this point, he had joined the Court of Special Sessions only two months earlier and was at age thirty-six by far "the junior man on the bench." At least one of Craddock's supporters picked up a hint of sympathy in him for dismissing the charges: He had actually silenced Comstock at one point when the vice crusader started regaling the court with his personal assessment of Craddock's dissolute character. Mayer, though, did nothing to challenge directly the judicial opinion of his senior colleagues, and by Monday, March 17, Craddock's fate was sealed.[41]

As Hinsdale pronounced the sentence—three months in prison— Craddock sat in "stoic silence," so the *New York Sun* reported, digesting the implications of her defeat. Staring straight ahead, she was led away to a holding cell in the Tombs in preparation for her lock-up in the Woman's Workhouse on Blackwell's Island, a thin islet in New York City's East River. Comstock, who had stood close by Craddock during the sentencing, rejoiced in having convicted another cankerous troublemaker—one more menace to the country's morals cut down to size. Her backers, by contrast, were rueful: Edward Bond Foote detected a "savage glee" in Comstock's broad smile at having "bagged his game."[42]

Nothing makes a martyr of an activist as much as a railroaded jail sentence, even a relatively short one of three months. The liberal presses were now ablaze with accounts of Craddock's trial and imprisonment. "Of all the farces I have ever witnessed," physician R. W. Shufeldt complained afterward in the *Boston Investigator*, "her trial in that court was certainly most farcical." It was "worthy only of a place in the court records of the Dark Ages, or the history of Romish inquisition." Another prominent civil liberties lawyer in Manhattan, Edward W. Chamberlain, lampooned the three judges involved. He pictured them patting each other on the back for having safeguarded society from "this refined delicate sensitive woman" and then later "retailing bawdy jokes at their clubs in the evening." Chamberlain placed Craddock in a martyr's gallery of persecuted freethinkers, including D. M. Bennett, the venerated editor of the *Truth Seeker* who had been sent to prison in 1878 for sending obscene literature through the mails. The comparisons soon got a lot grander when Stead chimed in from London about Craddock's imprisonment: "So it was with Socrates, so it was with Jesus Christ, and so it ever will be with all those who endeavor to incite their fellows to attain to a purer and nobler life."[43]

To Stead, ever the progressive reformer, one of the silver linings in Craddock's incarceration was the opportunity it presented for exposing and possibly correcting prison abuses. Not long into her time on Blackwell's Island, word began circulating in activist circles that she had been "violently and forcibly assaulted and her person outraged" by two "attendants" at the prison. This was not a story of rape, though certainly activist coverage was set up to suggest a moral equivalence; instead, it was a tale of compulsory vaccination. Craddock had never shown much interest before in this civil-liberties cause, but now the arguments of the Anti-Vaccination League (a branch had been organized in New York City in 1885) took on deep resonance: the right of the individual to refuse immunization, the right to conscientious objection to such governmental compulsion, and here the right even of the imprisoned to resist the "vaccine poison." From her cell at Blackwell's, she vociferously protested this violation of her body.

Like so many of her other efforts, Craddock's jail-bound attempts at reform earned her more punishment from the authorities. That Craddock so strenuously objected to vaccination made prison officials only more insistent; one of them told her that he would "vaccinate her every three days," so that he could be sure her blood was "contaminated." Another threatened her with the Black Cells, six solitary chambers in which unruly or insolent prisoners were thrown in total darkness without cot, chair, or blanket until they were "thoroughly mastered." "See here, Mrs. Craddock," the doctor in charge told her, "when you become a convict, you lose your civil rights."[44]

The horrors of Craddock's prison experience—the overcrowding, the dearth of toilet facilities and running water, the infestations of vermin, the wretched food, the prison dress, the conscripted labor—became physical marks of her status as a martyr among secular liberals. Though she shared this fate with other social radicals and Comstock targets—Emma Goldman had already done time on Blackwell's Island—that solidarity did little to soften the effects, physical and psychological, of being confined there. Craddock, a woman of education and culture, had been thrown into a three-tiered, four-to-a-cell, prison complex; she was one more convict indistinguishable from the drunkards, vagrants, prostitutes, and thieves with whom she now bunked. Craddock already knew, of course, what it was like to be treated as déclassé in polite society, but she nonetheless thought of the comforts and cleanliness of middle-class life as a birthright, as something that set her apart from the unwashed masses. Craddock found it difficult to endure the roughness of the workhouse without revulsion, and her supporters found it harder still to accept her treatment without outrage.[45]

As Craddock's three-month term wound down in mid-June, New York liberals geared up to celebrate her release from prison and to give her a hero's welcome. Edwin C. Walker, scandalous cohabitator with

Moses Harman's daughter and by now president of the Manhattan Liberal Club, made plans to fête Craddock with an indignation banquet at the Clarendon Hotel on Friday, June 20. Sparked to action by Craddock's conviction and looming federal trial, Walker, Foote, and company had spun off a new group, the Free Speech League, to hoist the banner for free expression. The Craddock dinner, honoring "the latest victim of Comstockism," attracted about one hundred attendees and served as the Free Speech League's inaugural event. From its humble beginnings with the Craddock banquet, the Free Speech League emerged over the next decade as an important antecedent of the American Civil Liberties Union (ACLU), which would be chartered eighteen years later in defense of pacifist activism during World War I. In advance of most other progressives, including the ACLU's Roger Baldwin, the Free Speech League would become an important legal resource for both Emma Goldman and Margaret Sanger in their joined causes for birth control and free expression.[46]

Predictably, the Free Speech League dinner for Craddock proved to be as much of an opportunity for the liberal movement to consolidate its indignant energy as it was a chance to honor a single martyr in its ranks. Walker presided at the dinner and introduced the main speaker, the labor radical Moses Oppenheimer. An ex-convict himself, Oppenheimer took the platform and offered a rousing defense of minority points of view in the face of tyrannical majorities. From there, the dinner unfolded as a mix of testimonials to Craddock's courage, blasts at "censorship by idiots," and tributes to a free press. Even as they warmly welcomed Craddock's release, several of the speakers found it necessary to keep her at arm's length. "Some say that her utterances are spiritualistic and unscientific," Walker admitted. "This may be true, but she is being prosecuted . . . because she expressed her views on a tabooed subject. Her opinions do not concern us; we simply stand for liberty." The free-speech principle did not depend on approval of Craddock's brand of sexology, but instead on the protection of her right to verbalize her ideas, however eccentric.

Walker's cautious remarks notwithstanding, Craddock appeared "greatly touched by the reception given her," and yet she also knew her audience. When it came time for her to speak, she steered clear of spiritualism, Divine Science, and yoga. Voicing her "confidence in the success of Liberalism and Freethought," she vowed to carry on the fight for free expression at her federal trial. It had been a long while since she had helped lead the American Secular Union or had lectured on sex worship at the Manhattan Liberal Club, but Craddock still knew how to work this particular crowd.[47]

Out of jail, but with the federal trial still on the horizon, Craddock returned that summer to her counseling work. It was in these months that she advised Eunice Parsons and her uncomfortable fiancé on how to overcome their divergent views on married sexuality. Craddock's legal predicament, though, shadowed even those face-to-face relationships as Eunice worried about the intertwined fates of her teacher and her writings. Comstock's behavior in this case, Eunice wrote Ida, "makes me *boil.*" "I hope you will win," she continued, "you *must*, for the sake of us young people, and the older ones too." Eunice was also fearful that she herself might become a target of investigation, since her local "Postmistress" knew that she was corresponding with Craddock and was clearly suspicious. Eunice had received copies of the contraband books through the mail and had circulated them among her friends. Until Craddock's writings were legally vindicated, she wanted to be very cautious; if victory could be achieved, then she was ready to become a publicist for the pamphlets. "Everyone will want them," Eunice told Ida in September, three weeks before the federal case went to trial in New York.[48]

Much of Craddock's time that summer was spent preparing for a climactic fight with Comstock in federal court. Her rise to liberal celebrity as a free-speech martyr had only served to make her a more prominent target for Comstock and to raise the stakes for the impending trial. As she wrote one of her supporters after her release from

Blackwell's Island, "I am making this stand not for my own liberty—that is only incidental—I am standing for the liberty of the press and freedom of religion. I have an inward feeling that I am really divinely led here to New York to face this wicked and depraved man Comstock in open court and to strike the blow which shall start the overthrow of Comstockism." By design and by necessity, Craddock would use her trial to fight for the broader principles for which she had long aligned herself.[49]

Craddock's mother, when she heard of her daughter's resolve to "roast Comstock" in the courtroom, was duly alarmed. Lizzie immediately wrote to Foote to nix the scheme by which her daughter would try to turn the tables on Comstock. "He is too well entrenched for anything she could say to affect him," Lizzie reasoned as she worried anew over her daughter's well-being. "And it would rebound and hurt her in the eyes of the Court." Instead, Lizzie wanted Ida to cut her losses and once again to plead insanity—surely, the asylum was better than prison, all the more for someone like her daughter with "a weakness of the brain."[50]

One thing, in particular, Craddock had to do that summer was find a new attorney. Pentecost, having become "quite pessimistic" about her prospects, had stepped aside for the federal case. Craddock could not have been sorry to see him go: Word was that several of her strongest supporters had been dissatisfied with his performance at the March trial for not being enough of "a fighter." They wanted to hand Craddock's case over to someone ready to spew more venom at Comstock, someone who would delight in the combat, and that was definitely Ida's inclination as well. Edward W. Chamberlain, a legal architect in the defense of both Moses Harman and Ezra Heywood, entered the breach created by Pentecost's departure. Having already weighed in on the travesty of Craddock's trial in the Court of Special Sessions, Chamberlain was fully primed for his latest free-speech battle. Once again, though, Craddock would go into a trial with a lawyer who set off the alarm bells of more upstanding citizens. Her legal opponents simply referred to her new defender as "Free-Love Chamberlain." Not that Chamberlain avoided name-calling: He dubbed Comstock "Smutty Tony" for his fixation with obscenity.[51]

When Craddock's case went to trial on October 10, no one in her camp seemed to think that she had much chance of prevailing. Perhaps in defending herself on the stand she would win the sympathy of jurors and effectively expose Comstock's abuse of power. That seemed like a remote possibility, given Comstock's lengthy run of courtroom successes, but Chamberlain and company were at least hoping for some good theater through which they could win favor in the court of public opinion, even if they lost in the court of law. They knew that Comstock could be made the fool—just as he had been when he performed his own laughable rendition of the Danse du Ventre. Perhaps this time, Chamberlain hoped, "our modern St. Anthony" would be revealed for what he was, a "pious scoundrel" and "loathsome rogue."[52]

Comstock's public image was not undercut the way that Craddock's defenders had wished—at least, not on the day of the trial. Judge Edward B. Thomas, sometime Republican politician and author of legal textbooks, reportedly saw Craddock much the way Comstock did—as a "very *dangerous* woman." He took the obscenity question to be the only one that mattered and ruled unilaterally on that issue: Craddock's writings were indeed "lewd, lascivious, [and] dirty." That determination left the jury to decide only whether she had placed the aforesaid material in the U.S. mail. Since no one disputed the fact that she had deposited her pamphlets at a Manhattan post office, Thomas's ruling rendered moot both Chamberlain's defense and Craddock's own explanations, including their overarching invocation of First Amendment freedoms. With only that very limited issue to determine—the obscenity laws had again simply swept aside the question of civil liberties—the verdict was obvious.

The judge, leaving little room for suspense in the jury's deliberations, had provided plenty of opportunity for Comstock to crow about the slam-dunk prosecution: The jury, he rejoiced, had been able to convict Craddock "without leaving their seats." It was, her backers howled, "a judicial outrage," "a complete overthrow of our jury system." The jury had been turned into "a mere ornament" with nothing to do but parrot the judge who had predetermined the outcome. For her part, Craddock remained defiant—she would exhibit no stoic silence this time. She declared, the *New York Sun* reported, that she would "continue in her educational mission in spite of a dozen Comstocks."

Craddock's sentencing date was set for a week later on October 17. Even as Chamberlain pledged to appeal the decision, Craddock fully expected, as an impenitent recidivist, to receive the harshest possible penalty—five years in prison. [53]

ON THE DAY OF CRADDOCK's sentencing, her long-suffering mother had planned to accompany her daughter to the courtroom. Lizzie still harbored hopes that Ida would end up in an insane asylum rather than in prison. Expecting to meet her at a Manhattan restaurant, Lizzie grew concerned when Ida did not appear. Had she taken flight again under a new pseudonym? Was she once more on her way to London with Stead as her rescuer? When it came to her mother, Craddock was something of an escape artist—and for good reason. Chamberlain had warned her just before the federal trial to continue to keep her distance from Lizzie and "not to be caught in a trap." "The disposition to rebuke you," he reported, "seems stronger than the mother love." Perhaps this missed appointment was simply another stealthy move on the part of a daughter who surely did not trust her mother's good intentions in wanting to serve as courtroom escort. "Oh, mother, I cannot, I will not consent to go to the asylum," Craddock swore to Lizzie the day before the sentencing, "as you are evidently planning to have me go."[54]

Used to tracking her daughter down, Lizzie headed over to Ida's room on West 23rd Street. She walked up to the stairs to the fourth floor to her daughter's small office; on the door was the tag, "Ida C. Craddock, Instructor of Divine Science." Perhaps her mother took a little comfort in that modest identification; at least, the card did not say "Student of Phallic Antiquities," "Expert in Sexology," or "Pastor of the Church of Yoga." Lizzie knocked, she knocked again, but there was no answer.

Lingering by the door, wondering where to look for her wayward daughter next, Lizzie noticed the smell of gas. Alarmed, she notified the police. When the officer arrived, he broke down the door. Craddock was lying in her bed in her nightgown with a rubber tube running from one of the building's gas jets toward her mouth. The windows were meticulously sealed, and the odor of gas filled the room. Ida's left wrist was slit open, and the blood had run into a pail on the floor.[55] At one point in her diary Craddock had recalled lines from Henry Wadsworth Longfellow's elegy for the poet Bayard Taylor: "Dead he lay among his books;/ The peace of God was in his looks." Now dead she lay among her books, what remained of them after Comstock's raid—and, whether or not the peace of God was upon her face, by now it was a little late for that grace.[56]

Though her room was strewn as usual with books and papers, it was nonetheless plain that Craddock had planned her death with tidy care. She had bundled up several packages for friends and left a long suicide note for her mother. She was unwilling, Ida explained in her letter to Lizzie, to let her lifework die a slow death in the penitentiary or in a hospital for the insane: "I maintain my right to die as I have lived, a free woman." Craddock knew, she confessed to her mother, that she had been "a hindrance to your respectability," but she tried to assuage Lizzie's pained disappointment with her by looking poignantly to the future. Ida rhapsodized about a social order in which subsequent activists had made marriage reform triumphant and about a spiritual world "where Anthony Comstocks and corrupt judges" were unknown. "Some day," Ida predicted to Lizzie with a sad yet hopeful air, "you will not be ashamed of me or my work. Some day you'll be proud of me."[57]

In taking her own life, Craddock had made two distinct gestures—one of reconciliation and another of unmitigated spite. On the one side, she had tried to right her relationship with her mother and to envelop the years of animosity in eternal love: "We shall be very happy together some day, you and I, dear mother; there will be a blessed reality for us both at last. I love you, dear mother; never forget that. And love cannot die." On the other side, Craddock was not looking for any appeasement in her long embattled relationship with Anthony Comstock. So, in addition to the carefully crafted suicide note to her mother, Craddock had composed a public letter attacking Comstock as a liar and hypocrite, addressed it to her lawyer Edward Chamberlain, and—with a fine sense of irony—placed it in the U.S. mail the night before she took her life. Craddock's sly parting shot at Comstock was not immediately known and had to wait a little longer to play itself out.[58]

On the day Craddock's body was discovered, headlines blared the news in the evening editions of the New York papers. "PRIESTESS OF YOGA A SUICIDE—Miss Ida Craddock, the Leader of a Peculiar Religious Sect, Kills Herself Rather Than Go to Prison," shouted New York's *Evening World*; "DEATH, NOT PRISON—Miss Craddock, Yoga Priestess, Kills Herself," reported the *Evening Sun*. The next day newspapers across the country picked up the story. "FEARING JAIL, SHE KILLS SELF—Miss Ida Craddock, High Priestess of Yoga, Inhales Gas—SHE WAS AN ADMIRER OF THE DANCE DU VENTRE," read the front-page headline in the *Atlanta Constitution*. So it went from Washington, D.C., to Denver to Salt Lake City to Los Angeles, lurid accounts of the death of a priestess.

In that first burst of coverage, it looked like Craddock's death would be safely pigeonholed as the suicide of a religious eccentric, the female "scholar," "pastor," and "sexologist" turned into an exotic and libidinous "priestess." "Phallic worship was to her a pure religion, and she did not hesitate to say so," the *Evening World* recalled of her New York lectures nearly a decade ago, alleging that her lewd presentations had almost raised riots among her listeners. There were some hints in the accounts that she had been "persecuted" for the oddity of her views—"a conglomeration of Oriental religions," as the *New York Times* described her "peculiar beliefs"—but there was a stronger sense that "the Craddock woman" was a crazy Free-Lover with a long arrest record whose objectionable activities had finally killed her off. Given "the woman's history," Comstock looked like a justified prosecutor.[59]

However much (or little) Lizzie grieved Ida's passing—she reported "feeling miserable as to health" because of all "this excitement and trouble"—the new spate of juicy publicity surrounding her daughter certainly compounded her sense of affliction. Rallying, Lizzie found Comstock's gloating outrageous and was especially sickened by his claim that her daughter had aimed to corrupt underage girls, a charge she knew in her bones to be a vicious twisting of Ida's "pure" intentions. She discreetly retrieved her daughter's body from the coroner and took it back to Philadelphia for a private funeral service in her own home. Craddock's long-time pastor from the Spring Garden Unitarian Church, Frederic Hinckley, presided and "said lots of good things about her and uttered some strong liberal views," so Lizzie reported to Edward Bond Foote, who had wanted to make sure Ida was given "a good send off."[60]

An earlier sermon of Hinckley's sheds some light onto how the pastor might have eulogized his departed congregant. In a funeral sermon four years earlier for Robert Purvis, a noted abolitionist and women's rights advocate, Hinckley had sung the praises of those "heroic men and women, who for conscience sake and for freedom's sake" were willing to antagonize the powers that be. "Farewell unselfish reformer, upright citizen, prophet of an enfranchised humanity," Hinckley had preached in Purvis's elegy. Perhaps Craddock's passing had offered another chance for him to extol those who were fighting to eliminate "artificial distinctions on account of sex," but, if so, his words were spoken without public fanfare. Lizzie had wanted a quietly inconspicuous funeral for Ida, and, at last, the mother could impose discretion upon the daughter.[61]

Craddock was buried in a plot at the Woodlands Cemetery in Philadelphia. Her mother, Lizzie Decker, joined her two years later; Lizzie's name took pride of place above Ida's on the obelisk that memorialized them both. Photograph by Rachel Lindsey.

Ida was peacefully laid to rest in a plot in Woodlands Cemetery, a lush Victorian funerary landscape just down the road from the University of Pennsylvania, on October 20, three days after her suicide. Her mother joined her daughter two years later in December 1904; buried side by side under the same obelisk, they ended up sharing a peculiarly phallic marker (at least as Ida would have seen it). Perhaps the combined monument and the tight proximity of their remains symbolized the heavenly resolution of their earthly conflicts, but Lizzie's name was chiseled above Ida's—as if to signal the restored order of maternal authority.

Notwithstanding the secluded funeral service that Lizzie had designed for her, Ida's death generated far more outraged protest than rest-in-peace calm. The indignation of activists directly involved in her case quickly rippled outward into wider liberal circles. The furor cast a shadow over Comstock's success and threatened to turn Craddock's conviction into a pyrrhic victory for the New York Society for the Suppression of Vice. Comstock was caught off-guard by this heated reaction; he had anticipated neither the effectiveness of Craddock's final communications nor the vehemence of her supporters in coming after him for payback. "Mrs. Craddock's death, horrible as it was, has resulted in some good," one of her advocates concluded shortly after her suicide. Namely, it had "put Comstock on the defensive," actually decidedly so.[62]

The Episcopal priest William Rainsford, who had mildly supported Craddock during her New York trials, was the first to throw Comstock off his game, calling him out two days afterward for his part in her suicide: "I would not like to be in your shoes," he wrote the vice crusader. "You hounded an honest, not a bad woman to her death. I would not like to have to answer to God for what you have done." Soon Rainsford escalated his attack, publicly calling for Comstock's removal from office. Comstock was absolutely dismayed to see a Christian minister turn on him like this. He called on Rainsford repeatedly to mend fences, but the rector remained aloof, disdaining Comstock as "a moral tyrant."

Comstock knew this mud-slinging breach was terrible for public relations—and also, potentially at least, for his finances. While he continued to enjoy federal authority, he always relied on a faith-based voluntary society to meet most of the expenses of his work. How could Rainsford, a well-placed cleric in a very wealthy congregation, attack him "without any regard to whether you divert from the support of this great cause, funds necessary to sustain it and carry it on"? When Rainsford still scorned him, Comstock threatened to have the priest arrested for criminal libel, a spectacle the media relished. Then, as an added damage-control measure, Comstock enlisted his Executive Committee, a powerhouse group of New York businessmen, to offer a public declaration of unqualified support for his handling of the Craddock case.[63]

As Comstock scrambled to defend himself, freethinking liberals were going on the attack across the board and were doing their best to turn "The Craddock Tragedy" into a cause célèbre. In a fortuitous coincidence Elizabeth Cady Stanton, the great elder of women's suffrage, died of heart failure on Sunday, October 26, at age eighty-five, nine days after Craddock's suicide. Despite the outpouring of somber reflection that Stanton's passing occasioned, that grief hardly distracted social radicals from the rage they were feeling over Craddock's demise at age forty-five. The day of Stanton's death a memorial service in Chicago gathered 1200 attendees at Handel Hall to honor Craddock and to blast away at Comstock. Alice Stockham spoke, and so did Juliet Severance, another physician who combined the cause of women's rights with spiritualist convictions.[64]

Both Stockham and Severance eulogized Craddock for having died a heroic death in her efforts to enlighten Americans on "tabooed subjects." Stockham's elegy survives only in snippets from press coverage of the event, but Severance's thoughts on Craddock's death were later published in full and offer a good sense of liberal ire:

> Are we a race of slaves that we tamely submit to having our mails rifled, the right of free thought and free speech trampled in the dust, the press muzzled under the pretense of subserving the interest of morality? . . . Shall we submit to a denial of free discussion and opportunity for education on sex matters, because forsooth some filthy minded idiot is of the opinion that it is obscene to discuss matters that pertain to every human life, and on which life depends? It is a momentous question. Ida C. Craddock was a pure-minded, intelligent

woman, working with a clean conscience for the good, as she believed, of humanity. . . . Poor outraged woman! driven to death to escape the tyranny of . . . the saintly Anthony Comstock.

The rhetoric was rapidly heating up in liberal circles: Craddock was "every inch a martyr," and Comstock an "unspeakable fiend."[65]

The next month the battle lines in the Comstock vs. Craddock affair got drawn even more sharply. Craddock had already been scoring posthumous points through published excerpts of the suicide note written to her mother, a letter presented as tender and touching—full of pathos—in journalistic commentary. Then Chamberlain released the open letter denouncing Comstock that Craddock had secretly mailed just before her suicide. Word of it had already begun circulating, but the letter appeared in full in the *Truth Seeker* only on November 1; shortly thereafter, it was republished in *Lucifer the Light-Bearer* as well. In this parting letter Craddock had taken one last swing at all "the salient features of Comstockism." She ridiculed Comstock's use of paid informers and decoy letters, his pursuit of a religious mission under the aegis of the federal government, his seizing and burning of books, and his manipulation of evidence. Most of all, she jeered at Comstock himself. "The man is a sex pervert," she diagnosed. "He is what physicians term a Sadist—namely a person in whom the impulses of cruelty arise concurrently with the stirring of sex emotion." How much longer would the American public allow that "unctuous sexual hypocrite" to "wax fat and arrogant" and to trample on First Amendment freedoms? How much longer would they allow him to suppress writings on sexology and impede their ability to obtain useful knowledge about their own bodies? In fine spiritualist fashion Craddock was managing, with Chamberlain as her designated intermediary, to speak from beyond the grave and to do so with prophetic force.[66]

Beyond its final blasting of Comstock, Craddock's public letter also situated her decision to take her own life within a freethinking tradition that cast the gesture as heroic and laudable rather than sinful and pathological. Her suicide could easily have sealed her reputation as damned reprobate and madwoman—church and state were both arrayed against self-murder as immoral, illegal, and insane. Instead her action took on the grandeur, courage, and genius of history's "Great Suicides." "I consider myself justified in choosing for myself, as did Socrates, the manner of my death," Craddock explained in her public letter. "I prefer to die comfortably and peacefully on my own little bed in my own room, instead of on a prison cot."[67]

As Craddock's invocation of Socrates suggested, she imagined suicide as possessing a distinctly pagan luster. "The greatest of the Greeks for five centuries were suicides," a freethinking tract of the period explained in defending suicide against its Christian status as a grievous sin against God. The agnostic orator Robert Ingersoll had claimed a few years before Craddock's demise that unjust imprisonment might well be one situation in which to choose the Greek path of noble suicide. "The grave," he said, "is better than the cell." At minimum, Ingersoll insisted, self-destruction should not provoke denunciation and contempt, but instead sympathy for those whose sufferings had become unbearable. Judgment, he said, should be reserved for those responsible for creating such wretched suffering—"the oppressors, the tyrants, those who trample on the rights of others, the robbers of the poor." For freethinking liberals and secularists, Craddock had managed to pack her final gesture with double power: It possessed a Socratic dignity and evoked righteous compassion—all the while casting a pall over the oppressor who had driven her to such desperation.[68]

Comstock did not let Craddock's self-representation stand unanswered. He returned fire with a public letter of his own on November 14 and followed up with a full self-defense in the vice society's *Annual Report* at the close of the year. Intensely frustrated over the public-relations headache her death had created for him, he continued to fume about Craddock's shamefulness, blasphemy, and insanity. At one point in discussing her case he reached for the unfortunate analogy of a mad dog; perhaps to some she seemed like "a small mad dog" safely left alone, but it was nonetheless "imperative that mad dogs of all sizes should be killed, before the children are bitten." He only meant that the obscene literature produced by rabid figures like her had to be destroyed, but the tactlessness of the comparison shows that Craddock's departing jeers, on top of her previous writings, had pushed Comstock's evangelical vigilance to a new level of score-settling vengeance.[69]

Comstock's outrage would not shield him from the equally intense fury of Craddock's supporters. In early December, three weeks after releasing his own public letter to the newspapers, Comstock ventured to the Brooklyn Philosophical Association to defend his work for the New York Society for the Suppression of Vice, but Craddock's suicide again derailed him. "Why did you convict Ida Craddock?" a half dozen voices had called out. When Comstock predictably went off on Craddock, much of the audience joined in the uproar, demanding that Comstock answer for hounding Craddock to her death. Manhattan Liberal Club president Edwin C. Walker rose to denounce him and declared the Bible to be littered with filth far worse than anything Craddock had ever published. Another old workhorse of liberal reform, Moncure D. Conway, joined the chorus, waxing eloquent about Craddock's brilliant "literary nudity" and reminding Comstock that questions of moral character are "not confined to sex only." After what he thought of as a stirring triumph for moral decency, Comstock was being called the real fiend—not Craddock. Enraged by the grilling, Comstock left the platform "pale with anger."[70]

Discomfited, Comstock nonetheless prevailed over critics of his conduct in the Craddock case—at least, he prevailed in the near term. He held onto his job, his power, and his esteemed board of well-positioned backers. The renewed calls for the repeal of his signature laws were once again turned back, and he was able to keep the heat on liberal obscenity peddlers for another decade and more—indeed, right up to his death in 1915. Despite his vice society's continued reign, Comstock's opponents had found a powerful weapon in the Craddock episode. "In the suicide of that bright, brainy woman, Ida C. Craddock," a correspondent had written excitedly to Moses Harman, "liberals have a gatling gun." If they failed to mow down Comstockian censorship in 1902, they certainly had dinged up the vice society's moral armor and roused many Americans to question Comstock's faithful endeavor "to do God's will" through relentlessly policing the postal system.[71]

If not quite a Gatling gun, Craddock's case had helped generate a new phase of liberal organizing in the defense of civil and religious liberties. Thanks in large part to her battle with Comstock, Manhattan liberals had organized the Free Speech League, which over the next two decades would significantly subvert the evangelical and legal certitude about the suppression of obscene literature. The very concept of obscenity would be witheringly criticized in these circles as an entirely subjective notion, an invention of the prudish observer. Obscenity, by this line of argument, was not a definable "quality of literature," but instead a fussy "contribution of the reading mind." That will-o'-the-wisp quality had made American obscenity laws hopelessly arbitrary in their application—Shakespeare could be plenty bawdy, so why were his plays more acceptable than Walt Whitman's poetry or James Joyce's fiction? Free-speech activists would also keep skewering obscenity's clichéd equation with blasphemy. Since that conflation was specifically employed to protect the Christian church and its clergy from offense, how could that not be a violation of church-state separation? Craddock's case had helped incite liberal activism in support of a much larger constitutional reassessment of the scope of free expression and religious liberty.[72]

The Craddock affair had also given new life to efforts to open up discussion of sexuality and reproduction in American culture. It had made that reform cause look courageous, even heroic; this was obviously a struggle that required gutsy activists, a reputation that Margaret Sanger would fully exploit in the next decade as she pushed forward with her birth-control campaign in the face of violent opposition. "The maxim that 'the blood of the martyrs is the seed of the church' holds good in other matters than religion," one physician wrote in 1903 with Craddock's example in mind. Comstock's "self-righteous zeal" in persecuting Craddock, the physician was sure, had only heightened public awareness of the sexual matters for which she had suffered. Three decades later in *Living My Life* Emma Goldman would recall Craddock as one of the country's "bravest champions of women's emancipation." Certainly, it was Craddock's Comstock-defying insistence on the importance of "sexual enlightenment" that Goldman had in mind.[73]

In elevating the causes of sex reform and civil liberties, Craddock's case loosened Comstock's hold on the moral high ground of public decency. The whole debacle had made Comstock look perverse, if not sadistic, for finding satisfaction in Craddock's self-destruction. A quarter century earlier Comstock had largely gotten away with reveling in the suicide of Madame Restell, a prominent provider of abortions and contraceptive devices in New York City. "A bloody ending to a bloody life," he had remarked remorselessly when Restell slit her own throat rather than face imprisonment on Blackwell's Island. Comstock found it much harder to take any glory in Craddock's demise. "Who is this highly moral American censor who is always averse to sex knowledge, sex literature?" another of Harman's correspondents asked rhetorically. The answer: He was a monster in the shape of a man, the "spawn of utter vileness," a Jack the Ripper whose weapon was not a knife but moral fanaticism. Mystical lover and metaphysical speculator, Craddock was an unlikely martyr for liberal secularism, but her "foul murder" had proven unusually effective in pounding Comstock in the fight for free speech, religious liberty, and sexual emancipation.[74]

CHAPTER SIX

One Religio-Sexual Maniac

—•◦•—

"MISS CRADDOCK WAS INSANE." So Clark Bell, the editor of *The Medico-Legal Journal*, opined in a one-sentence paragraph that opened his postmortem on the Craddock-Comstock affair in late 1902. Even though he shared the liberal viewpoint that Comstock had Craddock's blood on his hands, Bell was more interested in the mystic's madness than the crusader's fanaticism. A lawyer, Bell made the case against Craddock's soundness of mind in a lecture at the Manhattan Liberal Club just a couple of weeks after her suicide. He based his diagnosis on an extended interview the two had conducted of one another some months earlier: She had been looking into retaining him as counsel for one of her trials; he had been wondering about the wisdom of taking her on as a client; and they had ended up talking past one another. Informing Craddock that the only acceptable defense was an insanity plea, Bell had refused to take her case without her agreeing to confess that she was "the victim of an insane delusion." The issues that her struggle raised about civil and religious liberties, about free speech and "the advancement of woman," paled in his analysis before the question of her mental derangement.[1]

The lynchpin for Bell's diagnosis was Craddock's spiritualism—specifically, her experiences as a heavenly bride. In his lecture Bell recounted Craddock's basic claim to having a spirit husband—a notion that she had first divulged in late 1893 at the time of the Danse du Ventre controversy, but that she had hardly made the centerpiece of her public reflections on religion and sexuality thereafter. "She believed herself to be the wife of the departed spirit of a young man whom she had rejected as a suitor for her hand before his death," Bell explained of Ida's mystical love affair. "Her views of the marriage relation," he elaborated, "were based on what she had learned and experienced in her conjugal relations [with] her spirit husband, as tinged and colored by her distempered fancy." Whether Craddock's delusion warranted her confinement in a mental ward, Bell was as uncertain after her death as he was before it—but of her lunacy he was adamant. The angelic husband was the primary symptom of Craddock's disease—a disturbing apparition that Bell thought might have been dispelled through proper psychiatric treatment in or out of an institution.[2]

Even as experts like Bell focused on Craddock's spirit marriage for their diagnostic conclusions, other factors were clearly coloring posthumous accounts of her mental health. Thomas W. Barlow, the assistant district attorney in Philadelphia who had joined forces with Ida's mother to institutionalize her in 1898, revealed those various considerations in a letter he wrote two weeks after her death:

> Miss Craddock was insane; but her intellect was so brilliant, her powers of persuasion were so great, her control over her actions, when necessary, so apparently sane, that most people were deceived as to her real mental condition. She had for years fixed delusions, and she was a nymphomaniac, writing things and saying things which were lewd and obscene, the expressions of a disordered mind.

Barlow's postmortem appeared inadvertently ambiguous. Craddock had been brilliant, persuasive, and self-controlled; she had shown few outward signs of insanity; and, yet, underneath that rational exterior, she had been a sexual cauldron bubbling with crazy passions—a woman with too many obscene notions in her head and at least one too many spirits in her bed. By identifying Craddock as a nymphomaniac—an all-too evocative diagnosis in the era's psychosexual literature on women and nervous disorders—Barlow equated her pathology with a surging of uninhibited female desire. Nymphomania was a disease that usually revealed more about the fears and titillations of the medical men who deployed it than the ills of the patients who were diagnosed with it. (Satyriasis, the male counterpart to nymphomania, inevitably generated a small fraction of the interest that its female complement did.) Clearly, Barlow's lawyerly use of the term *nymphomaniac* in regard to Craddock was intended to be repressive, not healing—to bury her further, not to spare her reputation.[3]

Not all of Craddock's diagnosticians measured her mental health solely in terms of her spiritualist love life—and those who did not usually had brighter views of her general well-being. The physician R. W. Shufeldt, who had served as an expert witness in Craddock's defense before the Court of Special Sessions in New York, thought she was of perfectly sound mind. Having read her pamphlets and having met with her on several occasions, Shufeldt was far more impressed with Craddock's courage as an outcast sexologist than he was concerned about the religious experiences she claimed as inspiration for taking on that maligned public role. If she had simply been accorded the proper intellectual space to study medicine and biology as well as her constitutional right to free expression, Shufeldt was quite sure that Craddock would have been just fine. Utterly dismissive of Bell's legal opinion on Craddock's mental state, Shufeldt claimed to have no difficulty as a medical expert in placing her "taxonomically" among the sane.[4]

Shufeldt, like many of her most ardent supporters, was intent on remembering Craddock as a victim of Comstockery—a daring agent of sexual emancipation and social progress, "an earnest and noble woman." That reprise of Craddock's life, the valiant fighter against obscene tyrannies, had a lot of luster, but it was nonetheless hard pressed to hold the ground against the psychological sciences. Soon, indeed, it seemed to give way altogether. In the quarter century after the posthumous diagnoses that Bell and Barlow had offered in late 1902, Craddock's case was summarily entered into the "clinical record in abnormal psychology for the use of psychoanalysis and the psychiatrists." The martyr for civil liberties gradually morphed into the Freudian analysand—a transformation that threatened to make Craddock's psychopathology her only afterlife.[5]

No longer a struggling scholar, religious innovator, marriage reformer, or free-speech defender, Ida Craddock would become Ida C, a case history of a psychoneurotic. She would stand, in her own small way, as an American incarnation of Dora and Anna O, two of the foundational cases in the birth of psychoanalysis in fin-de-siècle Vienna. Even in death, though, Craddock remained one crafty madwoman. Knowing full well the power of psychiatric classification, she had been intent before she died on supplying the materials for a second opinion. Always the folklorist of her own experience, she had left behind a treatise on the history of heavenly brides—one that managed to talk back to those who would confine her solely to the annals of American psychoanalysis.

———— ·•· ————

BELL AND BARLOW had not been the first to pronounce Craddock insane. Her initial brush with bedlam had come in the aftermath of the Danse du Ventre controversy in early 1894, when she had quickly fled to London to escape her mother's plans to have her committed. "I have always had a horror of insane asylums," she declared at the time in explanation of her rushed departure from Philadelphia. "Suppose they should give me bromides, or douche me with cold water, or treat certain parts of my body with electricity?" she continued, well aware of the popularity of sedatives, hydrotherapies, and electrical stimuli as treatments for any number of disorders. "Why, they might make a mental wreck of me before they produced me in court." Her opponents managed to realize those fears for her only once—the three-month period from June to September 1898, the bulk of which she was confined at the Pennsylvania Hospital for the Insane. With the help of lawyer Carrie Burnham Kilgore, Craddock had won release, but thereafter the threat of renewed confinement—the "hounding" of her with "insane asylum papers"—was recurrent. [6]

To Craddock's supporters, these efforts to institutionalize her were a matter of political plotting rather than necessary treatment. "She was once incarcerated in a lunatic asylum, although not insane—an atrocity easily perpetrated," the physician Alexander Wilder remarked in February 1902. "That her notions are what many consider *outré*, I am aware; but that she is culpable or insane, I do not believe for a moment." One young woman, inspired by Craddock's example, put this charge more sharply. "Ah, Ida Craddock," she lamented in an "Infidel Sermon" published a short time after Wilder's assessment, "can the reading public conceive of the number of women who are bereft of liberty on account of some unorthodox opinion and confined in asylums by good Christian parents until they come to their senses, in other words, refute their original opinion for the orthodoxy stamped correct." The authorities' harassment of Craddock, from this perspective, was all about silencing her, not restoring her to health.[7]

Craddock's admirers were right that it did not take a lot to get a wayward family member committed in the late nineteenth century. Even with the statutes revised in Pennsylvania in 1883 to help prevent cases of unwarranted confinement, the process required only the signature of a near relation, endorsement from a magistrate or judicial officer, and certification from two physicians. Ida's mother had little trouble clearing the prescribed threshold for commitment papers in 1894 and again in 1898. Without good lawyers and well-connected supporters, Craddock might have been locked away among the incurably insane—a fate that her mother accepted as necessary for putting an end to her daughter's scandalous activities.

Ida's avowal of spiritual betrothal provided a crucial justification for her confinement, but the madness of that assertion was always impossible to separate from the threat she posed as a marriage reformer. "The charge against me, I afterwards learned, was the spirit husband; but this was only a pretext," Ida remarked the month after her release from the Pennsylvania Hospital for the Insane in 1898. "The real reason, unblushingly avowed by all parties, was my sex reform teaching. So the signing of a certificate by physicians was a farce. I was incarcerated on one charge, and really held on another, which did not appear in writing." Her spiritualist idiosyncrasies, in effect, offered her opponents another way of stopping her work on sexology. For the latter, she could be sent to jail for obscenity; for the former, she could be sent to the asylum for insanity. Craddock's claim to be a heavenly bride did nothing but compound her legal and medical vulnerabilities.[8]

American psychologists and asylum-keepers did not require a Freudian revolution to view Craddock's mixture of religion and eroticism through a medical lens. In nineteenth-century clinical accounts of mental disorders, "theomaniacs"—those who imagined themselves to be in heavenly communication (whether with angels, Jesus, or the Virgin Mary)—often overlapped with "erotomaniacs," those who fixated on an illusory love object. Both types tended toward singularly focused delusions; both were prone to visions or hallucinations; and both were liable to amorous excess, at least in their imaginations. No nineteenth-century medical psychologist would have been surprised by the proposition that earthly loves could be projected onto imaginary divine objects. And none would have blinked at the suggestion that women were especially prone to that kind of mistaken substitution. "Closely connected with salacity, particularly in women," one late nineteenth-century doctor remarked, "is religious excitement."[9]

One of the reasons why psychologists of the era easily recognized the connections between religion and sexuality was all the work that had already been done on sex worship and phallic symbolism—the very topics that had so absorbed Craddock. G. Stanley Hall, America's dean of the new psychological sciences at Clark University, wrote Freud a few years after their famed meeting in 1909 in Worcester, Massachusetts, that he was having a hard time applying Freud's "rather wild use of sex symbolism, e.g. that dreams of money mean spermatozoa, that every curve is feminine and every straight line masculine." Apprehensive about his own public reputation for uprightness, Hall worried that he and even more so Freud were in "much danger of repeating the extravagancies of the old students of phallicism." That was not a misplaced anxiety. Critics sneered at the psychoanalyst's ability to find sexual significance in any object. "Even the physician's stethoscope," one of the nation's leading neurologists, Francis Dercum, remarked incredulously in 1914, "is believed to be a phallic symbol." Freudian psychoanalysis gave the old studies of phallic worship a new lease on life, even as it seemed only to magnify their notoriety. Totems, taboos, fetishes, and phalluses—they all migrated out of Victorian anthropology into the modern psychology of religion.[10]

Beyond these wild encounters with the "primitive," the new psychologies were also shaped through heightened exposure to what William James labeled "the mystical classics." In creating a canon of spiritual guides and ecstatic visionaries—Teresa of Avila was always near the top of the list—researchers were able to establish, so they thought, a recognized baseline for sorting out the main features of mystical experience. Being in the canon did not always work to the mystic's benefit. "Psychic onanism"—that is how the Boston-based psychiatrist James S. Van Teslaar described what he found in culling this "devotional religious literature" for "data." In large measure, he concluded, "religious ecstasy and mysticism generally" were traceable to "aberrations of the erotic instinct." Whether the subject was Catholic mystics, aboriginal fetishists, or pubescent Protestants, the new psychologies of religion underscored the "close affinity between the sexual and religious emotions." As a German researcher portentously concluded in 1908, "We may describe the history of religions as the history of a special manifestation of the human sexual instinct."[11]

Not every psychologist was happy with this explicit sexual turn in exploring the religious consciousness. William James, indeed, was famously unhappy about it. In his classic account, *The Varieties of Religious Experience* (1902), James took direct aim at this intellectual "fashion" of explaining the religious emotions in sexual terms: "For the hysterical nun, starving for natural life, Christ is but an imaginary substitute for a more earthly object of affection," he wrote with a dismissive wave of the hand. "It seems to me that few conceptions are less instructive than this re-interpretation of religion as perverted sexuality." In his curt dismissal of the interdependent relationship between religion and sexuality, James ended up the odd man out. Even those colleagues who valued James's cautions against overly naturalistic interpretations of mystical experience conceded his error on this point. "We must surrender to the evidence," the Bryn Mawr psychologist James H. Leuba concluded in *The Psychology of Religious Mysticism* in 1925. "The virgins and the unsatisfied wives who undergo the repeated 'love-assaults of God' . . . suffer from nothing else than intense attacks of erotomania."[12]

If James marked one intellectual pole in debates over the psychosexual study of religion, Theodore Schroeder, more than any other expositor, staked out the antithesis: namely, "that all religion is ultimately reducible to sexual excitement and sexual ideas." A leading civil-liberties lawyer who doubled as a freelance psychoanalyst, Schroeder had already moved into the orbit of freethinking agnosticism and robust secularism as a young man. He had his own reasons for being skeptical about religion: His Roman Catholic mother had been disowned for marrying a Lutheran, and her treatment had left him permanently on guard against religious intolerance and utterly alienated from Christianity. Finishing his law degree at the University of Wisconsin in 1889, he thereafter began his legal career in Salt Lake City where he tangled repeatedly with both Mormons and their Protestant critics. The debates over Mormon polygamy especially piqued his "agnostic curiosity" and launched him into a psychosexual exploration of Mormon history and theology. Those initial fascinations honed his skills as both a freethinking polemicist and an avid collector. Within the decade, he had pulled together a massive repository of early Mormon and anti-Mormon materials. Schroeder became a lifelong compiler of cases to support his psychosexual theorizing about religion, and Craddock would surface as his favorite specimen.[13]

Souring on Salt Lake City, Schroeder moved to Manhattan in early 1903—in the winter immediately following Craddock's death. There he re-imagined himself as bohemia's legal advocate and emerged as a presiding force in the Free Speech League, an organization through which he quickly became aware of the lingering controversy surrounding Craddock's case. Over the next decade he cultivated associations with Emma Goldman, Lincoln Steffens, and Margaret Sanger, among other activists, and came to the legal defense of one social radical after another. All along he was willing to put his money (and his expertise) where his mouth was, and that was a good thing because he certainly liked to talk. Steffens, a vigorous muckraker in his own right, admired Schroeder's persistence in fighting injustices, large and small, but wearied of his self-assured verbosity: "I believe in Free Speech for everybody except Schroeder," Steffens half-jokingly remarked. By the 1910s Schroeder had become a player in both civil-liberties and psychoanalytic circles, but he had also developed a reputation for mule-headed tenacity in his intellectual labors. Once he had a thesis, he hammered it—and then kept hammering it. That proved especially true in his myriad studies designed to establish "the sexual origin of all religion and religious experiences."[14]

Over the course of his long career Schroeder had two consuming passions. The first was the total dismantling of anti-obscenity laws for the sake of free speech and a free press. That concern resulted in a series of publications, the most comprehensive of which was *'Obscene' Literature and Constitutional Law* (1911), a major work in the ongoing

Theodore Schroeder, free-speech lawyer turned psychoanalyst, painstakingly preserved Craddock's manuscripts in order to make her the primary case history in his psychosexual theory of religion's origins. Toying with the pen name "Lucifer" as a young man, he sported a goatee most of his life that seemed to fit him to the role of devil's advocate. Special Collections Research Center, Morris Library, Southern Illinois University, Carbondale.

liberal critique of Comstockian regulations of publishing and the postal system. His second obsession was establishing the sexual basis of all religious experience in order to advance both scientific knowledge and secular mores. Aligning himself with the highly regarded clinician William Alanson White and becoming—as part of his Freudian tutelage—one of White's first analysands, Schroeder emerged as a prolific contributor to the *Psychoanalytic Review* in the three decades after its founding in 1913. Publishing alongside Freud and Jung as well as Americans Isador Coriat and Karen Horney, Schroeder churned out more pieces for that banner journal than any of his more illustrious and better credentialed contemporaries.

Craddock got caught in the crisscrossing of Schroeder's dual preoccupations. No matter how much her court battles jibed with his liberal commitments to a free press, Schroeder's interest in her remained primarily sexual. In his copious work on censorship and constitutional

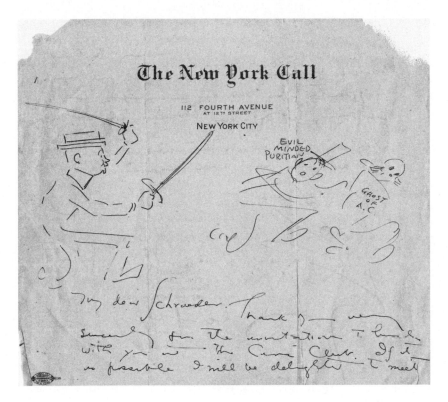

One of Theodore Schroeder's correspondents turned to caricature to capture Schroeder's manly zeal in chasing away America's puritanical and Comstockian bogeys. Special Collections Research Center, Morris Library, Southern Illinois University, Carbondale.

law, men like Moses Harman and D. M. Bennett held the starring roles, while women like Craddock and Alice Stockham rated cameos. Taking up the judicial claim that Craddock's *Wedding Night* was "unquestionably obscene"—indeed, "the most offensive of condemned literature"— Schroeder exploited the extremity of that estimate in a three-page review of her case: "If this is the worst, I am prepared to take my chances on lesser 'obscenity,'" he concluded after emphasizing the humanitarian impulse behind Craddock's booklet. That nod, though, was the most he ever made of her legal struggles in his various anthologies and casebooks on civil liberties. Put simply, Craddock's free-speech fight was not what Schroeder found attractive about her.[15]

Ida C served as the darling of Schroeder's other love, his psychosexual theorizing about religion, a subject upon which he planned multiple volumes with Craddock as his centerpiece (not to say centerfold). Toward that end, between 1915 and 1917, Schroeder published six installments of one of her manuscripts, the treatise on "Heavenly Bridegrooms," in the *Alienist and Neurologist*, on the conjecture that her mystical notions provided "an unintentional contribution" to his own psychosexual theories of religion's origins. Two decades later, still at work on his magnum opus on religion and sexuality, he remained preoccupied with Craddock, presenting her case history in the *Psychoanalytic Review* in 1936 under the title "One Religio-Sexual Maniac." Elsewhere he had started peddling his work on her under titles like "Ida's Theomania"; "Religious Erotism of Ida C"; "Puritanism through Erotomania to Nymphomania," and "Philosophy and Moral Theology of an Erotomaniac." As he assured potential publishers, "The material is very sexy, but its treatment is always coldly scientific." No doubt that frosty erudition is why, in one especially alluring variation, he proposed calling his volume on Craddock, "TRUE CONFESSIONS OF ONE SEXUAL AND RELIGIOUS MANIAC." The extent to which Craddock had become fused to Schroeder's inquiries was evident in the typographical error in one byline in 1917: It proclaimed the authors of the piece to be "Theodore and Ida C. Schroeder."[16]

Schroeder's psychosexual theory of religion's origins doubled down on all the reigning inquiries of the day. He saw, for example, ancient phallicism as the evolutionary fount of sexuality's sacramental aura: At the most primitive stage of human development, he claimed, "we find sex worship, with its exaggerated . . . estimates of the sacredness of sex." He also agreed with those psychologists who saw mysticism as masking deeper sexual urges and desires. Indeed, for Schroeder, passionate religious experience was at its heart a misinterpretation; it was actually

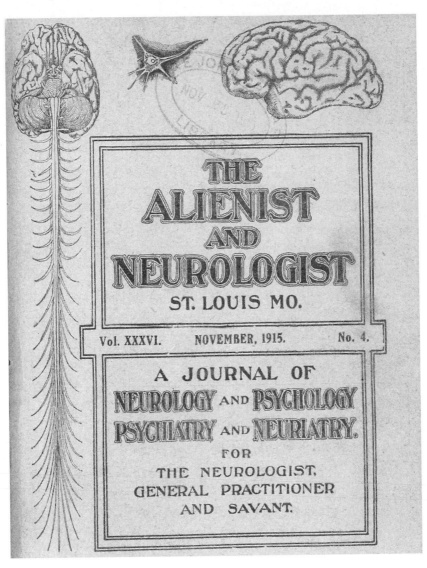

THE
ALIENIST
AND
NEUROLOGIST
ST. LOUIS MO.

Vol. XXXVI.   NOVEMBER, 1915.   No. 4.

A JOURNAL OF
NEUROLOGY AND PSYCHOLOGY
PSYCHIATRY AND NEURIATRY.
FOR
THE NEUROLOGIST,
GENERAL PRACTITIONER
AND SAVANT.

Schroeder began his publishing ventures on Craddock in 1915 in the Alienist and Neurologist, *a medical psychology journal based in St. Louis. Having previously featured the work of sexologist Havelock Ellis, the serial ran Schroeder's version of Craddock's work on heavenly bridegrooms in six parts over three years.*

an unrecognized sex ecstasy, a misidentified form of "psychic sexual orgasm." Schroeder's ultimate ambition was to demystify sexuality, to lead the march forward from the religious control of the body—whether exercised through sacraments or taboos—to "secularized sex." As Schroeder saw it, "sex-superstition is the most persistent of all superstitions," and modern civilization still suffered from this "mad overvaluation" of the sinfulness and sacredness of sex. "The secularization of sex," on Schroeder's terms, offered the consummate disenchantment of the world. Human feelings of love, intimacy, and desire would all be demythologized and then reinterpreted in terms of evolutionary psychology and biology.[17]

Schroeder presented himself as a secular liberator capable of freeing Americans from sexual repression, guilt, and shame. And he could free them too of the misdirected ecstasies of religious experience. "Religion as personal experience," he assured, "fades out, merges into pure secularism, when our libido is unrepressed through . . . continuous normal and satisfying self-expression." For Schroeder's secular reframing of experience, Craddock provided an especially instructive case of atavism, a revealing throwback to the ancestors. She was a latter-day exemplar of the original religious error, the primal confusion of sexual desire with religious feeling. In displaying that elemental mystification in such a vivid form, she offered the scientist a valuable window on "the psycho-sexual childhood of the race."[18]

The very blatancy of Craddock's regression, in Schroeder's view, made her the perfect case history for his larger ambition of advancing secular norms for modern sexuality. The practical advice of well-trained physicians would replace the mumbo-jumbo of ministers, Schroeder promised, in directing people's sex lives. Medical schools, substituting the science of sexology for the air of sacramental mystery, would eclipse churches and temples. And the scientific expertise of the male psychoanalyst would, in this instance, bare the bridal veil of the yoga priestess: To demystify Craddock's spirituality of the body was to offer a technical blueprint for seeing through religion's age-old distortion of sexuality. Once religion lost its power to regulate and consecrate sexuality, to gather the sublimated energies of sexual desire to its own ends, secular enlightenment would have its day. Sex and society would finally be free of religion's specter. Schroeder, like Freud, was intent on designing a future without religious illusion.

Schroeder's extensive musings on the psychosexual origins of religion may have been, as his critics often claimed, lifelessly naturalistic and dismally repetitious, but no one could dispute his success as a psychoanalytic provocateur. In 1915, the *New York Times Magazine* posed, in all seriousness and nonchalance, the question in a headline: "IS SEX THE BASIS OF RELIGION?" Schroeder, along with the psychiatrist James S. Van Teslaar, were the leading authorities for the piece, and it turned out that Van Teslaar had been inspired to take up the sexual psychology of religion primarily through Schroeder's published studies. Together the two investigators had discovered, the *Times* reported unblushingly, "the underlying sameness of all religions," that "at their 'very core' Christianity and the other great contemporary religions are what religion was at the beginning—'sex mysticism.'" By the 1910s and 1920s, the question of religion's sexual origins had achieved an avant-garde cachet among American intellectuals, and that topic increasingly exercised a middlebrow fascination as well. Schroeder had pressed that psychosexual explanation more insistently and irreverently than any other American writer. And no case history arrested his own attention more than Craddock's.[19]

———————

CRADDOCK'S FANTASIZED LOVE LIFE was consistently more involved than her mundane erotic relationships. As a young woman, she showed little propensity for courtship, let alone marriage. The main youthful infatuation she recalled was a "silly schoolgirl romance" with one of her Quaker teachers, "Miss Annie Shoemaker, whom I adored." Ida had regularly sent her roses every St. Valentine's Day "far into young womanhood," despite the teacher having always "pooh-poohed" her affections. Craddock even dated "the birth of my idealizing of sex" to a botany lesson that Shoemaker gave on plant fertilization. She remembered "Miss Annie" picking up the lesson book and remarking with a quiet dignity: "Girls, whenever I take up this subject, I feel as though I were entering a holy temple." From the sex life of plants Craddock made the initial leap to "the holiness of sex in human beings," and the spring for that was her intense affection for Annie: "I was head over ears in love with my teacher," Ida confessed.[20]

Until well into her twenties Craddock appeared far more comfortable with the intimacies of same-sex relationships—passionate bonds that were nourished and blessed in Victorian culture, particularly among women—than she did with potential male suitors. Her mother had offered her only stern advice in matters of courtship: namely, "that I must never, never allow a man to kiss me or put his arm about me, or even hold my hand—until the right man of all should come." Between her love for Shoemaker and her mother's exacting instructions, Ida claimed that until she was twenty-seven "all men were to me like shadows." Even then, she only took an interest in "a cut-and-dried old bachelor" whose very absence of ardor made him seem safe for flirtation. "I often asked myself if it were really love that I felt in attraction to this man," Craddock remarked, noting that she seemed mostly drawn to their contentious debates on "every question of the day" rather than to his straitlaced physical bearing. The two had kissed "on one or two rare occasions," Craddock admitted, but the gentlemanly bachelor was "too prim and careful to do much of it." Having grown up without a father or a brother and with all the cautions that hemmed in female respectability, Ida had been habituated to see men as shadowy (if not spectral) figures, and certainly her first courtship at age twenty-seven with this "dried mackerel," as one of his own friends described him, did not dramatically change that perception.

However incorporeal her relationship with this dyed-in-the-wool bachelor had been, Craddock nonetheless gained from it a new ease around men, even a fondness for them—what she described as a greater capacity to "esteem and honor manliness." Thereafter her love of Annie receded from view, and a number of men began to emerge as vital presences in her life. "I had learned, from my bachelor friend, enough of the pleasure of social relations with a person of the opposite sex to be aware that this is what I now needed," she reported. New male companions came into her life through church circles, book groups, and liberal clubs. During her stay in San Francisco in the late 1880s she took a particular interest in a young man named Euclid Frick. Casting her affection as a sisterly desire to shelter Frick from the city's corrupting influences, she emphasized that "there was never the slightest interchange of caresses between us." The warm feelings she expressed toward Frick were hardly those of a serious romance or even a simmering infatuation; they had instead the tone of a protective, older sibling—a woman nearing thirty looking out for a youth a decade her junior. The young man soon went off to medical school, became an army surgeon, and married someone else. Craddock for her part showed no regret over Frick's marriage to another, and he would not play an explicit role in her subsequent sexual fantasies.[21]

After her California sojourn in the late 1880s Craddock developed a strong working relationship with Richard B. Westbrook in leading the American Secular Union. That professional tie created a substantial partnership over the next couple of years, but there was no indication of any strong emotional connection between the two of them. Indeed, their collaboration quickly frayed once Craddock took up spiritualism and sexology; by 1894, Westbrook claimed to be opposing "tooth and nail her silly delusions" and was actively trying to prevent her from public discussion of "all sex questions." Needless to say, Craddock cooled on the relationship with Westbrook and instead kept up her close connections to his wife, Henrietta, who steadfastly refused to follow her husband in classing Ida among the deluded. "I have never considered you insane," she wrote her friend, "I have never considered any one insane simply because they knew more about something than I do."[22]

Other relationships with men offered more enduring sustenance than did Westbrook's curtailed sponsorship of Craddock's work. The old radical Moses Harman was a consistent sympathizer as was the physician Edward Bond Foote. The relationships with living men that Craddock most prized were intellectual companionships—at least, those were the only partnerships she cared to lift up:

> Some few men of my acquaintance there are (Heaven bless them!) who are like brothers to me. Chivalrous and protective toward me, they gladly let me either stand alone when I want to, or offer a helping hand when I am struggling to higher levels of wisdom. Instead of repressing my search for knowledge, they cheerfully offer to show the way to still wider fields than I had dreamed of. . . . I rest secure in the blissful consciousness that, however startling my questions and inferences, they will never sneer at them, never extract a double meaning from them, never rebuke my thirst for knowledge, never attempt a flirtation on the strength of the confidence I repose in them. . . . And again I say, heaven bless those men. If they did but know half the comfort they are to me in the temptations and trials of life.

After her limited experiment with physical intimacy with the old bachelor, Craddock never came close to finding "the husband whom soul and body cried out for"—at least, not in the mundane social world. Instead, she developed mutually respectful and rather cerebral companionships with a handful of men. If she was ever drawn to physical intimacies with any of them, she never let on.[23]

The most important man in Craddock's life was the editor and fellow spiritualist William T. Stead. He offered financial backing, intellectual enthusiasm, and religious rapport; indeed, he was the one confidante with whom she shared her spiritual diary about her intimacies with a heavenly bridegroom. He remained Craddock's stalwart defender to the very end, even writing a long letter to the U.S. Attorney General Philander Knox in an attempt to procure his office's intervention in her final showdown with Comstock. Years after her death, Stead was still maintaining his undying "loyalty to my dear friend," but that does not seem to have been a lover's fidelity. After her year-plus stay in London ended in mid-1895, the relationship between the two of them was carried on almost entirely through letters. Their strongest bond seems to have been their mutual sense of otherworldly communication— Craddock with Soph and Stead with his durable spirit contact Julia. Again if the two shared any other intimacies, even a furtive touch or flirtatious glance, neither was saying anything.

Stead's long-term faithfulness to Craddock was evident in the way he tried to protect her legacy from Theodore Schroeder's prying inquiries. When Schroeder started to collect materials on Craddock in 1906, Stead kept a wary distance and refused to hand over her manuscripts to him. He rightfully suspected that Schroeder intended to use "Miss C's experiences for the purpose of maintaining a theory which of all others would have been most abhorrent to her." Schroeder countered that his interest in her "spiritual sexuality" was strictly above board and that he very much shared Craddock's anti-censorship sentiments. Stead did not bite, and, when Schroeder supplied him with a copy of one of his early articles on "The Erotogenesis of Religion," Stead replied tartly that he had read the piece "with the greatest interest, but with profound disagreement with your conclusions." If Stead had not died prematurely— as a passenger onboard the *Titanic* in 1912—Schroeder might never have gotten his hands on the bulk of Craddock's papers. But, after Stead's death, the documents had ended up in the possession of his daughter Estelle, who shared her father's spiritualism, but not his protectiveness of Craddock. Shortly after the close of World War I, Estelle finally let

Schroeder have what he had been seeking for more than a decade—her father's cache of Ida's manuscripts.[24]

Once Schroeder got hold of Craddock's manuscripts—especially her "Diary of Psychical Experiences"—he set about rereading her sex life in psychoanalytic terms. Although Ida had always insisted that what she knew about sex she had learned through a combination of religious experience and medical study and not from sexual liaisons, Schroeder was unconvinced. However devoted he was to archiving Craddock's papers, he never felt particularly bound by the textual evidence they presented, and that liberty was particularly true of the stormy sex life he imagined for her. The pious biology lessons of Annie Shoemaker, Schroeder argued, had initially sparked her "erotomania," unleashing "the homosexual drive in all its intensity" and with "disastrous consequences" for her mental hygiene. Her mother's "intense puritanism," in turn, had prevented Ida from experiencing "a normal heterosexual interest" as a young woman and had also produced an "exaggerated guilt over masturbation," developmental problems that tilled the ground for her eventual insanity and suicide. Shoemaker had hallowed sex; her mother had tabooed it; and that ambivalence—the swinging between shame and awe—had left Craddock a neurotic wreck. "If only she had been taught to think of sex in a matter of fact, common sense, relatively objective fashion, with the holiness and sacredness thrown to the dogs," Schroeder concluded of Craddock's upbringing, "she might have become a very useful woman." Secularized sex, in other words, would have spared her the destabilizing emotional conflicts that arose from a religious culture that both mystified and demonized human sexuality.[25]

On her relationship with the desiccated bachelor, Schroeder took Craddock at her word: namely, that the liaison had belatedly awakened her heterosexual desires, but had failed to provide an adequate outlet for physical expression of those feelings. Craddock's self-confession about the frustrations of that relationship was perhaps the last moment of transparency Schroeder granted her. "An unbearable conflict between sexual desire and its fearful suppression," he suggested, was now turning her into a full-blown psychoneurotic. He speculated that at this point Craddock left Philadelphia for California, not out of a desire to escape her mother as she alleged, but in search of a resolution to her sexual tensions—as Schroeder put it, she was on a "quest for sexual experience." (The immediate impetus that Ida had specified for leaving home was a last-straw thumping she had received from Lizzie who had "in outbursts of passion, whipped me, many a time, for real or fancied offences.") Schroeder ran with the thin evidence of Ida's sisterly affection for Euclid Frick, the young man who had briefly boarded in the same house with her in San Francisco, and suggested that her newfound joy over her Golden State independence was actually a "honeymoon ecstasy."[26]

Schroeder based his conjecture of a San Francisco honeymoon mostly on a tiny Freudian slip he detected in one of Craddock's letters. In corresponding with her school friend Katie Wood, Ida had reported that she appreciated having a male boarder for the added sense of security it gave her after a burglar had broken into the house. Schroeder noticed that Craddock had changed the wording to specify that she did not like sleeping "in the house" alone by scratching out her original wording in which she said she did not like to sleep "there" alone. Schroeder took that correction to be a slip of the mask—an inadvertent admission that Craddock was actually sleeping "there" in the same bedroom with Euclid, her youthful boarder. For a woman who prided herself on frank talk about sex, it seems implausible that the evidence for her ecstatic sexual awakening in California would come down to that kind of grammatical clarification. Self-deception may have been intrinsic to her fantasized love life, but concealment was not. She was always more in danger of revealing too much, not too little.[27]

Schroeder's revelation of a Freudian slip in Craddock's letter turned out to have been his slip, not hers. He overlooked an obvious reference in the same letter to Euclid and Ida actually sleeping in separate rooms: Euclid comes trotting down the hall to her room when he hears her scream out in fright. Overeager in his psychoanalysis, Schroeder also omitted key details in presenting the burglary as something that happened in the neighborhood rather than in Craddock's own abode. The break-in had actually left the household feeling so vulnerable that Ida subsequently armed herself with a hatchet, Euclid with a revolver, and the housekeeper with a bat. The security Craddock was craving in this letter was not a lover's snuggle.

The honeymoon with Euclid Frick was just the beginning; thereafter, Schroeder's imagining of Craddock's sexual experience only got more vivid. In analyzing her role as corresponding secretary of the American Secular Union, Schroeder speculated that she had actually become the lover of the group's president, Richard Westbrook, whom he presented as a mystical ex-clergyman with a penchant for Tantric-inspired sex. As Schroeder commented, "This man was her constant support when later she got into much trouble with the police and the post office censorship. It seems highly probable, therefore, that he was also her instructor in a new sexual technique, over which she became so morbidly obsessed." There were many problems with this theory, not least that it was riddled with mistaken notions: Westbrook, a secular-minded skeptic, showed no interest in "unorthodox mysticism, especially that of the Far East"; he was an inconstant backer in Craddock's struggles with the censors, especially in comparison to his wife, who was one of her most consistent friends and who never showed the least worry about an affair of this sort; and he mostly kept his distance from the sex-radical wing among liberals and freethinkers. That Craddock and Westbrook were mystical companions and secret Free-Lovers, an amorous pair of co-conspirators sitting atop the secularist movement, was at best a long-shot proposition.[28]

The improbability of this relationship did not stop Schroeder from turning it into an imagined actuality: Westbrook was Craddock's love guru. He had introduced her to occult sexual techniques, which intensely pleasured her, and then he had deserted her, leaving her bereft: "What

Richard B. Westbrook was president of the American Secular Union while Craddock was serving as the group's corresponding secretary. Schroeder speculated that Westbrook, otherwise known for his scientific rationality, was actually Craddock's mystical sex guru. Portrait by Mary Elwell, 1900, Wagner Free Institute of Science.

is then more natural than that in these circumstances she should be driven to seek for relief, and the solution of her sex problem through some idealized fantasmal substitute, to replace the physical love of the mystical ex-clergyman?" Schroeder asked, already knowing the answer. "It seems probable that [Westbrook] had already prepared the way out, by teaching her the sexual technique and theology of the *Tantras*." The psychoanalyst's imagination of the "probable" was now running to its own phantasmal conjectures: Schroeder had no evidence for anything but a professional relationship between the two; he also had no evidence that Craddock had shown any awareness of Tantric materials at this point in her career, let alone that Westbrook had such curiosities and special talents. Westbrook was not the Omnipotent Oom.

What Schroeder did have was a theory about Craddock's psychoneurosis that required first her sexual satisfaction, then her sexual frustration, and then mystical substitution. Schroeder charted her hysterical descent this way: Craddock, once introduced to Westbrook's "very enticing technique," could not live without this ecstatically orgasmic practice, and yet, for whatever reason, Westbrook had stopped pleasuring her. That deprivation—"a period of sexual starvation, doubtless accompanied by masturbation with an increased feeling of guilt"—left her primed for a religious resolution of her madcap sexual urges. Haunted by memories of her past sexual ecstasies with the occult ex-clergyman and tormented by these no longer fulfilled desires, Craddock increasingly drifted away from objective realities into the world of unbridled sexual fantasy. Desperate, she began to sanctify that dreamland, to find the necessary compensation for the loss of Westbrook in "delusional intimacy with mystical or superhuman powers."[29]

Craddock was clearly not the only one floating off into sexual reveries and wish-fulfilling fantasies. Schroeder had turned Westbrook into a sex magus, Craddock into his Tantric consort, and the psychoanalyst into the revealer of buried secrets. In his role as Craddock's posthumous therapist, Schroeder had become thoroughly captivated by his own whimsical story of her descent into religio-sexual mania. He had, in effect, created a self-serving fantasy in which the secular psychoanalyst served as the antidote to the shamanic ex-clergyman. The enlightened scientist made himself the bearer of a new kind of male expertise that could demystify the hidden sexual conflicts that produced such female delusion. If Craddock had toppled down a spiritualist slope into psychosis—a tumble that carried her from lewd daydreams to nocturnal hallucinations—the secular therapist was in a position to secure others from the precipice of mental illness and moronic supernaturalism. Indeed, whatever else was to be gathered from the case history of Ida C, this much Schroeder thought quite clear: It showed that "puritanism and mysticism are really problems of mental hygiene."[30]

———•·•———

THE REAL ACTION in Craddock's sex life was in her imagination. During her early mediumistic efforts in 1892, she had begun to sense a clairaudient connection to various spirits, none more important than the shade of the young businessman who had courted her when she was in her late teens. Among the ghostly communications she heard from her departed suitor, now known as Soph, was that he still loved her and that he wanted another "chance to try to win me after I should come over to his land." So began Ida's renewed courtship with Soph, as if death no longer separated the two of them, as if romantic regret could be overcome. Though Ida could not see Soph—she saw his face only once in a half-awake moment, "the same face as on earth," but now "permeated with a wonderful spiritual light"—he nonetheless emerged as her "daily Borderland companion . . . quite near and dear to me." Here, in the gray areas of consciousness and coherence, Ida admitted to him and to herself that she loved him and that she wanted to be his wife—not merely in the world beyond the grave, but "right here and now." The idea of becoming the wife of an "unseen spirit lover" was, she knew, quixotic, perhaps even "quite a joke," but she found the prospect too alluring to resist. That there was a castle-in-the-air unreality to it all, she was ready to admit, but that there was also something "spiritualizing" and "uplifting" to this nuptial union, she was unwilling to deny.[31]

Contained within the poignant loneliness of Ida's phantasmal intimacy with her departed lover was a dense spiritualist relationship—one that proved no less sustaining and powerful for its hallucinatory immateriality. At times Soph functioned less as a spouse than an assisting angel or saint, helping her, for example, to find lost articles, such as "my pocket-knife, with buckskin purse cover" that she had misplaced. "Soph, indeed, seems at times a veritable St. Anthony of Padua in this respect," Craddock commented of his mundane interventions. At other times Soph seemed to represent a spirit of Yankee time-discipline: He exhorted her on the virtue of punctuality and even gave her internal prompts to make haste—"Now, dear love, you have but a few minutes left." He also helped her reach her appointments safely, serving as something of an angelic guardian. "Soph seems to make a point," she noted, "of escorting me to and from places, day and night." Adrift, as Craddock so often was in one city or another, the illusion of company and protection provided tangible relief from the reality of loneliness and vulnerability. "I rejoiced at having a husband who yearned to protect me," she wrote. As an angel or saint, Soph exercised quotidian powers of comfort and protection; he was a heavenly intermediary with an eye on Ida's everyday needs and burdens. Craddock was not looking for a redeemer but a companion. She needed saving from isolation, marginality, and harassment, not from sin.[32]

If Soph was a rather conventional angel in the help he offered, he was by no means a conventional husband—rather, he served as the mystical imagining of the ideal husband for the newly emancipated woman. Craddock's hallucinations, in other words, were also a dream of the transformation of marriage. "I love him more than ever," she reported of Soph at one point in her diary. "It begins to seem as though we were getting to be comrades." That expression of intimacy bespoke Craddock's companionate ideal for marriage—a union that was to be at once sexual and intellectual, physical and spiritual. At another point, for example, she imagined that Soph was staging a play in the other world and thrilled at her husband's artsy creativity:

> It seems like a fairy story that this cultured and artistic man should care for me as his life-companion—me, who [has] always passionately longed for the society of cultured people, but whose entire life, with the exception of my schooldays, has been mostly passed among my intellectual inferiors, the virtuous, respectable, kind-hearted, but oh, so dull people of the middle class. I get at times just hungry for a little association with people of brains and culture. . . . Sometimes I do wish the hour would hurry along when I can get over there and study and work up intellectually to become his true comrade.

Soph, the spirit husband, was the specter of the earthly husband Craddock never found, a companion who personified intellectual aspiration, emotional sensitivity, and sexual reciprocity. Craddock, in recording her relationship with Soph, had taken flight from reality as a way of imagining a new relational world for women of initiative and ambition like herself.[33]

If Craddock imagined Soph as an ideal companion, the relationship they enjoyed was never one of uncomplicated pleasures. Far from it. Even comrades had quarrels, bad sex, and petty miscommunications. After one "semi-hypnotic" encounter with Soph, for example, Craddock became annoyed about her saggy, uncomfortable bed and peevishly snapped: "I did think that a husband who couldn't get his wife a comfortable bed to lie on, no matter how plain, oughtn't to expect her to go to bed with him." During another of their spiritual (yet densely physical) embraces, Craddock found that Soph was "lacking in his usual ardor." She soon realized what the problem was: Despite having perfumed herself with a fragrance Soph liked before going to bed, Ida still had the odor of onions on her breath from dinner, and that was hindering Soph's passion. Though he remained tender and polite, his affections were simply not at their usual level. (In spiritualist cosmology, the spirit borderland had all the trappings of the physical world, and that necessarily included the full range of sensory perception—olfactory as much as the rest.) In imagining a spirit husband for herself, Craddock had projected a world that was both wildly idyllic and routinely flawed. The commonplaceness of so many of the problems the couple faced added a peculiar day-to-day realism to a journal ostensibly devoted to spiritual introspection and religious experience.[34]

While her relationship with Soph had its minor pitfalls, it also had much darker moments—ones that Craddock had prepared herself for, at least to some degree. She had studied enough about the history of witchcraft to expect a demoniacal and nightmarish underside to her experiences. The "Demon Lover" was every bit as much a part of the folklore that she had scrutinized as the "Angel Husband." "So many women with spirit lovers come to grief in time," she remarked, "and the lover becomes, apparently, diabolic." As her spiritualist experiences unfolded, Craddock definitely found out for herself that divine blessings were regularly paired with demonic ordeals—that bright moments of ecstasy could swiftly give way to dark nights of despair. Indeed, there were moments in her diary in which the whole pursuit of a heavenly bridegroom looked like it could end in sheer terror and madness. "It really looks like incipient insanity," Craddock wrote after a series of disturbing hallucinations that included tactile sensations of physical assault. Suffering from "chronic eczema," she considered her skin to be excessively sensitive, abnormally so; she suggested, indeed, that she had "the skin of a medium," a condition that allowed her to sense Soph's presence more keenly and yet also subjected her to horrible bouts of "fiendish touch." Several times in her diary such "infernal touches"— whatever they were and wherever they came from—left her feeling helpless and unstrung.[35]

Craddock's unhinging was especially evident in her recurring fears of improper sexual pleasures—fears that often left her conflicted and disoriented. She repeatedly excoriated herself for any imagined participation in "unnatural" practices—that is, for being involved in anything other than a fantasy of heterosexual intercourse. She remained particularly terrified of masturbation; the culture's epidemic fear of this "secret vice" recurrently seeped into her spiritualist experience. In valiantly trying to refuse the "base physical pleasure" of masturbation, Craddock's mystical piety regularly trembled with anxiety, if not panic. Given the invisibility of her lover, she lived in dread of being self-deceived not only about Soph's very presence, but also about the line between his supposed actions and her own: Were her hallucinatory fantasies, she occasionally worried, only a form of "mental masturbation"? That her angelic lover sometimes disregarded the rules against masturbatory forms of stimulation—say, offering more than a passing salute to the clitoris—only made the hypnotic fantasies harder for her to decipher. It did not help that one of the few authorities Craddock had immediately at hand for decoding masturbation was a notorious French treatise, Pierre Garnier's *Onanisme*, which detailed the dire effects of self-abuse on human health and civilization.[36]

To Schroeder, Craddock's spiritualized sexual reveries represented an obvious masturbatory practice as well as a compensatory device and coping mechanism. Dreaming up Soph ameliorated the guilt and inferiority complexes that had been produced through her illicit sexual pleasures, including the two torrid affairs he had ascribed to her. That Craddock remained enmeshed in her culture's sexual proscriptions, particularly those surrounding masturbation, was painfully clear; indeed, those interdictions at times produced mad levels of worry, melancholy, and self-reproach in her. Despite the psychic burdens she carried, though, the dreamworld Craddock inhabited by night was not simply depressing and fear inducing. Often enough, she managed to struggle through her panic over masturbation to achieve an acceptance of bodily delight—or, at least, a temporary abandonment to it: "Let the orgasm come," she heard Soph whisper to her at one point when worrying again about "a base masturbation," and this time she did: "I had succeeded beautifully."[37]

Craddock saw the intense conflicts she experienced—in body, mind, and soul—as a spiritual struggle that led not only to sexual pleasure, but also to mystical illumination. "I felt I had begun to care for God as, I think, the most mystical nuns must care for their divine Spouse, Christ," she related on New Year's Day 1902 near the end of her diary keeping. "I loved my husband, it was true, and was supremely happy in his mateship. But the Presence of God overwhelmed us both in the most beautiful and indescribable way." Of all the delusions on display—both Schroeder's and Craddock's—perhaps the most shocking was not Craddock's fantasy of an angel lover, but Schroeder's confidence in psychoanalysis to say all that needed to be said about Ida C's over-brimming imagination. The ecstasy of revelation versus the voice of reason—that is an old and almost tiresome choice, but fortunately it is not the end of this story. The scholarly Miss Craddock had already made sure of that.[38]

ONCE SOPH HAD COME BACK into her life, Craddock pursued various efforts at self-explanation: What exactly did she mean when she claimed to have a spirit for a husband? She played with different allusions and parallels—literary, artistic, and scholarly—as much to explain herself to herself as to anyone else. Hers proved a lush and beguiling project of self-interpretation.

Craddock's trusted confidante William Stead always warned her that the careful framing of her experience was of the essence; she needed, in his view, to emphasize that Soph was part of an elaborate dream-world; otherwise, she would simply be viewed "as stark, staring mad." As a well-read occultist, Stead had very explicit advice for Craddock on how to relate her mystical experiences to the outside world. "Instead of talking about a spirit husband," he counseled, "you should be most careful to say that you for many years had a very curious and vivid and consecutive series of dreams; that your dream-life had become to you quite as real as your waking life, and that in these dreams you lived the full life of a married woman." That slant, Stead thought, might "elicit sympathy" or, at least, "excite curiosity" rather than provoke derision and justify institutionalization. For Craddock to pursue the husband of her dreams was, in Stead's strategic estimate, a safer and saner construction than claiming outright to have found a spirit husband.[39]

Craddock was attracted to Stead's notion of placing the whole relationship with Soph in a dream state. Everyone knew, she once remarked, that "things happen in queer ways in dreams," and so that realm provided a creative, romantic, and even erotic license, a surreal sphere that nonetheless remained within the range of "normal experience." In exploring the possibility that her relationship with Soph was all taking place on a "dream plane," Craddock drew particularly on George Du Maurier's popular novel *Peter Ibbetson* (1891), a tale of two childhood companions who are painfully separated from one another and who yet remain soul mates into adulthood. Eventually, the star-crossed lovers, Peter and Mary, meet again, but she is already married, and he ends up in a jail cell for murdering her current husband, a pitiless aristocrat, in self-defense. Again tragically separated, they reconnect nightly in an idyllic world of dreams and thus keep their exalted union alive. (The story, adapted to stage and cinema, proved of enduring appeal; in 1935, it took on its most renowned incarnation, a feature film directed by Henry Hathaway and starring Gary Cooper and Ann Harding.) In a lover's world of elusive reminiscences and gossamer fantasies, Peter and Mary had discovered "a life within a life" through "the magic of dream-land."[40]

Not surprisingly, Craddock loved the story from the first time she encountered it. "Have you ever read Du Maurier's 'Peter Ibbetson'?" she gushed to her friend Katie Wood in 1898. "If not, I do want you to get it as soon as you can and read it over. I thought of you many times when I was reading his description of the happy days of his childhood, and thought of how much you would enjoy it. . . . To me, it is a lovely poem, some parts of which are worth reading over and over again." Soon, Du Maurier's novel had made its way into Craddock's own diary of spiritual experiences. (It helped, no doubt, that Mary was also a diary keeper; indeed, she was intent on preserving a voluminous record of her psychical excursions with Peter through their magical dream world.) In one passage in her journal Craddock spoke specifically of her efforts to "master the art of 'dreaming true,' like Peter Ibbetson." In one half-awake moment, as she was coming out of a dream, she heard Soph tell her explicitly: "Now, dear love, I want you to meet me in dream-life night after night, as Peter Ibbetson met his sweetheart." Craddock had a rich vocabulary for talking about her experiences—hypnotic trance, fantasy, hallucination, mental masturbation, waking vision, subjective consciousness, among other

This spirit photograph, taken in 1891, revealed a ghostly figure holding a wreath above William Stead's head. Victorian photography was haunted with specters and made Craddock's own angelic imaginings apiece with these wider cultural fascinations. Borderland 2 (1895): 310.

terms, were scattered through her diary—but Du Maurier's literary example had particular resonance for her. "Night after night," she recounted, "as I compose myself for sleep, I make a stern resolve to go over into dream-life wide awake, as Peter Ibbetson did."[41]

Craddock also looked to the visual arts for complementary imaginings of her dreamy relationship with Soph. The most obvious pictorial resource was spiritualist photography. Images of departed loved ones hovering as ghosts around the living would have been utterly familiar to her: William Stead sat for a spiritualist portrait as did Craddock's fellow sex radical Elmina Slenker. In one particularly emblematic episode, a spectral Abraham Lincoln had even appeared in a picture of Mary Todd Lincoln (the shade of the assassinated president placed his filmy hands on the shoulders of his grieving widow in a gesture of comfort). Though there is no record of Craddock posing for such a portrait, spirit photographs were commonplace icons in the late nineteenth century. Given her own interest in materializing the spiritual world—for example, through automatic writing, she thought that she had once received Soph's signature—it would be surprising if she had not at least considered obtaining an apparitional photograph of her husband. At one point in her diary she noted reading a book on spirit photography and had actually used one of its plates to imagine what a female spirit named Stéphanie looked like. Whether or not Craddock explored this particular medium through a studio visit, this much at least is apparent: Not only had she heard the spirits as interior voices, she had also caught tantalizing glimpses of them as spectral presences in Victorian photography.[42]

Ever a woman in pursuit of cultural elevation, Craddock drew inspiration primarily from the fine arts for the pictorial framing of her experience. She often gained a visual sense of Edenic innocence or heavenly splendor in the "picture galleries" of London and elsewhere. In one painting, for example, the look of "a youthful monk," whose gaze was rapt on the Madonna and Child, reminded her of Soph's worshipful eyes during their earthly courtship. "I stood and looked and looked at the picture," she marveled, "because it brought back so vividly the way Soph used to look at me." Soph was the monk, and she was the Virgin; Craddock always wanted her love life to be marked by purity and transcendence.[43]

Just as she took Du Maurier as a favored novelist, Craddock also had a beloved artist for her romantic imaginings: William Bouguereau, an acclaimed French salon painter of the period. Popular among American audiences from the 1870s through the 1890s, Bouguereau had staked his reputation on a scorn for the avant-garde, including the Impressionists and Post-Impressionists. By the time of his death in 1905, that was proving an increasingly bad wager. His works, the *New York Times* obituary sniffed, "possessed that prettiness which attracts the plutocratic merchant and the stock broker." The popularity of his art with "the American public of a couple of decades ago," the critic sniped, suggested a cultural "philistinism" only recently outgrown through a belated awakening to the contemporary.[44]

Philistine or not, Craddock would have stood by Bouguereau as a fine-art lens on her own erotic and religious intuitions—and as a fellow sufferer of persecution by Comstockian censors. For American audiences especially, Bouguereau personified the glorification of the nude in art and, as such, became another nemesis of Christian modesty. When, for example, Bouguereau's *Return of Spring* (1886) was exhibited in Omaha in 1890, a young Presbyterian man had felt a flash of righteous horror as he looked on the naked nymph. Fighting the "impure thoughts and desires" that the painting aroused, he asked himself "whether I should want my mother or sister to see that picture. And then I wondered what Christ would think of the picture if He stood before it. I felt that I ought to destroy it." So, this local Comstock seized a chair and smote "the canvas with all his might," leaving about a thirty-inch rent in the central figure and two of the cherubs who fluttered around her.[45]

The young evangelical's sudden iconoclasm epitomized the repressiveness that made Craddock despair for America's cultural and religious scene. The visual arts, as was the case with dance as well, seemed hopelessly impaired by the country's devotion to sexual reticence. In Craddock's view of the problem, Protestant tastemakers remained the chief culprits:

> The Church people are still the foremost opposers of the nude in art. This loathing for the sight of the human form divine, and the habit of thought which connects the naked body with sexual impurity, has had a most unfortunate effect upon art in America. . . . In statuary, men and women alike are adorned with a ridiculous fig-leaf, stuck like a postage stamp over where their genitals should be. Thus every exhibition of nude statuary becomes an object lesson to the rising generation in the idea that the sexual organs are something to be ashamed of, instead of something to rejoice in and glorify.

In some sense, Craddock and the chair-throwing Nebraskan saw Bouguereau's nudes the very same way—as a potent disturbance of Protestant mores and Victorian inhibitions. The visual power that she discerned in Bouguereau's artwork was the obverse of the overwhelming temptation that the twenty-five-year-old Presbyterian saw in the *Return of Spring*. The artist, in effect, offered a measure of both Comstockian and anti-Comstockian impulses, the danger and the appeal of unclothed desires.[46]

Craddock was intensely drawn to Bouguereau's vision of the mythic pair Cupid and Psyche. The artist had reprised their celebrated relationship in a number of canvasses and had produced two particularly provocative images of a youthful Cupid carrying an ecstatic and half-nude Psyche off into the heavens. To Craddock, Bouguereau's representation of the twosome brilliantly captured the rapturous tangle of body and spirit in which she and her angel husband were engulfed. Soph, Craddock analogized, "is like Bouguereau's Cupid . . . just that ethereal, heavenward-pointing direction of my entire being," while she was "like Psyche in that picture, still weighted down by this earthly body." At another point, she noted in her diary that Soph "seems to have the same feeling for me that is manifest in the face of the Cupid of Bouguereau's 'Cupid and Psyche'—a feeling which, although sexual, is unearthly, ethereal, transcendently fine and soft and pure." Bouguereau's artwork helped Craddock make sense of the dreams that had seized her, a pictorial embodiment of her fraught negotiations of the erotic and the spiritual. Bouguereau's entranced Psyche offered Craddock an archetypal myth through which to view her own experience; such fabled imagery allowed her to frame her disorienting visions apart from the familiar diagnoses—erotomania, theomania, and nymphomania—current in clinical psychiatry. Craddock thus imagined herself as a latter-day Psyche whose own longing, despair, and torment had ended in divine deliverance. Like her mythic double, Craddock felt that she too had been "carried into the realms of bliss on the bosom of Love."[47]

Craddock viewed one French artist in particular, William Bouguereau, as having the imaginative power to evoke the ravishing ecstasy of her religious experience. His Cupid and Psyche *(1889) captured the simultaneity of erotic passion and heavenly ascent that Craddock so prized. Private Collection, by permission of The Bridgeman Art Library International.*

Bouguereau's The Abduction of Psyche *(1895) combined wafting transcendence and blissful intimacy to even grander effect than his previous rendition had. From the collection of Frederick R. Koch.*

Craddock's fondness for the myth of Psyche and Eros pointed in the direction of her main project of self-explanation: That is, she turned again to scholarly inquiry, including folklore, comparative religion, and biblical interpretation. "The passion of the bookworm has always been strong within me," she noted in her diary after she had a dream in which a large "papier maché head" had shown forth, filled with "the goodies of learning." Those were certainly the sorts of sweets that Craddock was after when she began writing a "monograph" on the history of "Heavenly Bridegrooms" in May 1894, while conducting research at the British Museum. That book, she hoped, would prove that her own experience as a heavenly bride was not hopelessly crazy and unintelligible.

As with her large manuscript on phallic worship, Craddock's labor on "Heavenly Bridegrooms" was arduous. She pored over scriptural texts and patristic commentaries before making her way down to such books as Emanuel Swedenborg's *Conjugial Love* (1768), Walter Scott's *Demonology and Witchcraft* (1830), and E. B. Tylor's *Primitive Culture* (1871). A routine observation in her diary about one of her trips to the library provides some sense of how she was proceeding: "I had that day been collating quotations from Tertullian about angelic husbands, the last being taken from his treatise on *The Veiling of Virgins*. His insistence on veiling women perpetually, because, he said, it was through their beauty that the angels had fallen from heaven, had roused my indignation." Perhaps she was simply delusional—or, perhaps her contemporaries did not know the history of religion like she knew it. She pursued the delights of learning in order to lift her experiences out of isolated lunacy into comparative perspective.[48]

Through her research, she came to see the idea of divine betrothal as quite prevalent—within Christianity and well beyond it. "Every religion and folklore under the sun," she surmised, contained suggestive material on such intimate exchanges between heaven and earth. She wanted to craft "a sort of rough guidebook" to these angelic pathways, which, she was quick to note, led into the mythic core of Christianity itself through the Annunciation, the Holy Spirit's impregnation of the Virgin Mary, an event made manifest through the Angel Gabriel. As she remarked at the opening of her study, "The celestial being, who, whether God or angel, becomes the Heavenly Bridegroom of an earthly woman, is better known to the literature of the Christian Church than most people who are not theologians are aware." How easily, Craddock thought, Christians neglected those portions of the Bible, like the erotic poetry of the Song of Songs, that they found tricky or problematic.

Craddock especially wanted to draw attention to Genesis 6:2 in which the sons of God were said to have taken the daughters of men as wives. In the long history of biblical exegesis, Jewish and Christian, the passage had provoked endless controversy, but many expositors nevertheless took it to be an acknowledgment of sexual congress between angels and humans. Craddock, following that tack, traced the idea forward from the Book of Genesis to the commentaries of the early church fathers—Justin Martyr, Tertullian, and Augustine. Not that most of the early Christian interpretations of this angelic commerce impressed her, since the emphasis was placed on the vulnerability of the angels to corruption, the polluting enticements of women, the necessity of female modesty in dress, and the primacy of rigorous asceticism. This much, though, Craddock did like about the ancient commentaries: The confirmation that such divine-human encounter had for centuries been a serious theological preoccupation.[49]

After considering the history of early Christianity, Craddock went global: India, Mexico, China, Egypt, medieval Europe, and ancient Greece (the last, a chance to call to mind Psyche and Eros again). She pointed as well to "the Mohammedan Paradise," which "abounds in love-making," and pronounced it a vast improvement on the Christian heaven. That slant of vision dramatically reversed the received wisdom in which Christians were associated with sexual purity and Muslims with debased sensuality. As the German clinician Richard von Krafft-Ebing had observed in sharply contrasting the two religious traditions in his foundational work on sexual pathologies, "The picture of eternity seen by the faith of the Christian is that of a paradise freed from all earthly sensuality, promising the purest of intellectual happiness; the fancy of the Mussulman fills the future life with the delights of a harem full of houris." Upending the familiar Christian-Muslim hierarchy, Craddock was delighted to find voluptuous imaginings of paradise wherever she could.[50]

That Craddock turned to Islam for a positive example would hardly have been a winning argument in Protestant America. She had an answer, though, to the objection that her evidence came only from antiquated mythologies, Oriental superstitions, or Roman Catholic errors. Namely, she replied with contemporary evangelical examples— a woman from Rockford, Illinois; another from Wichita, Kansas; and a minister from Philadelphia, all of whom had a quite tangible sense of the divine-human relationship. Craddock even had a letter from an American convert who had come to know of such religious intimacies through the divine-healing movement, a faith-cure enterprise of decidedly evangelical character. The woman, as a newly betrothed bride of Christ, had written to another church sister to compare notes on their overlapping experiences, and that woman had, in turn, handed the letter over to Craddock. This "devout and pure-minded Christian" realized now that Jesus was Lord over her body as well as her soul: "The life abundant must flow into every part of His *purchased possession*, ere we are *fully* redeemed." Lest anyone think that her testimonial was merely figurative (admittedly, this was not likely to be a problem for Craddock), the woman insisted that her spiritual experiences were inseparable from the corporeal: "It should be plainly understood that the *union* [with Jesus] is as the sexual intercourse of husband and wife."[51]

Even as Craddock blithely multiplied her American Protestant examples, she knew that the notion of heavenly brides and bridegrooms was hard to make sound sensible. No matter how rich the historical record, the fact remained that it was "easy to dismiss all these stories, ancient, mediaeval, and modern, with contempt, as so many falsehoods, or, at best, self-delusions." Nevertheless, she maintained, "this mass of folklore belief is too overwhelming in quantity and too widely diffused to be dismissed lightly. Back of it all there must be some objective realities and some fire for all this smoke." In contrast to Schroeder's psychosexual theory in which secular science thoroughly supplanted religious experience, Craddock offered a mystical history of religion, a history with the angels left in. She was convinced that all this smoke pointed to the fire of the real—that something true about the divine world was actually being revealed in all these myths, epiphanies, and unions.[52]

When Schroeder serialized Craddock's book on heavenly bride-grooms in the *Alienist and Neurologist*, he thought that his own psychosexual schema fully absorbed her mystical history. For Schroeder, the sooner all talk of mystical union was recognized for what it was—a mislabeled sex ecstasy—the better; such experiences provided no special religious knowledge, only camouflage for bare sexual drives. The secular sophistication of Schroeder's posture was not necessarily an improvement on the mystifying blend of Craddock's position. Having penetrated the illusion, Schroeder had little else to say—as if the secularization of sex would take care of everything, as if nothing would be lost in the separation of body and spirit. Craddock seemed to come closer to the truth, to the reality, when she insisted that there was willy-nilly an open-ended exchange between religious and sexual experience, a fluidity of human emotions and sensations in which mixture was the rule: "Religion and sex-love, indeed, are but two reservoirs of emotion, which, standing side by side in every one's life, not only tend to frequently overflow into one another, but are also connected with one another below the surface by subtle and as yet not wholly discovered channels." In contrast to Schroeder's singular focus, Craddock multiplied the possibilities—including the arts and humanistic scholarship—for approaching the over-brimming relationship between Psyche and Eros.

In her range of curiosity and allusion, in her refusal of the foregone conclusion and the light dismissal, the madwoman outshone the psychoanalyst.[53]

Even at the time, a few commentators thought that Craddock had gotten the better of her posthumous editor. When Schroeder turned his series of articles into a stand-alone reprint in 1918, two reviewers of the volume looked at analyst and analysand side by side and decided sharply in the latter's favor. Rather than providing unintended support for Schroeder's psychosexual theory of religion's origins, Craddock's monograph had exposed the dullness of his editorial gloss. One of the reviewers was the notorious British magus Aleister Crowley, the extolled and excoriated genius of modern occultism. He had no trouble declaring a victor in this composite treatise: While Craddock's learning was "enormous" and her manuscript "remarkable," Schroeder's own reasoning displayed "exquisite nonchalance." Disallowing the tenacious American litigator the authority of scientific psychology, Crowley jabbed: "Only a lawyer could be so shameless. . . . One does not have even to disagree with him to see how worthless is his reasoning." Crowley embraced Craddock, "this most talented woman," as a fellow traveler pursuing the arcana of sex magic, but he also accorded her the scholarly palm she had so long sought. Craddock, by Crowley's lights, had become an adept practitioner of a go-between learning—one that moved back and forth between academic study and mystical retrieval.[54]

Perhaps the book on heavenly bridegrooms revealed Craddock's distinct voice—the scholar turned mystic, the mystic turned scholar. Yet, she always struggled with the question of her own agency and expressive freedom, and that was true with "Heavenly Bridegrooms" as in other aspects of her life: How much of its inspiration came from spirits and how much of it was a product of her hard work in the library? Was she once again a secretary rather than a scholar—as had been the case when she was forced to relinquish her college ambitions and turn to shorthand for a living instead? In working on this project she admitted feeling at times like whole paragraphs were being "dictated" by some outside intelligence. She almost resigned herself to a scribal rather than creative role, confiding in her journal: "I always did like to be a secretary." The desire, though, for her own authorship would soon rise again, and Craddock would reassert herself as a self-cultivated inquirer: These typescripts represented her intellectual labor; they were reflective of "my own standpoint," and nothing would have meant more to her than to get her research into print. "I could say good-bye to my husband with a far less aching heart, than to have my manuscripts perish out of the world, unpublished," she observed when contemplating the threatened destruction of her writings. She was ready to let "all this spook business go to the dogs" for the sake of her books. "I must live just to publish those manuscripts," she concluded. "The rest could go."[55]

Near the end of her life Craddock's self-resolve faltered once more. Feeling sick and downtrodden from her time in prison and on the cusp of a final court appearance, she worried anew that her experiences with Soph had been "a delusion, a lie." What if her spiritual life was "only hallucinative, through and through," she asked herself in despair? What if her mother—and the lawyers, doctors, and judges who agreed with her mother—were right, after all? "Oh God, to know only the truth, the truth!" she prayed in her next-to-last diary entry in late July 1902. "Truth, Truth, Truth is what I want." The ordeals of sensory confusion had started plaguing her again, and she was struggling hard to sort out illusion from reality, tormenting disease from spiritual training. Moments of coolness and clarity were few for her during that last summer in New York City; she often felt "desperate," like she "could endure no more."[56]

Craddock nonetheless kept grappling with her own demons (and angels). Trying once again to ward off the terror of disintegration, she reported in her final surviving diary entry, penned on August 26, two months before her suicide, that "a strangely serene and calm feeling" had come over her. It was an experience again mediated through her conjugal relationship with Soph, but it also sounded like a final assertion of renewed "elasticity and courage"—her own grasping of independence and creative voice: "I was in full control of myself, as queen of myself; and I WAS A WOMAN!" How long she held onto that assurance of self-possession, and whether she had it the night of October 16 as she methodically sealed up her room and turned on the gas, it is impossible to say. This much, though, is clear: Ida Craddock had made every effort to die a free woman and to be remembered as such.[57]

Epilogue

———⋅•⋅•⋅———

IN A POEM FROM HER COLLECTION *Lizzie Borden in Love* (2006),
Julianna Baggott imagines the birth-control pioneer Margaret Sanger,
tired and bereft, finding solace in addressing the ghost of Ida Craddock:

> *Ida, is it you? Gauzy as a bride, at long last,*
> *Do you instruct the virgins of heaven*
> *with pamphlets?*

Why, Sanger asks Craddock, did she "breathe poison" for Comstock,
"the angry man full of piss, . . . his brain a pink lard ham"? "Our enemy"
is now dead, Sanger relates, and yet she still feels Comstock's weight:
"Ida, tell me again how much we cannot speak of." In seeking to revive
her own spirits through invoking Craddock's spirit, Sanger divulges a
fantasy of "lewd flowers" rising "season after season" on Comstock's
grave, "a riotous orgy of fornication." Craddock's ghost, filmy and
wordless, becomes a conduit for the poet to channel Sanger's voice.[1]

The haziness of Sanger's encounter with Craddock, in Baggott's
portrayal, is about right: Most of the reformers of the next generation
barely knew how to engage spirit-minded comrades like Craddock or
Alice Stockham as flesh-and-blood allies. In her autobiography Sanger
expressed only surprise at the religious backers who seemed to come out
of the woodwork to defend her *Woman Rebel*, a monthly that quickly
fell under Comstock's ban as obscene literature in 1914. These
supporters represented groups, she said, "I had hardly known existed—

Theosophist, New Thought, Rosicrucian, Spiritualist, Mental Scientist." Another leading birth-control advocate of the 1910s, the physician William J. Robinson, to whom Sanger turned for support in publishing her book *Married Love*, was brusque and more specific. "Our radicals must be hard up indeed for pioneers," Robinson blasted in 1915, "when they have to drag in the name of Mrs. Ida Craddock, a poor weak-minded creature," worthy only of "a psychopathic asylum." He located her squarely among the "disreputables," a generation of Free-Love radicals and spiritualist outliers who had mostly—and thankfully, in Robinson's view—given way to forward-looking medical professionals and secular progressives.[2]

Sanger's surprise and Robinson's dismissal, like Theodore Schroeder's psychoanalysis, pointed to a broader secularizing of sexology that became only more pronounced as the twentieth century wore on. The creation of a secular sex revolution would gradually render the spiritual sex revolution of nineteenth-century reformers—John Humphrey Noyes, Victoria Woodhull, Lois Waisbrooker, Alice Stockham, Edward Carpenter, and Ida Craddock, among them—a bygone inheritance. "No Gods, No Masters" had been Sanger's slogan for the *Woman Rebel*, and a substantial portion of the twentieth-century movement for sexual emancipation would march forward under such secular banners. In 1979, when one of Craddock's long suppressed pamphlets was finally republished, the reviewer for the *New York Times* tellingly remarked: "If one excised from Ida C. Craddock's widely banned *Right Marital Living* its pious obeisance to religion, the plain and mostly accurate talk about orgasm and the 'marital embrace' would fit easily into a contemporary sex manual." In other words, if Craddock were to tally with the post-Kinsey, Masters and Johnson era of scientific sexology, her religion would need to be pared away.[3]

That excision of Craddock's religion was necessary not because sex had been successfully secularized by 1979. This was the very year, after all, that Jerry Falwell founded the Moral Majority, a conservative Protestant counterblast to the malign forces of secular humanism. Instead, Craddock's religion had to go because her cultural world—one in which metaphysical speculators and spiritual drifters were in the front ranks on sex-reform and civil-liberty causes—now sounded unimaginably foreign. It looked to the political left like Falwell was poised to become the new Comstock (and if not Falwell, then Donald Wildmon, who had two years earlier founded the National Federation for Decency, with its strong anti-obscenity agenda). Secular liberals were, amid the inklings of a new culture war, hard-pressed to envisage any form of religious piety as the handmaiden of sexual emancipation. With the rise of the Moral Majority and allied organizations, strict constructions of church-state separation and personal privacy—"Get Your Bible Off My Body" and "Focus on Your Own Damn Family"—seemed, once again, imperative for the protection of a liberal civil society. Even though Craddock and other disreputables had much to say about the joined privacy of religion and sex, they had become ghostly anomalies—social reformers who had championed the companionate equality of marriage partners, the importance of female passion and sexual pleasure, the liberalization of divorce laws, and the rights of reproductive control through an appeal to both secular principle and religious vision.

For all of the outrageous impossibilities that Craddock pursued, many of them now seem, a little more than a century later, like rather ordinary possibilities. Her vanguard ambition for the inclusion of women in the liberal arts, for example, has become utterly unremarkable as has her hope that women would be welcomed into the academy of scholars. Indeed, in 2004 the elite institution she had sought to integrate, the University of Pennsylvania, named as its eighth president the political philosopher Amy Gutmann. The issue at Penn, as elsewhere, has moved well past coeducation to the question of how to achieve greater gender equity in all faculty ranks, schools, and departments. Craddock's progressive enthusiasms for American higher education would hardly seem wild-eyed or brash now.

Even Craddock's enforced amateur status might appear at this point a credit rather than a debit. Having become disenchanted anew with William James's PhD octopus and Max Weber's spiritless specialists, contemporary intellectuals often romanticize the daring amateur, the independent voice who has somehow escaped the tireless self-monitoring of "proper, professional behavior." If anyone possessed "an unrewarded, amateurish conscience"—to borrow a laudatory phrase from Edward Said—it was Craddock. If anyone displayed an incorrigible dedication to her scholarly ideas apart from their respectability and marketability, it was Craddock. That creative amateurism made her exclusion from Penn and her marginality to professional societies no less painful; it made the renovated lavatory she had for an office in Philadelphia no more roomy or well-appointed. Perhaps Craddock would find it disconcerting to hear those who enjoy the perquisites of professionalization pining for the amateur's emancipation. The small consolation: What once made her a lightweight novice might now make her a bohemian hipster.[4]

Likewise, Craddock's teachings on the pleasures of heterosexual intimacy and the blessings of female passion look rather safe and restrained now. In many instances, indeed, she appears a taboo-preserving throwback as much as a full-orbed anticipation of the subsequent liberalization of sexuality in American culture. Perhaps, given her desire to promote sustained sexual encounters, she would be happy to hear the promises and four-hour perils of Viagra and Cialis advertisements so freely broadcast. Perhaps as well she would be pleased to see that evangelicals themselves have gotten into the act of celebrating the sexual delights of married couples with their own how-to manuals.[5] But, there would be much more to discourage her: the passing hook-ups of American youth culture, the mainstreaming of adult entertainment, and the globalization of the sex trade are all trends that would have made her cringe. Craddock, keenly aware of how much the commercialization of sex colored the perception of her own teachings, was not one to rejoice in the consumer's titillation. She preached a pro-sex, anti-censorship feminism only within the consecrated limits of heterosexual monogamy and only on the basis of the religious, medical, and social value of her work.[6] That *Playboy's* senior editor James Petersen presented her as the inaugurator of a freewheeling "Century of Sex," she would have found, to say the least, an irony-laden compliment.

As for the religious eccentricities of Craddock's Church of Yoga, these too seem rather mundane in hindsight. Articles on "Sex and Yoga: They're Good for the Soul" now land their authors in mainstream magazines rather than jail, and most health clubs and even many churches appear eager to help Americans realize their yogic potential.[7] The old ideal of a resolutely Christian America remains, to be sure, a live option on the right, but the cultural opening for both religious disaffiliation and post-Christian experimentation has markedly grown in the last generation. Roaming seekers, freethinking secularists, and outspoken atheists suffer few encumbrances in the religious marketplace—certainly, nothing with the bite of the blasphemy charge. So also the reversal of fates for obscenity and civil liberties: While many of the debates surrounding obscenity—including the definition of community standards and artistic value—remain intensely divisive, free literary expression largely trumped Comstockery at the Supreme Court level in the 1960s and 1970s. The obscenity charge could not silence Craddock, Sanger, or Havelock Ellis now nor could it keep Walt Whitman, James Joyce, D. H. Lawrence, or Henry Miller under wraps. Contemporary American writers—thanks to the court battles fought against censorship by pioneering mid-century publishers like Barney Rosset and Hugh Hefner—have little to worry about in the way of obscenity charges.

Not that Craddock herself would be blandly uncontroversial a century later. Religion, sex, gender, and politics—she pursued too many hot-button issues to avoid contention. Still, there are some advantages to having become a ghost in public memory. Unlike Sanger, whose legacy through Planned Parenthood continues to have polarizing political effects, Craddock floats only occasionally into view as a feminist forebear, a tragic free-speech martyr, a steamy occultist, or a sexologist ahead of her time. The diaphanous quality of those memories should not dissolve the grainy roughness of her life, the audacity and disrepute of it. Hers was a life lived on the borders—of solvency and sanity, of ostracism and vagrancy—and yet, even as she drifted from Philadelphia to London to Chicago to Denver to New York, Craddock was far from purposeless, always possessed as she was of a visionary's eye for uncanny perception and intense focus. An escape artist of the imagination, she tried to lift herself free on the paired wings of Eros and divine love. In soaring heavenward she became a spectacle of sin, sex, madness, and criminality, and immediately began a downward spiral. In the descent, as much as in the ascent, her struggles blazed with a sometimes searing light. Those flames have finally burned through the censor's filter.

ABBREVIATIONS

BI   *Boston Investigator*

DPE   Ida C. Craddock, "Diary of Psychical Experiences," box 2, f. 2-3, Ida C. Craddock Papers, Special Collections Research Center, Morris Library, Southern Illinois University, Carbondale, Illinois.

EBF   Edward Bond Foote

IC   Ida C. Craddock

ICP   Ida C. Craddock Papers, Special Collections Research Center, Morris Library, Southern Illinois University, Carbondale, Illinois.

LLB   *Lucifer the Light-Bearer*

RGP   Ralph Ginzburg Papers, 1848–1964, Mss 862, Wisconsin Historical Society, Madison, Wisconsin.

SML   Ida C. Craddock, "Story of My Life in Regard to Sex and Occult Teaching," box 2, f. 2, Ralph Ginzburg Papers, 1848–1964, Mss 862, Wisconsin Historical Society, Madison, Wisconsin.

SWC   Ida C. Craddock, "Sex Worship (Continued)," box 2, f. 5, Ida C. Craddock Papers, Special Collections Research Center, Morris Library, Southern Illinois University, Carbondale, Illinois.

TS   Theodore Schroeder

TSP   Theodore Schroeder Papers, Special Collections Research Center, Morris Library, Southern Illinois University, Carbondale, Illinois.

WTS   William T. Stead

NOTES

Preface

1. Nadine Brozan, "Chronicle," *New York Times*, Sept. 22, 1997, B7; Hugh M. Hefner, foreword to James R. Petersen, *The Century of Sex: Playboy's History of the Sexual Revolution, 1900–1999* (New York: Grove, 1999), x.

2. Brozan, "Chronicle," B7; Petersen, *Century of Sex*, 15–18; Emma Goldman, *Living My Life* (1931; Salt Lake City: Smith, 1982), 553. The scholarly literature on Craddock is limited and piecemeal. Four of the most notable works are Shirley J. Burton, "Obscene, Lewd, and Lascivious: Ida Craddock and the Criminally Obscene Women of Chicago, 1873–1913," *Michigan Historical Review* 19 (1993): 1–16, which particularly attends to the criminal case against Craddock in 1899; Evelyn A. Kirkley, *Rational Mothers and Infidel Gentlemen: Gender and American Atheism, 1865–1915* (Syracuse: Syracuse University Press, 2000), 92–98, which considers Craddock's role as a freethinker; Taylor Stoehr, ed., *Free Love in America: A Documentary History* (New York: AMS, 1979), 63–70, 302–315, 619–635, which helpfully contextualizes Craddock's teachings on sexuality; and Janice Wood, "Ida Craddock, Free Speech Martyr," in David B. Sachsman, S. Kittrell Rushing, and Roy Morris Jr., eds., *Seeking a Voice: Images of Race and Gender in the Nineteenth Century Press* (West Lafayette: Purdue University Press, 2009), 317–325, which highlights Craddock's 1902 battle with Comstock. See as well Shirley J. Burton, "Ida C. Craddock," in Rima Lunin Schultz and Adele Hast, eds., *Women Building Chicago, 1790–1990: A Biographical Dictionary* (Bloomington: Indiana University Press, 2001), 192–193; Robert P. Helms, "Ida C. Craddock," in Tom Flynn, ed., *The New Encyclopedia of Unbelief* (Amherst, NY: Prometheus Books, 2007), 220–221; and Inez L. Schaechterle, "Speaking of Sex: The Rhetorical Strategies of Frances Willard, Victoria Woodhull, and Ida Craddock," PhD diss., Bowling Green State University, 2005. The larger historiography on the sexual politics and religious debates of the era is immeasurably rich; those works that have provided me with especially important background and perspective include: Ann Braude, *Radical Spirits: Spiritualism and Women's Rights in Nineteenth-Century America*, 2nd ed. (Bloomington: Indiana University Press, 2001); Joy Dixon, *Divine Feminine: Theosophy and Feminism in England* (Baltimore: Johns Hopkins

University Press, 2001); John D'Emilio and Estelle B. Freedman, *Intimate Matters: A History of Sexuality in America*, 2nd ed. (Chicago: University of Chicago Press, 1997); Timothy J. Gilfoyle, *City of Eros: New York City, Prostitution, and the Commercialization of Sex, 1790–1920* (New York: Norton, 1992); R. Marie Griffith, *Born Again Bodies: Flesh and Spirit in American Christianity* (Berkeley: University of California Press, 2004); Helen Lefkowitz Horowitz, *Rereading Sex: Battles over Sexual Knowledge and Suppression in Nineteenth-Century America* (New York: Knopf, 2002); Kathi Kern, *Mrs. Stanton's Bible* (Ithaca: Cornell University Press, 2001); Joanne J. Meyerowitz, *Women Adrift: Independent Wage Earners in Chicago, 1880–1930* (Chicago: University of Chicago Press, 1988); Joanne E. Passet, *Sex Radicals and the Quest for Women's Equality* (Urbana: University of Illinois Press, 2003); Beryl Satter, *Each Mind a Kingdom: American Women, Sexual Purity, and the New Thought Movement, 1875–1920* (Berkeley: University of California Press, 1999); and Hal D. Sears, *The Sex Radicals: Free Love in High Victorian America* (Lawrence: Regents Press of Kansas, 1977).

3. DPE, 202. In her diary entry Craddock often used the abbreviation *MSS* for the word *manuscripts*. I have spelled it out for clarity's sake here and elsewhere.

4. Church of the Holy Trinity v. United States, 143 U.S. 457 (1892).

5. Kurt Vonnegut, "Worship," *New York Times*, April 13, 2007, A19. For a classic treatment of Protestant visions for a Christian nation, see Robert T. Handy, *A Christian America: Protestant Hopes and Historical Realities*, 2nd ed. (New York: Oxford University Press, 1984).

6. IC to Hugh Pentecost, Feb. 9, 1902, box 2, f. 2, RGP.

7. Hélène Cixous quoted in Amy Hollywood, *Sensible Ecstasy: Mysticism, Sexual Difference, and the Demands of History* (Chicago: University of Chicago Press, 2002), 3.

8. Walt Whitman, *Poetry and Prose* (New York: Library of America, 1996), 207.

9. Ibid., 242; TS, "Some Metaphysics of Sex," box 5, f. 21, ICP; George Santayana quoted in Robert D. Richardson, *William James: In the Maelstrom of American Modernism* (Boston: Houghton Mifflin, 2006), 160.

Chapter 1:
Belly-Dancing's Defender

1. IC, letter fragment to unidentified correspondent, n.d.; IC to Hugh Pentecost, Feb. 9, 1902, box 2, f. 2, RGP.

2. Heywood Broun and Margaret Leech, *Anthony Comstock: Roundsman of the Lord* (New York: Literary Guild of America, 1927), 49.

3. "Records of the New York Society for the Suppression of Vice, 1871–1953," 3: 126–127, Library of Congress, Manuscript Division; *The Thirtieth Annual Report of the New York Society for the Suppression of Vice* (New York: n.p., 1904), 14–15.

4. George E. Macdonald, *Fifty Years of Freethought: Being the Story of the Truth Seeker, with the Natural History of Its Third Editor*, 2 vols. (New York: Truth Seeker

Co., 1931), 2: 218. For the sinewy, hagiographic version of Comstock's life, see Charles Gallaudet Trumbull, *Anthony Comstock, Fighter: Some Impressions of a Lifetime of Adventure in Conflict with the Powers of Evil* (New York: Revell, 1913).

5. Anthony Comstock to Henrietta P. Westbrook, Feb. 28, 1902, box 2. f. 2, RGP; *The Twenty-Ninth Annual Report of the New York Society for the Suppression of Vice* (New York: n.p., 1903), 7, 9–25; "Comstock Tells His Part in the Ida Craddock Case," *Brooklyn Daily Eagle*, Nov. 14, 1902, newspaper clippings, box 20, f. 15, RGP.

6. IC to *New York Sun*, Feb. 21, 1902, box 2, f. 2, RGP.

7. IC to Pentecost, Feb. 9, 1902; IC to *New York Sun*, Feb. 21, 1902.

8. For a good account of the Columbian Exposition in light of other international fairs, see Robert W. Rydell, *All the World's a Fair: Visions of Empire at American International Expositions, 1876–1916* (Chicago: University of Chicago Press, 1984), 38–71.

9. Christopher Ricks, ed., *The Poems of Tennyson*, 3 vols. (Harlow, Essex: Longmans, 1987), 3: 242.

10. For documentation on these attractions, see J. W. Buel, *The Magic City: A Massive Portfolio of Original Photographic Views of the Great World's Fair and its Treasures of Art, Including a Vivid Representation of the Famous Midway Plaisance* (St. Louis: Historical Publishing Co., 1894), and Halsey C. Ives, *The Dream City: A Portfolio of Photographic Views of the World's Columbian Exposition* (St. Louis: Thompson, 1893).

11. IC, *The Danse du Ventre (Dance of the Abdomen) as Performed in the Cairo Street Theatre, Midway Plaisance, Chicago: Its Value as an Educator in Marital Duties*, 2nd rev. ed. (Philadelphia: n.p., 1897), 8–9; Kate Jordan, "The Danse du Ventre," *Atchison Daily Globe* (Atchison, KS), Jan. 1, 1894, 4.

12. "The Theatre in Cairo," *Current Literature* 13 (1893): 489; "Ahead of the Danse du Ventre: A Protest to be Made to Congress against the Indian Dances," *North American* (Philadelphia), Aug. 3, 1894, 8; "Gone Dance Crazy," *Chicago Tribune*, Aug. 6, 1893, 28. For broader consideration of the fair's Orientalist fantasies, see Zeynep Çelik, "Speaking Back to Orientalist Discourse at the World's Columbian Exposition," in Holly Edwards, ed., *Noble Dreams, Wicked Pleasures: Orientalism in America, 1870–1930* (Princeton: Princeton University Press, 2000), 76–97. On federal policies against Indian dancing in this period, see Clyde Ellis, "'There is No Doubt . . . the Dances Should Be Curtailed': Indian Dances and Federal Policy on the Southern Plains, 1880-1930," *Pacific Historical Review* 70 (2001): 543–569.

13. "Lady Managers Shocked," *New York Herald*, Aug. 5, 1893, 10; IC, "The Oriental Danse du Ventre of the Midway Plaisance," 1–2, Incoming Correspondence, Aug. 13, 1893, Bertha H. Palmer/Board of Lady Managers Papers, Chicago History Museum; F. W. Putnam, introduction in *Oriental and Occidental Northern and Southern Portrait Types of the Midway Plaisance* (St. Louis: Thompson, 1894), n.p.; "The 'Danse du Ventre,'" *St. Paul Daily News* (St. Paul, MN), Aug. 18, 1893, 4. On the mix of Putnam's own anthropological motives, see Rydell, *All the World's a Fair*, 55–65.

14. "The 'Danse du Ventre,'" *St. Paul Daily News* (St. Paul, MN), Aug. 18, 1893, 4; *The Twentieth Annual Report of the New York Society for the Suppression of Vice* (New York: n.p., 1894), 16; "Cairo Dances to Go," *New York World*, Aug. 5, 1893, 1.

15. Sol Bloom, *The Autobiography of Sol Bloom* (New York: G. P. Putnam's, 1948), 135.

16. "Cairo Dances to Go," 1. For Comstock's later orchestration of the arrest and prosecution of three of the Cairo Street dancers, see "Records of the New York Society," 2: 248.

17. "Comstock Shocked," *New York Recorder*, Aug. 7, 1893, 1, 11. Also see the account of Comstock's simulation in Broun and Leech, *Anthony Comstock*, 225–228.

18. "Opinions on the Danse du Ventre," *New York World*, Aug. 13, 1893, 17; IC, "Oriental Danse," 8–9. Craddock sent her plea to Bertha H. Palmer, head of the Exposition's Board of Lady Managers, which had shown interest in reforming the Midway entertainments. See IC, "Oriental Danse," and Ishbel Ross, *Silhouette in Diamonds: The Life of Mrs. Potter Palmer* (New York: Harper and Row, 1960), 95–96.

19. "Opinions on the Danse du Ventre," 17; IC, *Danse*, 4, 17, 35.

20. "Opinions on the Danse du Ventre," 17.

21. For an account of the Midway performances from the perspective of modern dance history, see Donna Carlton, *Looking for Little Egypt* (Bloomington: IDD, 1994). For the subsequent crosscurrents between religion and choreographic innovation, see Janet Lynn Roseman, *Dance Was Her Religion: The Spiritual Choreography of Isadora Duncan, Ruth St. Denis, and Martha Graham* (Prescott, AZ: Hohm, 2004).

22. Ives, *Dream City*, n.p.

23. "Sex-Modesty—The True and the False" and "The Danse du Ventre," in *LLB*, Dec. 22, 1893, 2; "Ida C. Craddock," *Freethinkers' Magazine* 7 (1890): 53.

24. IC, *Danse*, 4–5, 10, 19-20.

25. "Danse du Ventre in Brooklyn, N.Y.," *National Police Gazette*, March 31, 1894, cover, 7; IC, *Danse*, 13-14, 16; IC, "Oriental Danse," 1, 8.

26. "Danse du Ventre," *Yenowine's Illustrated News*, (Milwaukee, WI), Sept. 29, 1894, 2. The Museum of Modern Art has recently produced a four-disc DVD set entitled *Edison: The Invention of the Movies* in which two examples of the Danse du Ventre from 1895 and 1896 are reproduced. Blackhawk Films has compiled a VHS edition of "Edison primitives" that includes censored and uncensored versions.

27. DPE, 38.

28. Ibid., 55, 137, 171–172, 181, 185–186; Havelock Ellis, "Auto-Erotism: A Psychological Study," *Alienist and Neurologist* 19 (1898): 260–299. For Ellis's invention and its implications, see Thomas W. Laqueur, *Solitary Sex: A Cultural History of Masturbation* (New York: Zone, 2003), esp. 67–68.

29. DPE, 38.

30. IC, *Danse*, 33–34.

31. IC, *The Danse du Ventre (Dance of the Abdomen) as Performed in the Cairo Street Theatre, Midway Plaisance, Chicago: Its Value as an Educator in Marital Duties*

(Philadelphia: n.p., 1893), 5–6; IC, *Danse* (1897), 19. Given the fact that the majority of Craddock's published writings were outlawed, very few copies of her contraband pamphlets survive. Two copies of the 1893 edition of her *Danse du Ventre* are available in ICP, box 5, f. 8; a copy of the 1897 edition is in RGP, box 2, f. 2.

32. Kate Field, "Danse du Ventre as Gymnastics," *Chicago Tribune*, Sept. 8, 1893, 9; "Opinions on the Danse du Ventre," 17.

33. IC, *Danse* (1893), 11; George E. Macdonald, Editorial, Dec. 1893, newspaper clippings, box 20, f. 16, RGP. For Craddock's account of her subsequent work on the tract and her explanation of why she added that "little paragraph" on her spirit husband, see IC to EBF, Nov. 22, 1893 and IC to E. O. Walker, Dec. 13, 1893, ICP, box 1, f. 1.

34. IC, *Danse* (1893), 11.

35. TS, ed., "Heavenly Bridegrooms," *Alienist and Neurologist* 36 (1915): 436–437.

36. Anthony Comstock, *Traps for the Young*, ed. Robert Bremner (Cambridge, MA: Belknap Press of Harvard University Press, 1967), 240, 243.

37. IC to Pentecost, Feb. 9, 1902.

38. IC to EBF, June 6, 1898, box 2, f. 2, RGP; IC to Pentecost, Feb. 9, 1902.

Chapter 2: Not an Infidel, But a Freethinker and a Scholar

1. IC, *The Danse du Ventre (Dance of the Abdomen) as Performed in the Cairo Street Theatre, Midway Plaisance, Chicago: Its Value as an Educator in Marital Duties* (Philadelphia: n.p., 1893), 3–4; IC to EBF, Nov. 22, 1893, Dec. 20, 1893, box 1, f. 1, ICP.

2. Samuel P. Putnam, *My Religious Experience* (New York: Truth Seeker, 1891), 87–88.

3. Ibid., 87; IC to EBF, Nov. 22, 1893 and Dec. 20, 1893.

4. "A Very Shocking Time," *New York World*, Feb. 10, 1894, 2.

5. Ibid.; EBF and T. B. Wakeman, *The Manhattan Liberal Club: Its Methods, Objects, and Philosophy* (New York: n.p., [1894]), 5, 14–15; Richard B. Westbrook to EBF, Feb. 14, 1894, box 1, f. 1, ICP; "Observations," *Truth Seeker*, Feb. 17, 1894, 104. Macdonald based his editorialized estimate of Craddock's performance on an acquaintance's account; he regretted that he himself had missed "this chance to be corrupted."

6. IC to EBF, Nov. 22, 1893; "Lectures and Meetings," *Truth Seeker*, Feb. 17, 1894, 105; "Lectures and Meetings," *Truth Seeker*, Feb. 3, 1894, 69; "Lectures and Meetings," *Truth Seeker*, Feb. 10, 1894, 89. Little at all survives of Craddock's own impressions of her New York lectures. She notes them in passing in DPE, 43, and in "Record of Cases in Oral Instruction," box 4, f. 8, ICP.

7. Voltairine de Cleyre, "The Past and Future of the Ladies' Liberal League," *Rebel*, Oct. 20, 1895, 18; Nov. 20, 1895, 31.

8. De Cleyre, "Ladies' Liberal League," Nov. 20, 1895, 32; Jan. [20], 1896, 43; IC to James B. Elliott, July 14, 1894, box 1, f. 1, ICP.

9. DPE, 40. All of Craddock's book manuscripts are considered in detail in this chapter or the ones that follow, except for IC, "Human Traits in Animals," box, 4, f. 7, ICP. This 137-page typescript, "a plea for love and good fellowship toward animals," included reflections on everything from animal rights to the metaphysical questions of whether animals have souls and whether they can perceive ghosts (p. v). Its preface is dated July 1, 1899.

10. The sparse details about the father and the family's business were gleaned from city directories at the Philadelphia City Archives as well as local newspapers. For sample advertisements, see *North American* (Philadelphia), Dec. 22, 1857, 3; *Philadelphia Inquirer*, Jan. 23, 1864, 8. Theodore Schroeder records the story that the father had the freethinking expectation that his daughter would receive no Christian training, a secular pedagogy that her mother then disregarded, but it is a shadowy claim. See TS, "Puritanism through Erotomania to Nymphomania," box 5, f. 30; TS, "Miscellaneous Notes," box 6, f. 7, ICP.

11. IC, "The Marriage Relation," 121–122, box 3, f. 3, ICP.

12. IC to WTS, July 11, 1895, box 1, f. 1, ICP. Lizzie Craddock subsequently remarried and took on the new surname, Decker; her surviving correspondence is all from the period after she became Lizzie Decker. Ida was grown by the time her mother remarried Thomas B. Decker (about 1880), and she makes no mention whatsoever of her stepfather (who predeceased her and her mother in 1896). In other words, the only familial relationship of obvious consequence to Craddock was the one with her mother.

13. SML, 1; "Ida C. Craddock," *Freethinkers' Magazine* 8 (1890): 52-53; "Ida C. Craddock's Mother Speaks," *LLB*, Nov. 20, 1902, 354; "Mrs. Lizzie Decker Suddenly Stricken: General Temperance Advocate Passed Away after Attending National Convention of W.C.T.U.," *Philadelphia Inquirer*, Dec. 8, 1904, 4; "Bequests to Charity," *Philadelphia Inquirer*, Dec. 15, 1904, 14; DPE, 50.

14. IC, "Marriage Relation," 151; IC to Katie Wood, n.d. June 1879; July 11, 1877; June 5, 1879; box 1 f. 1, ICP. The first two letters that survive are from the summer of 1877; there are four from 1879; and three from the late 1880s. Hence the bulk of documentation for Craddock's life is from the period after she became controversial as a freethinker and then as a spiritualist marriage reformer.

15. "Ida C. Craddock," 52; Catherine Wood, "Miss Ida C. Craddock," March 30, 1903, box 1, f. 2, ICP. In the 1890 profile of Craddock that appeared in the *Freethinkers' Magazine*, it was reported that she had attended Friends' Central School and graduated second in her class. The last detail about her class rank cannot be confirmed from surviving records, but her attendance at Friends' Central can be traced. Records show Craddock's enrollment from the February term of 1873 through the February term of 1876. Katie Wood's memory served on this point at least: Craddock was a rarity in paying extra tuition to study all three offered

languages (French, German, and Latin). See Girls' Department, Roll of Pupils, 1845–1874, and Girls' Department, Register, 1874–1889, Friends' Central School Archives, Wynnewood, Pennsylvania. For Craddock's estimate of how her Quaker education shaped her, see IC, "Ashamed of Being Called 'Infidel,'" *BI*, April 22, 1891, 3.

16. IC, "Goethe's Faust Translated by Bayard Taylor," *Saturday Evening Post* (Philadelphia), March 30, 1878, 8.

17. *Catalogue of the Trustees, Officers, and Students of the University of Pennsylvania, 1879–80* (Philadelphia: Collins, 1879), 18–19.

18. "Ida C. Craddock," 53. For a very helpful overview of the larger history, see Barbara Miller Solomon, *In the Company of Educated Women: A History of Women and Higher Education in America* (New Haven: Yale University Press, 1985), esp. 43–61.

19. "Minutes of the Trustees of the University of Pennsylvania, 1882–1892," 2, 10-13, 26, University Archives, University of Pennsylvania. For the outlines of Craddock's case within the larger institutional history of Penn, see Edward Potts Cheyney, *History of the University of Pennsylvania, 1740–1940* (Philadelphia: University of Pennsylvania Press, 1940), 305–306.

20. "Minutes," 12–13, 136; "Miss Anthony," *Philadelphia Inquirer*, Feb. 20, 1883, 3. Craddock's case received some brief mention in the newspapers. See *Philadelphia Inquirer*, Nov. 12, 1882, 3; *Dallas Weekly Herald*, Nov. 16, 1882, 5.

21. IC to Wood, Dec. 8, 1887, box 1, f. 1, ICP.

22. Ibid.; SML, 2.

23. SML, 2; IC, *Primary Phonography: An Introduction to Isaac Pitman's System of Phonetic Shorthand* (Philadelphia: n.p., 1882), iv.

24. Henry Atlee Ingram, *Illustrated Girard College* (Philadelphia: n.p., n.d.), 10, 22; "Girard's Will and Girard College Theology," *Freethought: A Liberal Journal*, Jan. 5, 1889, 4; "The Girard College Theft," *Freethought: A Liberal Journal*, Jan. 19, 1889, 35–36; Richard B. Westbrook, *Girard's Will and Girard College Theology* (Philadelphia: n.p., 1888), 13–20. Voltairine de Cleyre took up the Girard cause in her essay "Secular Education" (1887). See Sharon Presley and Crispin Sartwell, ed., *Exquisite Rebel: The Essays of Voltairine de Cleyre—Anarchist, Feminist, Genius* (Albany: State University of New York Press, 2005), 186.

25. Westbrook, *Girard's Will*, 53. On the Westbrooks, see "Richard B. Westbrook," *Freethinkers' Magazine* 7 (1889): 184–188; *In Memoriam Richard Brodhead Westbrook* (Philadelphia: Wagner Free Institute of Science, 1899); Henrietta Payne Westbrook, *The West-Brook Drives* (New York: Eckler, 1902). On Craddock's connection to the Wagner Free Institute, see "Ida C. Craddock," 53, and "Minutes of the Board of Trustees," 89–030, 1:34–75, Archives of the Wagner Free Institute of Science, Philadelphia.

26. SML, 3–4; IC to Katie Wood, Oct. 1, 1889, box 1, f. 1, ICP.

27. IC to Wood, Oct. 1, 1889. On her interest in involvement with Bellamy's followers, see also IC, "The Advantages of a Badge" and "Nationalism and Christian Socialism," *Nationalist* 3 (1891): 407.

28. IC to Wood, Oct. 1, 1889. On her election, see "The National Secular Congress," *Freethought: A Liberal Journal*, Nov. 9, 1889, 707–708.

29. *Equal Rights in Religion: Report of the Centennial Congress of Liberals, and Organization of the National Liberal League, at Philadelphia on the Fourth of July, 1876* (Boston: National Liberal League, 1876), 7–8; George Macdonald, "History of the American Secular Union," undated clipping, ZAE, p.v. 391, New York Public Library.

30. Macdonald, "History"; Anthony Comstock, *Traps for the Young*, ed. Robert Bremner (Cambridge, MA: Belknap Press of Harvard University Press, 1967), 158–167, 185–207; *The Third Annual Congress of the National Liberal League* (New York: D. M. Bennett, 1879), 89–97.

31. IC, "How to Make Freethinkers of the Young," *Freethinkers' Magazine* 9 (1891): 392; IC, "Ashamed of Being Called 'Infidel.'" 3.

32. Otto Wettstein, "'The Torch of Reason,' vs. the Pansy," *BI*, March 25, 1891, 3; "Miss Craddock Answers Mr. Wettstein," *BI*, April 1, 1891, 3; SML, 4; Abraham Schell, "R. B. Westbrook and the American Secular Union," *BI*, Feb. 11, 1891, 3. Craddock's pansy has been recently revisited as a symbol of freethought, again within a gender-inflected context. See Annie Laurie Gaylor, *Women without Superstition* (Madison, WI: Freedom from Religion Foundation, 1997), xii.

33. "A Book of Ethics for Use in the Public and Private Schools," *Philadelphia Inquirer*, Oct. 12, 1891, 5; Richard B. Westbrook and IC, "The Prize Awarded," *BI*, March 11, 1891, 3.

34. IC, "Church Taxation," *BI*, April 30, 1890, 3; IC, "Our 'Church Taxation' Pamphlet," *BI*, June 11, 1890, 3; IC, *The Army of the American Secular Union* (Philadelphia: n.p., 1890), 5–6. The only surviving copy of this last-named pamphlet is at the New York Public Library, ZEY p.v. 8 #5, but it also appeared as a piece in the *BI*, Aug. 20, 1890, 3. Her other promotional pamphlet was simply entitled *American Secular Union*; she referred to it as "The Flag and Pansy Leaflet" in *BI*, March 18, 1891, 3. It offered a reiteration of the Nine Demands of Liberalism, a history of the organization, a call for new members, and a defense of her "pansy badge." Copies survive at the Wisconsin Historical Society and in "Religion—Anti-Religion—American Secular Union," Vertical Subject File, Labadie Collection, University of Michigan.

35. IC, "How to Make Freethinkers," 386–395. The same essay was reprinted two months later in *BI*, Sept. 9, 1891. For a positive response that suggested the difficulties of carrying Craddock's plan out, see "Liberal Sunday Schools," *BI*, Feb. 4, 1891, 4. For wider efforts to raise young freethinkers, see Joanne E. Passet, "Freethought Children's Literature and the Construction of Religious Identity in Late-Nineteenth-Century America," *Book History* 8 (2005): 107–129.

36. "A Few Words from Miss Craddock," *Truth Seeker*, Feb. 14, 1891, 100; "Is It Unsectarian?" *American Sentinel*, Nov. 20, 1890, 361–362; "Fourteenth Annual Congress," *BI*, Sept. 10, 1890, 3; IC, "Call to Liberal Societies," *BI*, Jan. 7, 1891, 3. This moderating role was most fully displayed in *The Fifteenth Annual Congress of the*

American Secular Union, Held in Philadelphia October 31, 1891 (Philadelphia: Loag, [1891]), 12–20, 24–28, and Robert C. Adams, "The American Secularists," *Secular Thought*, Nov. 21, 1891, 247–248.

37. SML, 4; *Fifteenth Annual Congress*, 17–19, 24–25.

38. SML, 4. For one of Wakeman's call to arms, see T. B. Wakeman, *The Comstock Postal Law Unconstitutional* (New York: Truth Seeker, [1878]).

39. *Woman's National Liberal Union Convention for Organization Held February 24–25, 1890* (Washington, D.C., n.p., [1890]), 3; IC, "The Coming Convention of Liberal Women," *Truth Seeker*, Feb. 1, 1890, 69. The latter also appeared in *Freethought: A Liberal Journal*, Feb. 15, 1890, 102–103. Craddock's endorsement contrasted sharply with Westbrook's hostile response to Gage after she refused him welcome at the convention: "You are the President of another society," she reportedly told him, "and I don't mean to be the bob-tail of anybody's kite." See Richard B. Westbrook, "The Gage Gathering," *BI*, March 19, 1890, 3. Craddock would have been a better emissary for the American Secular Union, but she apparently was unable to attend; she is nowhere mentioned in the minutes of the meeting itself. See Matilda Joslyn Gage, ed., *Woman's National Liberal Union: Report of the Convention for Organization* (Syracuse: Masters and Stone, 1890).

40. IC, "How to Make Freethinkers," 389–394. The details of Craddock's curriculum in the ensuing paragraphs all come from this essay.

41. IC, "Some Notes on Alaskan Myths," *Truth Seeker Annual and Freethinkers' Almanac for 1891* (New York: Truth Seeker, 1891), 38–47 (quotation on p. 42).

42. Helen H. Gardener, *Men, Women, and Gods, and Other Lectures* (New York: Truth Seeker, 1885), 52–53.

43. Elizabeth Cady Stanton, *The Woman's Bible* (Boston: Northeastern University Press, 1993), 1: 10; 2:8.

44. See Alexander Wilder, introduction in F. Max Müller, *India: What Can It Teach Us?* (New York: Funk and Wagnalls, 1883), xiii–xviii.

45. Louis Henry Jordan, *Comparative Religion: Its Genesis and Growth* (Edinburgh: Clark, 1905), xiii, 10, 166–169. Jordan makes a long list of the "tangible achievements" of the new science (pp. 369–414) from which I have gathered the examples used in this paragraph.

46. Morris Jastrow, *The Study of Religion* (New York: Scribner's, 1901), vi, 56. For curricular developments at Penn and elsewhere, see Morris Jastrow, "Recent Movements in the Historical Study of Religions in America," *Biblical World* 1 (1893): 24–32. On Jastrow's intellectual journey, see Harold S. Wechsler, "Pulpit or Professoriate: The Case of Morris Jastrow," *American Jewish History* 74 (1985): 338–355.

47. "Ida C. Craddock," 53. For the relationship among gender, amateurism, and professionalization, see especially Bonnie G. Smith, *The Gender of History: Men, Women, and Historical Practice* (Cambridge, Mass.: Harvard University Press, 1998). Religion is tangential to Smith's purposes, but her remarks on Gage, Stanton, and Jane Ellen Harrison are relevant (see pp. 180–181, 191–192, 202–205, 209–210).

48. William James, "The Ph.D. Octopus," *Harvard Monthly* 36 (1903): 1–9.

49. Evidence for the two missing chapters comes from internal references to them within these three parts. See IC, "Sun and Dawn Myths," 28, 35–36, 40, box 3, f. 2, ICP; IC, "Lunar and Sex Worship," 90, box 1, f. 6, ICP. The surviving type-script for "Lunar and Sex Worship" is signed and dated September 25, 1902; the other two sections are undated. It is clear that she was working on this topic from at least the early 1890s and parts of the surviving manuscript would appear to be directly connected to the public lectures she gave on the subject in 1893 and 1894. In short, she worked on this book over a long period.

50. Richard Payne Knight, *A Discourse on the Worship of Priapus* (1786) reprinted in Ashley Montagu, ed., *Sexual Symbolism: A History of Phallic Worship* (New York: Julian, 1957), 21.

51. Ibid., 27, 50. For Knight's slipping of sex worship into ostensibly safer top-ics, see Richard Payne Knight, *The Symbolical Language of Ancient Art and Mythol-ogy* (New York: Bouton, 1876), 12–13, 98, 141–142. For the world of antiquarian collectors and anticlerical radicals that Knight inhabited, see Giancarlo Carabelli, *In the Image of Priapus* (London: Duckworth, 1996), and G. S. Rousseau, "The Sor-rows of Priapus: Anticlericalism, Homosocial Desire, and Richard Payne Knight," in G. S. Rousseau and Roy Porter, eds., *Sexual Underworlds of the Enlightenment* (Chapel Hill: University of North Carolina Press, 1988), 101–153. For attention to Knight's work on "phallicism" in the context of nineteenth- and early-twentieth-century occultism, see Bradford Verter, "Dark Star Rising: The Emergence of Mod-ern Occultism, 1800–1950," PhD diss., Princeton University, 1997, 71–87, and Joscelyn Godwin, *The Theosophical Enlightenment* (Albany: State University of New York Press, 1994), 1–25.

52. SWC, 124–125. For the closeted copy at the British Library as of 1836, see George Ryley Scott, *Phallic Worship: A History of Sex and Sexual Rites in Relation to the Religions of All Races from Antiquity to the Present Day* (London: Luxor, 1966), xix. On the history of the British Museum's "Secretum," see Carabelli, *In the Image of Priapus*, esp. 1–11; Peter Fryer, *Private Case—Public Scandal: Secrets of the British Museum Revealed* (London: Secker and Warburg, 1966); David Gaimster, "Sex and Sensibility at the British Museum," *History Today* 50 (2000): 10–15; and Dominic Janes, "The Rites of Man: The British Museum and the Sexual Imagination in Vic-torian Britain," *Journal of the History of Collections* 20 (2008): 101–112. In addition to the curatorial practices at the British Museum, those at the National Museum in Naples were crucial to developing restricted collections of "phallic antiquities" (in this case, excavated artifacts from Pompeii). Indeed, the ostensibly "secret" antiquities in Naples were crucial in the very creation of the category of "pornog-raphy" in the nineteenth century. See Michael Grant, *Eros in Pompeii: The Erotic Art Collection of the Museum of Naples* (New York: Stewart, Tabori, and Chang, 1997), and Walter Kendrick, *The Secret Museum: Pornography in Modern Culture* (Berke-ley: University of California Press, 1996), 2–32. Curator Wendy Woloson at the

Library Company of Philadelphia looked for records on secret cases and special requests from the period for me, but she found no official notice of Craddock's application. Indeed, she reported that shelf lists and accession records from the period make no mention of the Ridgway ever owning a copy of Knight's *Discourse*. However, on further inspection, Woloson found the volume "conveniently" misidentified. Hence, more than a century later, the secret copy that Craddock somehow identified has finally been made an accessible part of the collection. It is highly unlikely that Craddock gained access to the carefully restricted holdings at the British Museum. There is record of an American graduate student, Edmund Buckley, then working on his PhD in comparative religion at the University of Chicago, applying for and obtaining access to Richard Payne Knight's collection in 1893, but no similar record exists for Craddock. Her admission materials mention only a desire to do "research work in books on occultism and mysticism." She avoided any mention of sex worship in her application letters of April 13, 1894 and Nov. 30, 1898 (the first letter was under the pseudonym Irene Sophia Roberts and the second under her given name; William Stead endorsed both applications). See Reading Room Records, Reader's Tickets/A51154 and A63473, Central Archives, the British Museum; Edmund Buckley to Principal Librarian, Aug. 24, 1893, Pre-1896 In-Letters, Department of Prehistory and Europe, the British Museum. For Buckley's work, which includes an account of the extensive "precautions" he had to overcome to get access to the British Museum's collection, see Edmund Buckley, *Phallicism in Japan* (Chicago: University of Chicago Press, 1895), 7–9. Buckley, in turn, showed his own caution in emphasizing that his study was for limited circulation as "an academic monograph"; the "general reader," he feared, might find its frank discussion of phallicism "unduly stimulating," which was, he insisted, wholly contrary to his "scientific purpose" (p. 4).

53. Thomas Wright, *The Worship of the Generative Powers during the Middles Ages of Western Europe* reprinted in Montagu, ed., *Sexual Symbolism*, 7.

54. J. G. R. Forlong, *Rivers of Life, Or, Sources and Streams of the Faiths of Man in All Lands*, 3 vols. (London: Quaritch, 1883), 1: 93; 3: "Synchronological Chart."

55. Robert Allen Campbell, *Phallic Worship* (St. Louis, 1887; London: Kegan Paul, 2002), 16. Campbell was an American elaborator of the British sources.

56. Forlong, *Rivers of Life*, 1: 3; J. G. R. Forlong, introduction in Hodder M. Westropp, *Primitive Symbolism as Illustrated in Phallic Worship or the Reproductive Principle* (London: Redway, 1885), iii; Hargrave Jennings, *Phallism: A Description of the Worship of the Lingam-Yoni in Various Parts of the World, and in Different Ages* (London: n.p., 1892), iv. Providing a space for men only to discuss taboo subjects—including phallic worship—had been one of the main reasons the Anthropological Society of London had set itself up in opposition to the Ethnological Society of London in 1863. The latter group had decided to admit women. See George W. Stocking Jr., "What's in a Name? The Origins of the Royal Anthropological Institute (1837–1871)," *Man* 6 (1971): 380. To the extent that Craddock had female

company at all in this domain of inquiry, it was a very sparse group. Elizabeth Evans mentioned fertility worship in passing in her *History of Religion* in 1892; the seer Madame Blavatsky alluded to phallic symbolism in a few spots in *Isis Unveiled* in 1877 and wrote a very critical review essay on Hargrave Jennings' studies of the subject in 1896. In a company of amateurs and scholars that boasted dozens of male authorities by 1900, Craddock is the only woman of the period that I have found who wrote an entire treatise on "phallicism" and "sex worship." Also of note, though, is the work of Eliza Burt Gamble on ancient religion, which is discussed below. For a massive survey of the relevant literature, see Roger Goodland, *A Bibliography of Sex Rites and Customs: An Annotated Record of Books, Articles, and Illustrations in All Languages* (London: Routledge, 1931).

57. SWC, 8–9, 19–20, 27, 37.

58. Westropp and Wake, *Ancient Symbol Worship*, 32.

59. Forlong, *Rivers of Life*, 1: 280, 450; 3: "Synchronological Chart."

60. DPE, 191; IC, "Marriage Relation," 185. See also IC, "Sun and Dawn Myths," 37–38; IC, "Lunar and Sex Worship," 85. The joining of such mythological observations to a rigid race hierarchy—based on the philological divisions of Aryan, Semitic, and Turanian—was especially evident in James Fergusson's *Tree and Serpent Worship*, which, in turn, was strongly critiqued as a philological and anthropological pipedream in [John McLennan], "Tree and Serpent Worship," *Cornhill Magazine* 19 (1869): 626–640. On this point, Craddock was more in line with McLennan's stand than Fergusson's.

61. Campbell, *Phallic Worship*, 16; Westropp and Wake, *Ancient Symbol Worship*, 31.

62. SWC, 104, 116, 125; IC, "Lunar and Sex Worship," 23-24, 80. Cynthia Eller has scrutinized most fully the ongoing feminist fascination with a matriarchal past. See her *The Myth of Matriarchal Prehistory: Why an Invented Past Will Not Give Women a Future* (Boston: Beacon, 2000), along with her forthcoming project focused on the nineteenth-century background.

63. IC, "Lunar and Sex Worship," 23–25, 32, 76; SWC, 63, 99, 168.

64. IC, "Lunar and Sex Worship," 62, 89–90; SWC, 95.

65. SWC, 193–195, 206–207; Walt Whitman, *Poetry and Prose* (New York: Library of America, 1996), 236.

66. SWC, 162.

67. Eliza Burt Gamble, *The God-Idea of the Ancients: Or, Sex In Religion* (New York: G. P. Putnam's Sons, 1897), iii–v, 206–216. Gamble's labors have not received much attention, especially her work on religion, but see Rosemary Jann, "Revising the Descent of Woman: Eliza Burt Gamble," in Barbara T. Gates and Ann B. Shtier, eds., *Natural Eloquence: Women Reinscribe Science* (Madison: University of Wisconsin Press, 1997), 147–163, and Penelope Deutscher, "The Descent of Man and the Evolution of Woman," *Hypatia* 19 (2004): 35–55.

68. J. E. Harrison, "The Pillar and the Maiden," *Proceedings of the Classical Association* 5 (1907): 65–67, 77; Sandra J. Peacock, *Jane Ellen Harrison: The Mask and*

the Self (New Haven: Yale University Press, 1988), 204–212, with Harrison's critique of phallic elements quoted on p. 205.

69. For an illuminating example of Parsons's early work on religion and gender, see Elsie Clews Parsons, "The Religious Dedication of Women," *American Journal of Sociology* 11 (1906): 610–622. For Craddock's membership in the American Folklore Society, see the *Journal of American Folklore* 9 (1896): 317; 10 (1897): 340; 11(1898): 313. During that time she made only one very modest contribution to the journal's "Notes and Queries" section. See IC, "The Tale of the Wild Cat: A Child's Game," *Journal of American Folklore* 10 (1897): 322–324.

70. Jane Ellen Harrison, *Alpha and Omega* (London: Sidgwick and Jackson, 1915), 128.

71. IC to Katie Wood, July 5, 1901; IC to WTS, Sept. 10, 1901; IC to unidentified correspondent, Nov. 1, 1901, box 1, f. 1, ICP; DPE, 215.

Chapter 3:
Pastor of the Church of Yoga

1. "Religious News" and "Religious Announcements," *Chicago Tribune*, July 12, 1874, 6. See the same columns in *Chicago Tribune*, Aug. 16, 1874, 6; Sept. 6, 1874, 6; Jan. 10, 1875, 6; Jan. 17, 1875, 6. The best source for the country's religious demographics remains Edwin Scott Gaustad and Philip L. Barlow, *New Historical Atlas of Religion in America* (New York: Oxford University Press, 2001).

2. "Religious Announcements," *Chicago Tribune*, Dec. 17, 1899, 30. Likewise, see "Religious Announcements," *Chicago Tribune*, Nov. 26, 1899, 32; Sept. 21, 1890, 34; Sept. 10, 1893, 36; Dec. 10, 1893, 39; March 7, 1897, 38; June 17, 1900, 14.

3. Ibid., Dec. 17, 1899, 30; Feb. 25, 1900, 31.

4. IC to Katie Wood, Aug. 19, 1877, box 1, f. 1, ICP.

5. E. H. Stokes, ed., *Ocean Grove, Its Origin and Progress, as Shown in the Annual Reports Presented by the President* (Philadelphia: Haddock and Son, 1874), 67, 73–74.

6. Ibid., 10–11, 62–63. For a history of Ocean Grove, see Troy Messenger, *Holy Leisure: Recreation and Religion in God's Square Mile* (Philadelphia: Temple University Press, 2000).

7. IC to Katie Wood, June 5, 1879, box 1, f. 1, ICP.

8. IC, "Heavenly Bridegrooms," 6–7, box 4, f. 1, ICP.

9. Ibid.

10. "News of Friends," *Friends' Intelligencer and Journal* 45 (1888): 396; DPE, second part, 7.

11. For Quaker divisions and denominational history in the period, see Hugh Barbour and J. William Frost, *The Quakers* (New York: Greenwood, 1988), 203–229. For the broader Quaker influences on Whitman and company, see Leigh Eric Schmidt, *Restless Souls: The Making of American Spirituality* (San Francisco: Harper, 2005), esp. 233–236.

12. DPE, 19–20, 43, 177; "Ashamed of Being Called 'Infidel,'" *BI*, April 22, 1891, 3. For additional testimony to the Quaker influence on Craddock's spiritual temper, see WTS to Philander Knox, Sept. 24, 1902, box 2, f. 2, RGP.

13. SWC, 19–20. The Spring Garden Unitarian Society subsequently closed, and its records have apparently been lost, but a small cache of the church's newsletters from the period have survived at Andover-Harvard Theological Library, Harvard Divinity School, Harvard University. One of these offers a directory of members and affiliates, and Craddock appears on that list of members (as do her allies, Richard and Henrietta Westbrook). See Spring Garden Unitarian Church, *The Message* 1 (March 1898): n.p. The congregation's representation of itself as a model for the "Liberal Church" is on full view in the *Year Book of the Spring Garden Unitarian Society* (Philadelphia: Buchanan, 1887), 5–6, 21–22.

14. "'Freethought' and Free Thought," *American Sentinel*, Dec. 27, 1890, 379.

15. Frederic A. Hinckley, *Beckonings of the Spirit* (Philadelphia: n.p., 1890), 18; Frederic A. Hinckley, "What Do Unitarians Believe?" *The Message* 1 (March 1898): n.p.

16. Frederic A. Hinckley, *The Relation of the Sexes* (Washington, D.C.: Society for Moral Education, 1887), 7, 10; Frederic A. Hinckley, *The Deeper Meanings* (Boston: Ellis, 1894), 46. The church's role as host to various reformers can be tracked in the pages of the *Philadelphia Inquirer*, Feb. 20, 1883, 3; Dec. 10, 1883, 2; May 25, 1885, 2; Nov. 19, 1885, 3; Oct. 25, 1886, 3; Feb. 15, 1888, 3; April 5, 1888, 3; Jan. 26, 1889, 2; March 3, 1890, 3; March 28, 1891, 5; March 7, 1892, 5; Nov. 7, 1896, 1. Sessions on the "Study of Emerson," led by Hinckley, are noted each month in Spring Garden Unitarian Church, *The Message* 1 (Dec. 1897-July 1898): n.p. Two other noteworthy liberals, Charles Ames and William L. Nichols, successively led the church prior to Hinckley taking over in 1896.

17. "Ida C. Craddock," *Freethinkers' Magazine* 8 (1890): 53–54; "A Few Words from Miss Craddock," *Truth Seeker*, Feb. 14, 1891, 100. Details of Craddock's ongoing involvement as "an active member" of the Unitarian church come from one of her mother's letters. See Lizzie Decker to EBF, Oct. 21, 1902, box 2, f. 2, RGP.

18. See H. H. Furness Jr., ed., *Preliminary Report of the Commission Appointed by the University of Pennsylvania to Investigate Modern Spiritualism in Accordance with the Bequest of the Late Henry Seybert* (1887; Philadelphia: J. B. Lippincott, 1920). For broader background on spiritualism and psychical research in the period, see Alan Gauld, *The Founders of Psychical Research* (New York: Schocken, 1968), and R. Laurence Moore, *In Search of White Crows: Spiritualism, Parapsychology, and American Culture* (New York: Oxford University Press, 1977).

19. DPE, 120–121; IC to Katie Wood, March 15, 1887; Oct. 1, 1889. Specifically, Craddock mentions reading Margaret Oliphant, *Two Stories of the Seen and Unseen* (Edinburgh: Blackwood, 1885); William Denton and Elizabeth M. F. Denton, *The Soul of Things; Or, Psychometric Researches and Discoveries* (Boston: Walker, Wise, and Co., 1863), and Edmund Gurney, Frederic W. H. Myers, and Frank Podmore, *Phantasms of the Living*, 2 vols. (London: Society for Psychical Research, 1886).

20. SML, 4; IC to Wood, March 15, 1887.

21. William James, *Essays in Psychical Research* (Cambridge: Harvard University Press, 1986), 362.

22. DPE, 17. For experiments with various spirit-writing machines, see Paul Carus, "Spirit or Ghost: Comments upon Spiritism and Spiritistic Interpretations of Psychical Phenomena," *Monist* 12 (1902): 397–398. Despite receiving "innumerable most remarkable answers" through these devises, Carus was skeptical of the results that he and a professor of physics obtained, seeing instead subliminal influences and wishfulness at work. The point is the currency and respectability of such experiments—respectable at least in so far as one remained disbelieving.

23. *Columbus Enquirer-Sun*, July 31, 1892, 6.

24. SML, 4.

25. Ibid., 4–5. "Our Gallery of Borderlanders" was a regular feature of the spiritualist journal *Borderland* (1893–1897).

26. SML, 4–7; DPE, 213.

27. SML, 5–7; DPE, second part, 16.

28. SML, 4–7; DPE, 213.

29. SML, 5.

30. IC to James B. Elliott, July 14, 1894, box 1, f. 1; IC, "Miscellaneous Notes," box 6, f. 7, ICP. Within these assorted notes is a three-page fragment of a longer document (now apparently lost) in which Craddock describes how she eluded her mother's "plan to abduct me by force" and place her in an asylum. The long spiral of shame and anger in her mother's relationship with her was given especially full review in a letter from IC to Katie Wood, July 5, 1901, box 1, f. 1, ICP.

31. WTS, *If Christ Came to Chicago!* (Chicago: Laird and Lee, 1894), 445; "A Visitor's Criticism of Philadelphia," *Philadelphia Inquirer*, March 6, 1894, 4. On Stead's career, including his trip to Chicago and his spiritualist inquiries, see Frederic Whyte, *The Life of W. T. Stead*, 2 vols. (New York; Houghton Mifflin, 1925), 1: 324–340, 2: 39–53, 63–64. For a biography organized largely around his fascination with mediumistic phenomena, see Estelle W. Stead, *My Father: Personal and Spiritual Reminiscences* (London: Heinemann, 1913). On his American campaign, see Joseph O. Baylen, "A Victorian's 'Crusade' in Chicago, 1893–1894," *Journal of American History* 51 (1964): 418–434.

32. IC, "Miscellaneous Notes." On their meeting through an unnamed editorial friend, see WTS to Knox, Sept. 24, 1902. It is possible they were introduced to each other in Chicago in the wake of the World's Fair, but a Philadelphia introduction appears much more likely. Stead initially published some of his communications from Julia Ames in *Borderland* and then later collected them in *Letters from Julia* (1897), which, in turn, was expanded into *After Death: A Personal Narrative* (1914).

33. IC, "Miscellaneous Notes."

34. DPE, 19.

35. Ibid., 19–20, 49. Craddock highlights her dress-reform efforts in IC, "The Marriage Relation," 35–38, box 3, f. 3, ICP.

36. DPE, 19–20, 33; Irene Sophia Roberts to the Principal Librarian, April 13, 1894, Reading Room Records, Reader's Ticket/A51154, Central Archives, the British Museum.

37. DPE, 112. On Freer's colorful career, see Trevor H. Hall, *The Strange Story of Ada Goodrich Freer* (London: Duckworth, 1980). For the holdings of "The Borderland Library," see *Borderland* 1 (1894): 582–584. The other intellectual companion that Craddock noted making in London was Richard Harte, a solidly accomplished writer on marriage customs as well as the "new theology" of liberal universalism. See DPE, 11, 115, 123, and Richard Harte, *The New Theology Being Some Outspoken Letters to a Lady* (London: Allen, 1894).

38. DPE, 20, 37, 47, 60, 145, 176.

39. Ibid., 93, 99, 104–105, 131.

40. Ibid., 144, 156, 172–174. Alma Gillen's American network can be seen in her very scarce journal called *Expression;* the lone surviving issue—one from the third volume and dated October 1900—is housed in the Special Collections of the Syracuse University Library. Her metaphysical principles were set out especially in Alma Gillen, *The Law of Expression, Or, The Order of Creation* (London: n.p., 1895). For a superb history of the gendered dimensions of New Thought, see Beryl Satter, *Each Mind a Kingdom: American Women, Sexual Purity, and the New Thought Movement, 1875–1920* (Berkeley: University of California Press, 1999).

41. DPE, 174.

42. Ibid., 156, 187; Alma Gillen, *The Passion of Passions* (London: n.p., 1896), 88. For an express example of Craddock's positioning herself in relation to New Thought or Divine Science, see her handbill "The Mental Scientists Versus Marriage," n.d., box 2, f. 2, RGP.

43. DPE, 116–117, 187.

44. Ibid., 207–208. Her firing from the Highway Bureau was picked up in the Philadelphia newspapers. See the clippings in box 20, f. 15, RGP.

45. DPE, 222.

46. IC, *The Heaven of the Bible* (Philadelphia: Lippincott, 1897), 56–57, 66; "Religious," *Literary World*, April 17, 1897, 132; "Books of the Week," *Outlook*, April 17, 1897, 1044; "The Heaven of the Bible," *Borderland* 4 (1897): 212–213.

47. IC, "Heavenly Bridegrooms," 73.

48. DPE, 35-36, 108, 187, 191. The correspondence with Dharmapala apparently does not survive but is mentioned in her diary.

49. IC, "Heavenly Bridegrooms," 56–57.

50. DPE, 209.

51. IC, "The Marriage Relation," 129.

52. Vivekananda's renunciations, including his inclination to bowdlerize Ramakrishna's biography and teachings, have been the subject of a growing body of

scholarship. Jeffrey J. Kripal's controversial work—despised by many devotees of Ramakrishna and Vivekananda, lauded by many scholars—has been especially significant in this regard. See Jeffrey J. Kripal, *Kālī's Child: The Mystical and the Erotic in the Life and Teachings of Ramakrishna* (Chicago: University of Chicago Press, 1995), 8–9, 25–27. Also see Hugh B. Urban, *Tantra: Sex, Secrecy, Politics, and Power in the Study of Religion* (Berkeley: University of California Press, 2003), and Carrie Tirado Bramen, "Christian Maidens and Heathen Monks: Oratorical Seduction at the 1893 World's Parliament of Religions," in Tracy Fessenden, Nicholas F. Radel, and Magdalena J. Zaborowska, eds., *The Puritan Origins of American Sex: Religion, Sexuality, and National Identity in American Literature* (New York: Routledge, 2001), 191–212. For broader background on the movement, see Carl T. Jackson, *Vedanta for the West: The Ramakrishna Movement in the United States* (Bloomington: Indiana University Press, 1994). For the particular importance of Vivekananda's *Râja Yoga*, see Elizabeth de Michelis, *A History of Modern Yoga* (London: Continuum, 2004), 149–180, and for wider American appropriations of yoga since the turn of the twentieth century, see Catherine L. Albanese, "Sacred (and Secular) Self-Fashioning: Esalen and the American Transformation of Yoga," in Jeffrey J. Kripal and Glenn W. Shuck, eds., *On the Edge of the Future: Esalen and the Evolution of American Culture* (Bloomington: Indiana University Press, 2005), 45–79.

53. DPE, second part, 15, 17–18; Swami Vivekananda, *The Complete Works of Swami Vivekananda*, 8 vols. (Calcutta: Advaita, 1989), 1: 122, 137. Vivekananda later subsumed his New York lectures on Râja Yoga, initially published separately, into his broader work on *Vedanta Philosophy* (1899).

54. IC, "Marriage Relation," 129–130; [Hargrave Jennings], *Phallic Miscellanies; Facts and Phases of Ancient and Modern Sex Worship* (n.p.: n.p., 1891), 1. This singular association of Hinduism with sexuality, picked up especially from the late eighteenth-century work of William Jones, was widespread in the nineteenth-century literature on phallic worship. For another paradigmatic instance, see Edward Sellon, *Annotations on the Sacred Writings of the Hindüs, Being an Epitome of Some of the Most Remarkable and Leading Tenets in the Faith of that People Illustrating their Priapic Rites and Phallic Principles*, 2nd ed. (London: n.p., 1902), 12, 59.

55. IC, "Marriage Reform," 129, 136–137.

56. Srischandra Basu, trans., *The Esoteric Science and Philosophy of the Tantras, Shiva Sanhita* (Calcutta: Prakas, 1893), 35–37.

57. IC, "Marriage Relation," 129, 136–137; Basu, *Esoteric Science*, 35–37. Craddock singled out the ninth section of chapter four as the one that most attracted her attention and picked up the "inaccessible glory" phrase from the translated text itself.

58. Basu, *Esoteric Science*, 28–29, 35–37; DPE, 115, 127; second part, 56; IC, "Marriage Relation," 136–137. On subsequent appropriations, see Urban, *Tantra*, 203–263, and Hugh B. Urban, *Magia Sexualis: Sex, Magic, and Liberation in Modern Western Esotericism* (Berkeley: University of California Press, 2006), 81–108.

59. DPE, second part, 22, 56. It is impossible to reconstruct Craddock's Sunday meetings in any detail. A few titles of her talks survive: "Man and Woman as They Were, As They Are, as They Ought to Be"; "Object of the Church of Yoga"; "How to Take a Spiritual Bath," and "The Apple Mythos," but little more than that is available. See *Chicago Tribune*, Dec. 17, 1899, 30; Jan. 14, 1900, 31; Jan. 21, 1900, 46; Jan. 28, 1900, 36; Feb. 25, 1900, 31. It is also impossible to know the size or composition of her audience. Several of those whom she advised on marriage relations were attendees of her church. She did mention that Lillian and Virna Harman, daughter and granddaughter of the sex radical Moses Harman, attended at least one of her Sunday meetings at this time. See DPE, second part, 19.

60. Basu, *Esoteric Science*, 12, 35–37.

61. Ibid.; IC, "Yoga Applied to the Married Life: A Course of Instruction," circular, n.d., box 2, f. 2, RGP.

62. On Bernard, see Urban, *Tantra*, 209–215; Hugh B. Urban, "The Omnipotent Oom: Tantra and Its Impact on Modern Western Esotericism," *Esoterica* 3 (2001): 218–259: and Robert Love, *The Great Oom: The Improbable Birth of Yoga in America* (New York: Viking, 2010). Craddock's designation as "high priestess and pastor of the Church of Yoga" was picked up across the country at the peak of her legal travails in 1902. See, for example, *Montgomery Advertiser* (Montgomery, AL), Oct. 18, 1902, 1; *Columbus Enquirer-Sun* (Columbus, GA), Oct. 18, 1902, 1, plus the newspaper clippings in box 2, f. 2, RGP. Another religious character in Chicago, William Walker Atkinson, who was also known as Yogi Ramacharaka, represented a similar New Thought/yoga hybrid, but again he pursued his experiments in the wake of Craddock's venture, not before. See William Walker Atkinson, *Law of the New Thought* (Chicago: Psychic Research, 1902), and Yogi Ramacharaka, *Fourteen Lessons in Yogi Philosophy and Oriental Occultism* (Chicago: Yogi Publication Society, 1908). It is certainly possible, though, to read Craddock's Tantric turn retrospectively in terms of previous occultist explorations of divine androgyny and erotic mysteries during the second half of the nineteenth century. See, for example, the varied sources collected in Joscelyn Godwin, Christian Chanel, and John P. Deveney, eds., *The Hermetic Brotherhood of Luxor: Initiatic and Historical Documents of an Order of Practical Occultism* (York Beach, ME: Weiser, 1995).

63. There were many other fine candidates for the rank of quintessential seeker at the turn of the century. For another good example, see Thomas A. Tweed, "Inclusivism and the Spiritual Journey of Marie de Souza Canavarro (1849-1933)," *Religion* 24 (1994): 43–58.

64. Upton Sinclair, *The Profits of Religion: An Essay in Economic Interpretation* (Pasadena: n.p., 1918), 250–253, 255; Otoman Zar-Adusht Hanish, *Inner Studies: A Course of Twelve Lessons* (Chicago: Sun-Worshiper Publishing Co., 1902), 68, 72, 91. See also Otoman Zar-Adusht Hanish, *Health and Breath Culture According to Mazdaznan Philosophy (Sun-Worship)* (Chicago: Sun-Worshiper Publishing Co., 1902). Exposure of his German background came a decade after Craddock's

association with him. See "Father Exposes Dr. Hanish," *Chicago Tribune*, May 18, 1912, 3.

65. Hanish, *Inner Studies*, 157, 163–165, 172–173; IC, "Telepathy between the Sexes," Feb. 27, 1900, 17, box 5, f. 1, ICP. For Craddock's specific concurrence with Hanish, see IC to S. L. Krebs, Oct. 19, 1901, box 1, f. 1, ICP. That Hanish had been a consumer of Craddock's *Right Marital Living* before publishing his own advice is evident from his appearance in April 1900 in her "Address Book of Customers for Books and Pupils of Divine Science," box 7, f. 4, ICP.

66. "'Dr.' Hanish on Trial," *Chicago Tribune*, June 5, 1904, 7; "Fanatic Leaves Maniac Trail," *Los Angeles Times*, Nov. 16, 1907, 12; "Hanish in Jail," *Chicago Tribune*, March 5, 1912, 1; "Seek Jurors for Sun Cult Trial," *Chicago Tribune*, Nov. 22, 1913, 13; "Hanish Loses on Decoy Letters," *Chicago Tribune*, Nov. 25, 1913, 8; "Expose Secrets of Hanish Cult," *Chicago Tribune*, Nov. 26, 1913, 3; "Jurors Thrilled by Hanish Book," *Chicago Tribune*, Nov. 27, 1913, 3; "Sun Cult Jurors Get Case Today," *Chicago Tribune*, Nov. 28, 1913, 3; "Convicts Hanish of Immorality," *Chicago Tribune*, Nov. 29, 1913, 3; "Six Months for Hanish," *Washington Post*, Dec. 16, 1913, 4. The charges against Hanish, which came to include "statutory offenses" against children, only got more damning in later years. See "Law's Fierce Light upon Sun-Worshippers," *Los Angeles Times*, Jan. 11, 1920, II, 1.

67. IC to WTS, Sept. 10, 1901, box 1, f. 1; IC, "The Marriage Relation," box 3, f.6, ICP. That she continued to offer her Tantric-inspired lessons once in New York City is evident from the circular produced there to advertise her services. See IC, "Yoga Applied to the Married Life," but this handbill promised private classes and individual instruction, not regular Sunday meetings. By then, she had a congregation of readers, not hearers. But, as she put it, "Does either law or custom prohibit one from being the pastor of a congregation of readers?" See IC to Editor *Sun*, Feb. 21, 1902, box 2, f. 2, RGP.

68. "Alleged Misuse of Mails: Woman Held on Charge of Circulating Forbidden Literature," *Philadelphia Inquirer*, Feb. 19, 1902, 1; "Chose Death Before Prison," *New York Times*, Oct. 18, 1902, 2.

69. IC to WTS, Sept. 10, 1901.

Chapter 4: An Expert in Sexology

1. IC, "Record of Cases in Oral Instruction," 22, 26–29, 35, box 4, f. 8; Eunice O. Parsons to IC, Sept. 3, 1902, box 1. f. 2, ICP. In the case notes the nurse is identified simply as Miss E. O. P., but, judging from Craddock's correspondence for September 1902, this case is identifiable as Eunice O. Parsons; five letters from Parsons to Craddock survive from that month and line up closely with the case record. Craddock's long list of questions for her clients are preserved in "Regeneration and Rejuvenation of Men and Women, through the Right Use of the Sex Function," box 4, f. 5, ICP.

2. "The Wedding Night and Right Marital Living," advertising circular, n.d., box 7, f. 5, ICP; IC, "Regeneration and Rejuvenation," 6; IC, "Records of Cases of Marital Reform Work," 24, box 5, f. 12, ICP.

3. "Ida Craddock's Letter to Her Mother," *Truth Seeker*, Oct. 25, 1902, 680. For indications of the cover (and coverage) that sympathetic physicians provided her, see *Medical World* 15 (1897): 440; *Massachusetts Medical Journal* 20 (1900): 557–558; and *Minneapolis Homœopathic Magazine* 9 (1900): 284–285.

4. The presumed norms of liberal privatization—Protestant Christianity in the domain of religion and heterosexual marriage in the domain of sexuality—have now been the subject of considerable critique. For that debate and for the recognition of the interconnections between the freedoms of religion and sexuality, see Janet R. Jakobsen and Ann Pellegrini, *Love the Sin: Sexual Regulation and the Limits of Religious Tolerance* (New York: New York University Press, 2003), esp. 103–126. It is worth underlining that Protestant Christianity was not necessarily the norm being drawn upon by those marriage reformers most tenacious for liberal freedoms and privacy.

5. Moses Harman and his circle are at the center of Hal D. Sears, *The Sex Radicals: Free Love in High Victorian America* (Lawrence: Regents Press of Kansas, 1977). Harman's explanation of his journal's title is quoted on p. 55. See also William Lemore West, "The Moses Harman Story," *Kansas Historical Quarterly* 37 (1971): 41–63. For the prior generation upon which Harman's group built, see John C. Spurlock, *Free Love: Marriage and Middle-Class Radicalism in America, 1825–1860* (New York: New York University Press, 1988).

6. Sears, *Sex Radicals*, 74–76, 88; Moses Harman, "A Free Man's Creed," *LLB*, April 7, 1897, 106.

7. "The Danse du Ventre" and "Sex Modesty—The True and the False," *LLB*, Dec. 22, 1893, 2; "Letter to a Prospective Bride," *LLB*, Aug. 18, 1897, 259; "Two New Books by Ida C. Craddock," *LLB*, Sept. 22, 1897, 299; "Mrs. Craddock," *LLB*, Oct. 30, 1902, 331; DPE, second part, 19. For her ongoing support in the journal, see "Ida C. Craddock," *LLB*, Jan. 28, 1899, 28; "Right Marital Living," *LLB*, Aug. 19, 1899, 252; "Right Marital Living," *LLB*, Feb. 17, 1900, 43; "The Wedding Night," *LLB*, Aug. 11, 1900, 245.

8. For broad analysis of the communitarian intersection with sexual innovation, see Lawrence Foster, *Religion and Sexuality: Three American Communal Experiments of the Nineteenth Century* (New York: Oxford, 1981).

9. John Humphrey Noyes, *Male Continence* (Oneida, NY: Oneida Circular, 1872), 8, 11–12; "Sex Modesty," 2. Craddock's early debt to Noyes is especially evident in her *Helps to Happy Wedlock: No. 1 for Husbands* (Philadelphia: n.p., 1896), 5–9, and IC, "Male Continence," May 1895, box 6, f. 7, ICP.

10. The works of Miller and Chavannes are both anthologized in Taylor Stoehr, ed., *Free Love in America: A Documentary History* (New York: AMS, 1979), 588–618.

11. IC, *Helps*, 16; IC, "To Wives and Mothers," circular, [1897], box 2, f. 2, RGP; Alice B. Stockham, *Karezza: Ethics of Marriage* (Chicago: Stockham, 1903), 24, 27.

For Stockham's career in its New Thought context, see Beryl Satter, *Each Mind a Kingdom: American Women, Sexual Purity, and the New Thought Movement, 1875–1920* (Berkeley: University of California Press, 1999), 134–149, 230–231, and R. Marie Griffith, *Born Again Bodies: Flesh and Spirit in American Christianity* (Berkeley: University of California Press, 2004), 91–94. On Stockham's free-speech travails, see the file on her in box 22, f. 16, RGP, and Alice B. Stockham to TS, August 27, 1906, box 5, f. 17, RGP. Especially at issue was a small, fifteen-page booklet of hers on *The Wedding Night*, which was suppressed. No copy has survived. For Stockham's wider publishing program, see *Catalogue of the Publications of the Stockham Publishing Company* (Chicago: Stockham, n.d.).

12. Stockham, *Karezza*, vii, 64–65, 129–130.

13. Ibid., 69; IC, *Helps*, t.p., 16. For Craddock's overlap with Social Purity activism, see Carl N. Degler, *At Odds: Women and the Family in America from the Revolution to the Present* (New York: Oxford University Press, 1980), 268–269, 277–278, 281, 288–289.

14. Stockham, *Karezza*, 16–18, 20; Lois Waisbrooker, *Bible Truth Bursting its Shell* (n.p.: n.p., n.d), 24; Lois Waisbrooker, *A Sex Revolution* (Topeka: Independent Publishing Co., 1894). Waisbrooker, a spiritualist and a sometime collaborator with Moses Harman, was also a target for Comstock, and that has helped make her pamphlets scarce. See the file on her in box 6, f. 2, RGP; the holdings in the Labadie Collection, University of Michigan; and also Joanne E. Passet, *Sex Radicals and the Quest for Women's Equality* (Urbana: University of Illinois Press, 2003), 113–121. Victoria Woodhull, one of Comstock's most notorious foils, had also made this spiritualizing move a recurrent plea in her controversial lectures of the 1870s: "Let the sexual act become the holiest act of life, and then the world will begin to be regenerated, and not before" (p. 51). See Victoria Claflin Woodhull and Tennessee C. Claflin, *The Human Body the Temple of God; Or, The Philosophy of Sociology* (London: Hyde Park Gate, 1890), 1–2, 51–53, 500, 529, 548–549, 555–556, 567.

15. Edward Carpenter, *Love's Coming-of-Age: A Series of Papers on the Relations of the Sexes* (Chicago: Kerr, 1912), 14, 62. This copied passage from Carpenter is in IC, "Miscellaneous Notes," box 6, f. 7, ICP. See also IC, "The Marriage Relation," 86–87, 117, 119, 124, 196, box 3, f. 3, ICP.

16. Edward Carpenter, *Days with Walt Whitman: With Some Notes on his Life and Work* (London: Allen, 1906), 49–50; Edward Carpenter, *From Adam's Peak to Elephanta: Sketches in Ceylon and India* (London: Sonnenschein, 1903), 179–181; Alice B. Stockham, *Hindu Wedding Bells and Taj Mahal* (Chicago: Stockham, n.d.); Alice B. Stockham, introduction in Edward Carpenter, *A Visit to a Gñani* (Chicago: Stockham, 1900). On Carpenter's devotedness as a Whitman disciple, see Michael Robertson, *Worshipping Walt: The Whitman Disciples* (Princeton: Princeton University Press, 2008), 167-188. Another radical literary figure of the period who appealed to Craddock (and Carpenter) was the Canadian novelist Grant Allen, author of *The Woman Who Did* and *The New Hedonism*. Craddock

especially drew on his Darwinian defense of the sex instinct. See IC, "Marriage Relation," 6–10.

17. IC, *The Danse du Ventre* (Philadelphia: n.p., 1893), 1, 5.

18. IC, *Advice to a Bridegroom* (Philadelphia: n.p., 1897), 1. Copies of Craddock's pamphlets of sexual counsel are very, very rare. *Advice to a Bridegroom* survives only in the form of a fragmentary typescript at the New York Public Library, the published version of the pamphlet having been lost entirely. That it was actually published seems evident from several ads that she placed for it in *LLB* in early 1898. The other pamphlets survive in the Ralph Ginzburg Papers at the Wisconsin Historical Society and in the Rare Book and Special Collections at the Library of Congress. Tellingly, even the main collection of Craddock Papers at Southern Illinois University has none of the outlawed pamphlets beyond two copies of the 1893 version of the *Danse du Ventre*. For the medical preview of the one tract, see IC, "Right Marital Living," *Chicago Clinic* 12 (1899): 197–200. For notice of its September appearance, see "Books Received," *Chicago Tribune*, Sept. 23, 1899.

19. IC, "Address Book of Customers for Books and of Pupils in Divine Science," box 7, f. 4, ICP. Many of her customers were identified by initials only, but of the little more than 500 who can be identified by sex, the ratio was nearly 3 men to 2 women.

20. IC, *Letter to a Prospective Bride* (Philadelphia: n.p., 1897), 3–4, 8, 10, 15–17; IC, "The Marriage Relation," 1, 69.

21. "The Wedding Night and Right Marital Living," advertising circular, n.d., box 7, f. 5; IC, *Right Marital Living* (Chicago: n.p., 1899), 30–38, 43, 46, 48; IC, "Telepathy Between the Sexes," 14, box 5, f. 1, ICP; IC, "Marriage Relation," 22, 31, 34–35, 76, 78–80. For popular examples of the more euphemistic advice literature of the period, see Mary Wood-Allen, *What a Young Girl Ought to Know* (Philadelphia: Vir, 1905); Mary Wood-Allen, *Almost a Man* (Ann Arbor: Wood-Allen, 1895); Lyman Beecher Sperry, *Confidential Talks with Young Men* (Chicago: Revell, 1898); Lyman Beecher Sperry, *Husband and Wife: A Book of Information and Advice for the Married and the Marriageable* (New York: Revell, 1900). For wider surveys of American sex manuals, see Michael Gordon, "From an Unfortunate Necessity to a Cult of Mutual Orgasm: Sex in American Education Literature, 1830-1940," in James M. Henslin, ed., *Studies in the Sociology of Sex* (New York: Appleton, 1971), 53–77; Peter Laipson, "'Kiss without Shame, for She Desires It': Sexual Foreplay in American Marital Advice Literature, 1900-1925," *Journal of Social History* 29 (1996): 507–525; Jessamyn Neuhaus, "The Importance of Being Orgasmic: Sexuality, Gender, and Marital Sex Manuals in the United States, 1920–1963," *Journal of the History of Sexuality* 9 (2000): 447–473. On the evangelical Protestant sources of the ideology that Craddock was critiquing, see Nancy F. Cott, "Passionlessness: An Interpretation of Victorian Sexual Ideology, 1790–1850," *Signs* 4 (1978): 219–236.

22. IC, "Cases of Marital Reform Work," 39; IC, *Letter*, 8; IC, *Right Marital Living*, 46.

23. IC, *Right Marital Living*, 37. For the ongoing debate with Edward Bond Foote about ejaculation, see IC to EBF, Nov. 3, 1896; EBF to IC, Sept. 8, 1899; EBF to IC, Dec. 28, 1900, box 1, f. 1, ICP.

24. IC, *The Wedding Night*, 3rd ed. (New York: n.p., 1902), 9; IC, "Marriage Relation," 74–75; IC, *Right Marital Living*, 37–38.

25. IC, *Advice*, 3–4; IC, "Marriage Relation," 74–75, 80–81, 218–220; Havelock Ellis, *Studies in the Psychology of Sex*, 6 vols. (Philadelphia: Davis, 1924), 1: 280. For a brilliant history of the anxieties about masturbation and the social sources of those fears, including the terror of the individual imagination running amok in its solipsistic fantasies, see Thomas W. Laqueur, *Solitary Sex: A Cultural History of Masturbation* (New York: Zone, 2003).

26. IC, "Marriage Relation," 74–75, 215.

27. Ibid., 80–82.

28. IC, *Right Marital Living*, 22–25, 38. The vernacular examples celebrating "fucking" are taken from John D'Emilio and Estelle B. Freedman, *Intimate Matters: A History of Sexuality in America*, 2nd ed. (Chicago: University of Chicago Press, 1997), 83. Some sex radicals (notably Ezra and Angela Heywood) embraced this straight-talking vernacular, but Craddock and Stockham did not use the f-word. On how the Heywoods used the term, see Sears, *Sex Radicals*, 177–178.

29. IC, "Marriage Relation," 1, 4, 26; IC, *Letter*, 18.

30. IC, "Marriage Relation," 115.

31. IC, "Cases of Marital Reform Work," 1, 5.

32. Ibid., 20, 22–23.

33. Ibid., 9.

34. Ibid., 34–35.

35. Ibid., 6–8.

36. IC, "Oral Instruction," 31–33.

37. IC, "Cases of Marital Reform Work," 4–5.

38. Ibid., 2, 24. Craddock did not identify the religious background of about half of her pupils. Of those that she did, it was a very diverse lot, but far from strictly representative of the American denominational map. No Methodists, the largest Protestant body at the time, were identified among her clients, and she had a high percentage of pupils from the typically more liberal side of the spectrum: Unitarianism, spiritualism, and New Thought.

39. Ibid., 31–32.

40. Ibid., 37–38; IC, "Oral Instruction," 7, 14.

41. IC, "Oral Instruction," 25–26.

42. Ibid., 27. On the vast expansion of the sex industries in entertainment, prostitution, and publishing, see Timothy J. Gilfoyle, *City of Eros: New York City, Prostitution, and the Commercialization of Sex, 1790-1920* (New York: Norton, 1992); Donna Dennis, *Licentious Gotham: Erotic Publishing and its Prosecution in Nineteenth-Century New York* (Cambridge, Mass.: Harvard University Press, 2009); and

Joanne J. Meyerowitz, *Women Adrift: Independent Wage Earners in Chicago, 1880–1930* (Chicago: University of Chicago Press, 1988), xviii–xx, 39–41, 142.

43. IC, "Cases of Marital Reform Work," 16–19.

44. IC, "Oral Instruction," 34; IC, "Cases of Marital Reform Work," 9–10.

45. IC, "Oral Instruction," 10.

46. IC, "Marriage Relation," 207–208.

47. Ibid., 241–243.

48. Ibid., 159, 161, 171. The companionate ideal, to which Craddock gave expression, continued to provoke outrage well into the twentieth century. See Rebecca L. Davis, "'Not Marriage at All, but Simple Harlotry': The Companionate Marriage Controversy," *Journal of American History* 94 (2008): 1137–1163.

49. IC, "Marriage Relation," 179, 190; Waisbrooker, *Bible Truth Bursting Its Shell*, 8; Victoria C. Woodhull, "Tried as by Fire; Or, The True and the False, Socially," in Madeleine B. Stern, *The Victoria Woodhull Reader* (Weston, MA: M and S Press, 1974), 16–17, 25, 28. Though Craddock shared their logic, other sex radicals, including Waisbrooker, Woodhull, and Ezra Heywood, offered more sustained reflection on this point—how the rights of religious privacy needed to be extended to the "sacred seclusion" of the bedchamber. See also E. H. Heywood, *Cupid's Yokes: Or, The Binding Forces of Conjugal Life* (1877), reprinted in Martin Blatt, ed., *The Collected Works of Ezra H. Heywood* (Weston, MA: M and S Press, 1985), 22–23.

50. IC, "Marriage Relation," 3, 121.

51. IC, "Memoranda: Indictment in Chicago," 4, box 2, f. 2, RGP; IC, "Cases of Marital Reform Work," 6, 9, 19; IC, "Oral Instruction," 30.

52. IC, "Oral Instruction," 10–11.

53. IC, "Marriage Relation," 122.

Chapter 5: Every Inch a Martyr

1. "Records of the New York Society for the Suppression of Vice, 1871–1953," 3: 64, 126–127, Library of Congress, Manuscript Division. For a sustained analysis of these records and of obscenity cases in New York during Comstock's ascendancy, see Elizabeth Bainum Hovey, "Stamping Out Smut: The Enforcement of Obscenity Laws, 1872–1915," PhD diss., Columbia University, 1998. For a statistical breakdown on Comstock's arrestees—by religion, ethnicity, occupation, age, and so forth—see Richard Christian Johnson, "Anthony Comstock: Reform, Vice, and the American Way," PhD diss., University of Wisconsin, 1973, 154–168, 183–197.

2. In many ways, the most informative biography of Comstock remains the old standard of Heywood Broun and Margaret Leech, especially since the authors had access to Comstock's diaries, which were later lost or intentionally destroyed (by his successors at the New York Society for the Suppression of Vice). See Heywood Broun and Margaret Leech, *Anthony Comstock: Roundsman of the Lord* (New York: Boni, 1927). For a more recent biographical treatment, see Anna Louise Bates,

Weeder in the Garden of the Lord: Anthony Comstock's Life and Career (Lanham, MD: University Press of America, 1995); for a good sociological treatment of Comstock's crusade, especially in terms of class formation, see Nicola Beisel, *Imperiled Innocents: Anthony Comstock and Family Reproduction in Victorian America* (Princeton: Princeton University Press, 1997); for the spread of Comstock's Protestant cause from New York to Boston, see P. C. Kemeny, "'Banned in Boston': Moral Reform Politics and the New England Society for the Suppression of Vice," *Church History* 74 (2009): 814-846; for women reformers who joined in the anti-obscenity campaigns for maternalist and feminist reasons, see Leigh Ann Wheeler, *Against Obscenity: Reform and the Politics of Womanhood in America, 1873-1935* (Baltimore: Johns Hopkins University Press, 2004); and for placing Comstock's anti-obscenity campaign within the larger panoply of evangelical Protestant efforts to use the federal government to reconstruct morality, see Gaines M. Foster, *Moral Reconstruction: Christian Lobbyists and the Federal Legislation of Morality, 1865–1920* (Chapel Hill: University of North Carolina Press, 2002), esp. 47–71. Richard Johnson discovered the fate of Comstock's diaries and related papers, the loss of which makes the vice society's arrest records the primary archival material surviving on Comstock's crusade. See Johnson, "Comstock," 5.

3. On the legal and literary contexts for the obscenity rulings, see especially Helen Lefkowitz Horowitz, *Rereading Sex: Battles over Sexual Knowledge and Suppression in Nineteenth-Century America* (New York: Knopf, 2002), 404–436, and Edward de Grazia, *Girls Lean Back Everywhere: The Law of Obscenity and the Assault on Genius* (New York: Random House, 1992). The impact of the *Hicklin* standard on American jurisprudence is well known; less noticed is the irony that the original British case involved a Protestant pamphlet attacking supposed Roman Catholic immoralities—namely, *The Confessional Unmasked: Showing the Depravity of the Romish Priesthood, the Iniquity of the Confessional, and the Questions Put to Females in Confession.* The irony of a Protestant fount for the prevailing legal measure of obscenity was not lost on Theodore Schroeder. See TS, *'Obscene' Literature and Constitutional Law* (New York: n.p., 1911), 55–56.

4. Charles C. Moore, *Behind the Bars; 31498* (Lexington: Blue Grass Printing, 1899), 216–219, 290–294. For the pamphleteering possibilities of Ingersoll's closing argument in the Reynolds case, see Robert G. Ingersoll, *Trial for Blasphemy* (New York: Farrell, 1888). For cursory summaries of the Kneeland, Reynolds, and Moore cases, see Leonard W. Levy, *Blasphemy: Verbal Offense against the Sacred, from Moses to Salman Rushdie* (Chapel Hill: University of North Carolina Press, 1995), 414–422, 506–512. For the counter-argument to Levy's emphasis on the decline of blasphemy jurisprudence, see Sarah Barringer Gordon, "Blasphemy and the Law of Religious Liberty in Nineteenth-Century America," *American Quarterly* 52 (2000): 682–719. Gordon stresses the strength of American blasphemy laws, flowing from the precedent of People v. Ruggles in New York in 1811, and the judiciary's protective stance toward a generalized Christianity throughout the nineteenth century. As

Gordon also indicates, blasphemy had long been associated with libertinism; in other words, the basis for the slippage between obscenity and blasphemy ran deep. For the English parallels, including the conflation of blasphemy with indecency, see Joss Marsh, *Word Crimes: Blasphemy, Culture, and Literature in Nineteenth-Century England* (Chicago: University of Chicago Press, 1998), esp. 207–215.

5. Moore, *Behind the Bars*, 221–243. The *Blue-grass Blade* carried at least five articles on Craddock's case in 1902. See, for example, "Organize! Organize!" *Blue-grass Blade*, Nov. 9, 1902, 4; "Another Victim of Ignorance and Tyranny," *Blue-grass Blade*, Nov. 16, 1902, 2.

6. IC, "Brief Account of My Indictments," 5, box 2, f. 2, RGP; IC to [WTS], undated fragment, [1899], box 2, f. 2, RGP.

7. For the belated application in the 1940s of an individual civil liberties approach to church-state relations, see David Sikkink, "From Christian Civilization to Individual Civil Liberties: Framing Religion in the Legal Field, 1880–1949," in Christian Smith, ed., *The Secular Revolution: Power, Interests, and Conflict in the Secularization of American Public Life* (Berkeley: University of California Press, 2003), 310–354. For especially perceptive analyses of the limits of free-exercise jurisprudence in the nineteenth and early twentieth centuries, see Sarah Barringer Gordon, *The Mormon Question: Polygamy and Constitutional Conflict in Nineteenth-Century America* (Chapel Hill: University of North Carolina Press, 2002), and Tisa Wenger, *We Have a Religion: The 1920s Pueblo Indian Dance Controversy and American Religious Freedom* (Chapel Hill: University of North Carolina Press, 2009).

8. Anthony Comstock, *Traps for the Young*, ed. Robert Bremner (Cambridge, MA: Belknap Press of Harvard University Press, 1967), 158.

9. Anthony Comstock, *Frauds Exposed; Or, How the People Are Deceived and Robbed, and Youth Corrupted* (New York: Brown, 1880), 388–495; Comstock, *Traps for the Young*, 184–185, 199; Anthony Comstock, "Lawlessness of the Liberal Leagues," *Our Day: A Record and Review of Current Reform* 1 (1888): 393–398; Anthony Comstock, "Indictable Art," *Our Day: A Record and Review of Current Reform* 1 (1888): 48.

10. DPE, 207–209.

11. Ibid.

12. Advertisement, *Philadelphia Inquirer*, April 25, 1897, 15; DPE, 209.

13. DPE, 209, 215.

14. Ibid., 209. The dates and details of the postal complaints against Craddock are recorded in U.S. v. Ida C. Craddock, Case 31, Aug. 1898, Records of U.S. District Court, Eastern District of Pennsylvania, National Archives and Records, Philadelphia.

15. IC, "Memoranda: Indictment in Chicago," 2–4, box 2, f. 2, RGP; IC, "To My Patrons and Well-Wishers," Dec. 1897, box 2, f. 2, RGP; "Miss Craddock Resigns" and "Why She Resigned," newspaper clippings, 1897, box 20, f. 15, RGP; "Daily Doings in City Hall," *North American* (Philadelphia), Nov. 16, 1897. For notices that she

was circulating her pamphlets, see *LLB*, Aug. 18, 1897, 259; Sept. 22, 1897, 299. Craddock preferred to blame office politics, particularly her refusal to pay assessments to the city's corrupt political machine, as the source of her firing. That might have been the case, but her pamphleteering on behalf of sex reform caught most public notice.

16. IC to EBF, June 6, 1898, box 2, f. 2, RGP.

17. Ibid.; TS, "Notes on Ida C," box 20, f. 16, RGP; IC, "Memoranda," 5; IC, "Brief Account"; IC to Katie Wood, July 5, 1901, box 1, f. 1, ICP. Schroeder seems to have gotten at least a bare overview of Craddock's medical evaluations of 1898; he certainly tried hard to gain access to her records through directly contacting the authorities involved in her case. These asylum records, though, were officially off limits to Schroeder, and, by Pennsylvania state law, any materials naming specific patients remain closed to researchers. For Schroeder's efforts, see Owen Copp to TS, Feb. 10, 1913; Edward A. Strecker to TS, March 14, 1923, box 1, f. 4, ICP. On the legal process of official medical certification, see *Information Respecting Friends Asylum for the Insane and Requirements for Admission* (Philadelphia: Buchanan, 1897), 17, and *The Annual Report of the Department for the Insane of the Pennsylvania Hospital* (Philadelphia: Ferris, 1889), 38–42. Finally, it should be noted that Craddock's diary is scant for the period from September 1897 to October 1898, so the story here has to be pieced together mostly through correspondence.

18. IC to Katie Wood, Oct. 8, 1898, box 2, f. 2, RGP.

19. Ibid. The date of Craddock's release from the Pennsylvania Hospital for the Insane was Sept. 7, 1898, roughly coincident with the agreement to drop the indictment. On the dates of her confinement, see Owen Copp to TS, Sept. 20, 1913, box 1, f. 4, ICP.

20. IC to Wood, Oct. 8, 1898; DPE, 190.

21. This London debacle is traceable in IC to Katie Wood, Dec. 2, 1898; Dec. 9, 1898; Dec. 13, 1898; and Dec. 20, 1898, box 1, f. 1, ICP.

22. IC, "Memoranda," 1-2, 4. Specifics on the Chicago case are recorded in U.S. v. Ida C. Craddock, Case 3078, Oct. 1899, Criminal Records and Dockets, U.S. District Court, Northern District of Illinois, National Archives, Great Lakes Region, Chicago. See also Shirley J. Burton, "Obscene, Lewd, and Lascivious: Ida Craddock and the Criminally Obscene Women of Chicago, 1873-1913," *Michigan Historical Review* 19 (1993): 1–16.

23. Clarence Darrow, *The Story of My Life* (New York: Scribner's, 1932), 11, 398–399. The designation "attorney for the damned" comes from Arthur Weinberg, ed., *Attorney for the Damned: Clarence Darrow in the Courtroom* (Chicago: University of Chicago Press, 1989). Craddock's case, a plea bargain, has obviously not made the canon of Darrow's celebrated courtroom feats.

24. IC, "Brief Account," 2, 4–5. Comstock was subpoenaed as the figurehead of the whole anti-obscenity campaign, but Craddock pointed to the Western Society for the Suppression of Vice as the behind-the-scenes force in this instance. It was

housed in Chicago's YMCA building and headed by Comstock's equally vigilant comrade-in-arms R. W. McAfee. See "Right Marital Living," *LLB*, Feb. 17, 1900, 43.

25. "Right Marital Living," *LLB*, 43; IC to [WTS], undated fragment; IC, *The Wedding Night*, 3rd ed. (New York: n.p., 1902), 13. The three objectionable passages (pp. 6–7, 12–13, 17–18) were specified in the federal indictment in New York in March 1902, which is discussed below. A copy of the expurgated Denver edition of *Right Marital Living* has not survived, but an excerpt from the new preface was reprinted in the *Lucifer* article cited above. Craddock also discusses it in the undated fragment of a letter to Stead noted above.

26. IC, "Brief Account," 5–7; *Washington Post*, April 25, 1901, 2. The relevant police court records have not survived.

27. IC, "Brief Account," 7; IC to Moses Harman, in *LLB*, Aug. 10, 1901, 239.

28. On her financial squeeze, see IC to Katie Wood, [Aug. 1, 1901], box 1, f. 1; IC, "Account of Expenses," Aug.-Sept. 1901, box 1, f. 3; IC to WTS, Sept. 10, 1901, box 1, f.1, ICP.

29. The note on her landlord's son and his two friends is in her "Account of Expenses." On the role of her Baptist landlord, E. D. Garnsey, see IC to Hugh O. Pentecost, March 12, 1902, box 2, f. 2, RGP. On decoy letters and her New York arrest, see IC to Hugh O. Pentecost, Feb. 9, 1902; IC to Editor *Sun*, Feb. 21, 1902, box 2, f. 2, RGP, and IC to Hugh O. Pentecost, Feb. 4, 1902, box 1, f. 1, ICP.

30. *Twenty-Ninth Annual Report of the New York Society for the Suppression of Vice* (New York: n.p., 1903), 10–11.

31. Ibid.; Anthony Comstock to Henrietta Westbrook, Feb. 28, 1902, box 2, f. 2, RGP. Details on the New York case are recorded in U.S. v. Ida C. Craddock, Criminal Case C-2738, March-Oct. 1902, U.S. Circuit Court for the Southern District of New York, National Archives, Northeast Region, New York City. The detail on her limited print runs is from IC to Pentecost, March 12, 1902. The *Truth Seeker* later printed a copy of what they said was a failed decoy letter that Comstock sent to Craddock under the assumed name of "Miss Frankie Streeter." See "Comstock and His Methods," *Truth Seeker*, Nov. 8, 1902, 710. The journal included a letter from Craddock refusing to send her pamphlets to a minor without parental consent. See IC, "Craddock's Reply," *Truth Seeker*, Nov. 8, 1902, 710.

32. IC to Editor *Sun*, Feb. 21, 1902; "Alleged Misuse of Mails: Woman Held on Charge of Circulating Forbidden Literature," *Philadelphia Inquirer*, Feb. 19, 1902, 1; "Dr. Rainsford Sent Approval," *New York Sun*, Feb. 19, 1902, 7.

33. IC to Editor *Sun*, Feb. 21, 1902; "Alleged Misuse of Mails," 1; "Dr. Rainsford Sent Approval," 7.

34. R. W. Shufeldt, "Critique of the Trial of Ida C. Craddock," *BI*, April 5, 1902, box 20, f. 15, RGP.

35. IC to Editor *Sun*, Feb. 21, 1902; IC to Pentecost, Feb. 4, 1902 and Feb. 9, 1902; Shufeldt, "Critique of the Trial"; IC to EBF, June 18, 1902, box 1, f. 2, ICP; Hugh O. Pentecost, "One-Ideaed People," *Truth Seeker*, Nov. 22, 1902, 738–739.

For Pentecost's polemics against religion, see Hugh O. Pentecost, *What I Believe* (New York: Twentieth Century, 1891); Hugh O. Pentecost, "Persistence of Superstition," *Truth Seeker*, Jan. 25, 1902, 58; and Hugh O. Pentecost, "Superstitions of Liberals," *Truth Seeker*, Oct. 17, 1903, 658–659.

36. EBF, "Comstock versus Craddock," *LLB*, Feb. 27, 1902; EBF, "Comstock versus Craddock," *Truth Seeker*, Feb. 22, 1902, 120; EBF, "Craddock Fund," box 1, f. 3, ICP; EBF, "Comstock vs. Craddock—Again," *Truth Seeker*, March 15, 1902, 168. Foote's piece appeared in various radical publications and as a stand-alone circular. For a copy of the latter, see box 20, f. 16, RGP. Foote received dozens of letters and donations in favorable response to it, the evidence for which survives in ICP.

37. "Mrs. Craddock Goes to Jail," *New York Sun*, March 18, 1902, 5; R. W. Shufeldt, "Letters from Gotham," *BI*, newspaper clippings, box 2, f. 2, RGP. The other two doctors who were subpoenaed as defense witnesses were Elmer Lee and George Knipe, New York physicians who were supportive of her labors. See IC to EBF, March 12, 1902, box 1, f. 1, ICP. Another medical authority, Byron Robinson, chimed in with a letter of endorsement from Chicago. There were conflicting reports about whether the three-judge panel allowed the doctors to testify as expert witnesses on Craddock's behalf. Shufeldt's first-person account claims he took the stand, and he was still complaining three years later about the discourtesies he suffered "in the witness chair" during her trial. See R. W. Shufeldt, "The Medico-Legal Consideration of Perverts and Inverts," *Pacific Medical Journal* 48 (1905): 385–386. But, see also Cyrus W. Coolridge, "Ida Craddock and Anthony Comstock," *BI*, newspaper clippings, box 20, f. 16, RGP, where it is claimed the doctors were prevented from testifying. By Shufeldt's account, his testimony was cut short, and he was not allowed to answer a question put to him directly by Craddock. Only the docket books survive for the Court of Sessions for this period, so the official legal documents for this trial are very thin. For an account that squares with Shufeldt's version of events, see "Ida Craddock's Case," *Truth Seeker*, March 29, 1902, 199–200.

38. "Mrs. Craddock Goes to Jail," 5.

39. Ibid.; "Mrs. Craddock Sentenced," *New York Times*, March 18, 1902, 7; "Ida C. Craddock Convicted," *LLB*, April 3, 1902, 89-90; Elizur Brace Hinsdale, *Autobiography with Reports and Documents* (New York: J. J. Little, 1901), 16, 81–83; "John Most Gets Year in Jail," *Philadelphia Inquirer*, Oct. 15, 1901, 16; "Family Ties Sundered," *New York Times*, April 30, 1884, 2. On Most's radicalism, see Beverly Gage, *The Day Wall Street Exploded: A Story of America in its First Age of Terror* (New York: Oxford University Press, 2009), 41–68.

40. "Mrs. Craddock Goes to Jail," 5; EBF, "Convicted of 'Blasphemy': Craddock Crushed and Comstock Crowing," *Truth Seeker*, April 12, 1902, 230–231. For biographical information on McKean, see "Justice McKean Dead," *New York Times*, June 14, 1908, 11.

41. Shufeldt, "Critique of the Trial"; Edward W. Chamberlain, "The Persecution of Craddock," *LLB*, May 1, 1902, 120–121.

42. "Mrs. Craddock Goes to Jail," 5; EBF, "Convicted of 'Blasphemy': Craddock Crushed and Comstock Crowing," 230–231; "Craddock's Case," 199–200; "Mrs. Craddock Sentenced," *New York Times*, March 18, 1902, 7; Shufeldt, "Letters from Gotham"; Shufeldt, "Critique of the Trial"; Edward W. Chamberlain, "The Persecution of Craddock"; *Twenty-Ninth Annual Report*, 7.

43. Shufeldt, "Critique of Trial," 5; Chamberlain, "Persecution," 121; Edward W. Chamberlain, "The Blackmailing of Mrs. Craddock," *LLB*, July 17, 1902, 210.

44. Edward W. Chamberlain, "Craddock Assaulted," *LLB*, May 22, 1902, 148; Moses Harman, "Mrs. Craddock's Workhouse Experience," *LLB*, Aug. 14, 1902, 243–244; IC to EBF, May 12, 1902 and June 1, 1902; IC to Hugh O. Pentecost, March 19, 1902; Henrietta Westbrook to EBF, April 10, 1902, box 1, f. 2, ICP; "The Work-House—Blackwell's Island," *Harper's New Monthly Magazine* 33 (1866): 696. For an excellent examination of the political and social consequence of the anti-vaccination movement among late Victorian liberals, see Nadja Durbach, *Bodily Matters: The Anti-Vaccination Movement in England, 1853–1907* (Durham: Duke University Press, 2005).

45. IC, "'In Durance Vile': Mrs. Craddock's Story of Her Imprisonment under the Reign of Comstock," *Truth Seeker*, Aug. 9, 1902, 504–505.

46. "Defense Fund," *LLB*, June 19, 1902, 181; "By the Way," *LLB*, July 3, 1902, 196; Cyrus W. Coolridge, "The Craddock Dinner," *LLB*, July 10, 1902, 201–202; "The Craddock Dinner," *Truth Seeker*, June 28, 1902, 409. There were other free-speech cases of moment, including one involving a group of social radicals in Home, Washington, that sparked Foote and Walker to organize the Free Speech League, but Craddock's jailing, release, and federal trial were the most immediate precipitating events. See, for example, how the connection is made in Philip G. Peabody to EBF, May 16, 1902, box 1, f. 2, ICP. For an excellent overview of free-speech activism in this era, including the importance of the Free Speech League's cutting-edge radicalism, see David M. Rabban, *Free Speech in its Forgotten Years* (Cambridge: Cambridge University Press, 1997), esp. 64–76. For particular delineation of the father-son duo behind much of this early activism, see Janice Ruth Wood, *The Struggle for Free Speech in the United States, 1872–1915: Edward Bliss Foote, Edward Bond Foote, and Anti-Comstock Operations* (New York: Routledge, 2008).

47. Coolridge, "Craddock Dinner," 201–202; R. W. Shufeldt, "The Release of Mrs. Craddock," *BI*, July 5, 1902, newspaper clippings, box 20, f. 15, RGP.

48. Eunice O. Parsons to IC, Sept, 21, 1902; Sept. 25, 1902; and Sept. 30, 1902, box 1, f.2. ICP.

49. E. Elmer Keeler, "The Wedding Night," *The Clinic* (Syracuse, NY), newspaper clippings, box 20, f. 16, RGP.

50. Lizzie S. Decker to EBF, March 29, 1902 and May 9, 1902, box 1, f. 1–2, ICP.

51. IC to EBF, June 18, 1902; Hugh O. Pentecost to EBF, Nov. 5, 1902, box 2, f. 2; Edward Chamberlain to Lizzie Decker, Nov. 17, 1902, box 2, f.2, RGP.

52. "A Spiritualist to Editor," *LLB*, Dec. 25, 1902, 394; Chamberlain to Decker, Nov. 17, 1902.

53. The details on the federal trial are from: "Mrs. Craddock Convicted," *New York Sun*, Oct. 11, 1902, 9; "Ida Craddock Convicted Again," *Truth Seeker*, Oct. 18, 1902, 661; "Ida C. Craddock's Last Words," *LLB*, Nov. 13, 1902, 344–346; *Twenty-Ninth Annual Report*, 12; Coolridge, "Craddock and Comstock," 11; "The Craddock Tragedy," *Torch of Reason*, Nov. 6, 1902, 4.

54. Edward W. Chamberlain to IC, Sept. 10, 1902, box 2, f. 2, RGP; "Ida Craddock's Letter to Her Mother," *Truth Seeker*, Oct. 25, 1902, 680.

55. "In Jail's Shadow Ida Craddock Died," *New York Herald*, Oct. 18, 1902; "Priestess of Yoga a Suicide," *Evening World* (New York), Oct. 17, 1902; "Another Comstock Victim: Ida C. Craddock Driven to Suicide by the Mendacious Anthony," unidentified newspaper clipping. All three of these accounts are from newspaper files in box 20, f. 16, RGP. See also "Escapes Prison by Death," *New-York Tribune*, Oct. 18, 1902, 6. Her death was widely covered in the newspapers, and the reported details were not entirely consistent. Did she cut both of her wrists? Was the rubber tube in her mouth or at her side? Did one police officer come to her mother's aid or two? But, the basic outline of events is evident from multiple sources.

56. DPE, 190. Craddock recalled the lines as being from James Russell Lowell, but they are from Longfellow.

57. "Letter to Her Mother," 680.

58. Ibid.

59. "Priestess of Yoga a Suicide," Oct. 17, 1902; "Death, Not Prison," *Evening Sun* (New York), Oct. 17, 1902, newspaper clippings, box 2, f. 2, RGP.

60. Lizzie Decker to EBF, Oct. 21, 1902, box 2, f. 2, RGP; "Ida C. Craddock's Mother Speaks," *LLB*, Nov. 20, 1902, 354.

61. Frederic A. Hinckley, *Sermon Preached at the Funeral of Robert Purvis* (Washington, DC: Judd and Detweiler, 1898), 5–6, 10.

62. Coolridge, "Craddock and Comstock," 11.

63. *Twenty-Ninth Annual Report*, 13, 15; "Attacks Anthony Comstock," *New York Times*, Oct. 29, 1902, 16; "Says Comstock Hounded Woman to Suicide," *Chicago Tribune*, Oct. 28, 1902, 5; W. S. Rainsford, *The Story of a Varied Life: An Autobiography* (New York: Doubleday, 1922), 339, 342; "Threatens Dr. Rainsford," *New-York Tribune*, Nov. 4, 1902, 1; "Vice Society for Comstock," *New York Sun*, Nov. 4, 1902, 3.

64. "Memorial of Ida C. Craddock," *LLB*, Nov. 6, 1902, 340. For an example of the Stanton-Craddock conflation at the time, see "Stanton, Austin, Craddock, the Humanitarian Trinity," *Blue-grass Blade*, Nov. 30, 1902, 3.

65. "Memorial of Ida C. Craddock," 340; "The Craddock Tragedy: What Should Be Done About It," *Torch of Reason*, Nov. 6, 1902, 4; Edwin C. Walker, "The 'Trial' and Death of Ida C. Craddock," *LLB*, Oct. 30, 1902, 328–329: Juliet H. Severance, "Thoughts on the Death of Ida Craddock," *Truth Seeker*, Nov. 1, 1902, 698; "George Macdonald on the Craddock Case," *LLB*, Dec. 11, 1902, 377; "Ruminations," *LLB*, Nov. 13, 1902, 348.

66. "Ida Craddock's Last Words: Like Socrates, She Chooses for Herself the Manner of Her Death," *Truth Seeker*, Nov. 1, 1902, 694–695; "Craddock's Last Words," *LLB*, Nov. 13, 1902, 344–346.

67. "Craddock's Last Words," 345.

68. Robert G. Ingersoll, *Is Suicide a Sin? Robert G. Ingersoll's Famous Letter, Replies by Eminent Men, and Col. Ingersoll's Brilliant Rejoinder, Prefaced by a Startling Chapter, Great Suicides of History!* (New York: Eckler, n.d.), 5, 16, 65. Hugh Pentecost, who continued to dislike his former client, took the contrarian view in dismissing the nobility of her final act, labeling her a "quitter": "If you have a gospel worth preaching at all, it is worth preaching until somebody else kills you. Do not give it up." See Pentecost, "One-Ideaed People," 739.

69. *Twenty-Ninth Annual Report*, 17.

70. "Comstock Tells His Part in the Ida Craddock Case," *Brooklyn Daily Eagle*, Nov. 14, 1902, newspaper clippings, box 20, f. 15, RGP; Anthony Comstock, "Public Morals and the Law," *Brooklyn Daily Eagle*, Nov. 14, 1902, 6; "Warm Time for Comstock at Philosophical Society," *Brooklyn Daily Eagle*, Dec. 8, 1902, newspaper clippings, box 14, f. 1, RGP; "Mr. Comstock Denounced," *New York Times*, Dec. 8, 1902, 2; "Comstock Knocked Out," *Richmond Dispatch*, Dec. 9, 1902, 11; Cyrus W. Coolridge, "Anthony Comstock under Fire," *LLB*, Jan. 1, 1903, 401–402; "Comstock in Cold Type," *Truth Seeker*, Dec. 27, 1902, 822–824. Conway had become interested in the Craddock case only after her death, but he then displayed a hearty enthusiasm for her heroic witness. See Moncure D. Conway, "The Inner Heritage of Secularism," *Twenty-Sixth Annual Report of the American Secular Union and Freethought Federation* (New York: Truth Seeker, 1902), 86–89. Walker used the December encounter over the Craddock case as the jumping off point for a full-scale attack on Comstock's censorship apparatus. See Edwin C. Walker, *Who is the Enemy; Anthony Comstock or You?* (New York: n.p., 1903), 6–10, 32–33.

71. Flora W. Fox, "Repeal the Comstock Laws," *LLB*, Nov. 20, 1902, 354; "Livesey Hits Comstock," *Brooklyn Daily Eagle*, Nov. 13, 1902, 9.

72. TS, *'Obscene' Literature and Constitutional Law*, 56, 271.

73. Emma Goldman, *Living My Life* (1931; Salt Lake City: Smith, 1982), 553.

74. Broun and Leech, *Comstock*, 156; "Instruction in Sexual Matters for the Laity," *North American Journal of Homœopathy* 18 (1903): 514; "Repeal the Comstock Law," *LLB*, Dec. 25, 1902, 394; Conway, "Inner Heritage," 87; James F. Morton Jr., "The Fight for Free Speech," *LLB*, Nov. 12, 1903, 345.

Chapter 6: One Religio-Sexual Maniac

1. [Clark Bell], "Ida Craddock and Anthony Comstock," *Medico-Legal Journal* 20 (1902): 429–433; "Comstock and the Craddock Case," *New-York Tribune*, Nov. 8, 1902, 2. Bell previously outlined his reasons for refusing her case in a letter to EBF, March 3, 1902, box 1, f. 1, ICP.

2. Bell, "Craddock and Comstock," 429–433.

3. *Twenty-Ninth Annual Report of the New York Society for the Suppression of Vice* (New York: n.p., 1903), 19. In defining erotomania and nymphomania many clinicians defined the former as a mental disease that took over the imagination and the latter to be a physiological, organically grounded disease that was given overt bodily expression. In practical usage, however, the two categories regularly shaded from one into the other. Theodore Schroeder would employ the terms with the clinical distinction in mind in analyzing Craddock: "Here I am using 'erotomania' as meaning a psychogenetic erotic obsession. By nymphomania I mean a pathological organic basis for an erotic obsession." See TS, "Puritanism through Erotomania to Nymphomania," 1, box 5, f. 30, ICP.

4. R. W. Shufeldt, "Letter from Gotham," *BI*, newspaper clippings, box 2, f. 2, RGP; R. W. Shufeldt, "Critique of the Trial of Ida C. Craddock," *BI*, newspaper clippings, box 20, f. 15, RGP; R. W. Shufeldt to IC, Jan. 27, 1902, box 1, f. 1, ICP.

5. "Memorial for Ida C. Craddock," *LLB*, Nov. 6, 1902, 340; Shufeldt to IC, Jan. 27, 1902; TS, "One Religio-Sexual Maniac," *Psychoanalytic Review* 23 (1936): 26–45; TS, "The Physical Side of Marriage," 2, box 6, f. 3, ICP.

6. IC, "Miscellaneous Notes," 16, box 6, f. 7; IC to Katie Wood, Dec. 9, 1898. For contemporary accounts of nervous disorders and prevailing therapies by two prominent physicians with ties to the Philadelphia hospital where Craddock was treated, see Francis X. Dercum, ed., *A Text-Book on Nervous Diseases* (Philadelphia: Lea, 1895); H. C. Wood, *Nervous Diseases and Their Diagnosis* (Philadelphia: Lippincott, 1887). For background on the hospital's history and its practices, including religious correctives in treating insanity, see Nancy Tomes, *A Generous Confidence: Thomas Story Kirkbride and the Art of Asylum-Keeping, 1840–1883* (Cambridge: Cambridge University Press, 1984), esp. 48, 85, 88, 98-100, 221–222.

7. Alexander Wilder to EBF, Feb. 26, 1902, box 1 f. 1, ICP; "An Infidel Sermon," *Blue-grass Blade*, July 12, 1903, 2.

8. IC to Katie Wood, Oct. 8, 1898, box 2, f. 2, RGP.

9. J. E. D. Esquirol, *Mental Maladies: A Treatise on Insanity*, trans. E. K. Hunt (Philadelphia: Lea and Blanchard, 1845), 320–342; Conolly Norman, "Mania," in D. Hack Tuke, ed., *A Dictionary of Psychological Medicine*, 2 vols. (Philadelphia: Blakiston, 1892), 2: 765. For the broader debates about the pathologies of religious experience, including mediumistic phenomena, see Ann Taves, *Fits, Trances, and Visions: Experiencing Religion and Explaining Experience from Wesley to James* (Princeton: Princeton University Press, 1999); Ann Braude, *Radical Spirits: Spiritualism and Women's Rights in Nineteenth-Century America*, 2nd ed. (Bloomington: Indiana University Press, 2001), esp. 142–161; Leigh Eric Schmidt, *Hearing Things: Religion, Illusion, and the American Enlightenment* (Cambridge, MA: Harvard University Press, 2000); Molly McGarry, *Ghosts of Futures Past: Spiritualism and the Cultural Politics of Nineteenth-Century America* (Berkeley: University of California Press, 2008), esp. 121–153; and Christopher G. White, *Unsettled Minds:*

Psychology and the American Search for Spiritual Assurance, 1830–1940 (Berkeley: University of California Press, 2009).

10. G. Stanley Hall to Sigmund Freud, Sept. 26, 1913, in Saul Rosenzweig, ed., *Freud, Jung, and Hall the King-Maker: The Historic Expedition to America (1909)* (St. Louis: Rana House, 1992), 373–374; Francis X. Dercum, "An Evaluation of the Psychogenic Factors in the Etiology of Mental Disease, Including a Review of Psychanalysis," *Journal of the American Medical Association* 62 (1914): 753. Hall wrote revealingly of his attractions to—and his apprehensions about—Freudian claims in his autobiography. See G. Stanley Hall, *Life and Confessions of a Psychologist* (New York: Appleton, 1923), 406–414. For the definitive biographical study of Hall, including his intricate dance with Freud, see Dorothy Ross, *G. Stanley Hall: The Psychologist as Prophet* (Chicago: University of Chicago Press, 1972).

11. William James, *The Varieties of Religious Experience* (1902; New York: Penguin, 1982), 419; James S. Van Teslaar, *Sex and the Senses* (Boston: Badger, 1922), 249, 253; Havelock Ellis, *Studies in the Psychology of Sex*, 7 vols. (Philadelphia: Davis, 1921–1928), 1: 310–311, 315. Ellis quotes Iwan Bloch's 1908 work, *Sexualleben unserer Zeit*, on p. 315. For an insightful examination of the psychological literature on mysticism in the context of European religious and intellectual history, see Cristina Mazzoni, *Saint Hysteria: Neurosis, Mysticism, and Gender in European Culture* (Ithaca: Cornell University Press, 1996).

12. James, *Varieties*, 10–12; Josiah Moses, *Pathological Aspects of Religions* (Worcester, MA: Clark University Press, 1906), 18–19, 22; James H. Leuba, *The Psychology of Religious Mysticism* (New York: Harcourt, Brace, 1925), 151.

13. James Bissett Pratt, *The Religious Consciousness: A Psychological Study* (New York: Macmillan, 1920), 111; TS, "Evolution of a Psychologist of Religion," box 1, f. 2, TSP. Schroeder's career as free-speech lawyer has received a lot more attention than his role as psychoanalyst of religion. See especially David M. Rabban, *Free Speech in its Forgotten Years* (Cambridge: Cambridge University Press, 1997), 47–55, 198–200. For an overarching biographical perspective, see David Brudnoy, "Liberty's Bugler: The Seven Ages of Theodore Schroeder," PhD diss., Brandeis University, 1971. For an early appreciation of his labors as a psychologist, see Maynard Shipley, "A Maverick Psychologist," *New Humanist* 6 (1933): 37–40. For subsequent notice of him as one of America's most insistent Freudian critics of religion, see Nathan G. Hale Jr., *Freud and the Americans: The Beginnings of Psychoanalysis in the United States, 1876–1917* (New York: Oxford University Press, 1971), 270–271, and Jon H. Roberts, "Psychoanalysis and American Christianity, 1900–1945," in David C. Lindberg and Ronald Numbers, eds., *When Science and Christianity Meet: From Augustine to Intelligent Design* (Chicago: University of Chicago Press, 2003), 234.

14. Steffens quoted in Hutchins Hapgood, *A Victorian in the Modern World* (New York: Harcourt, Brace, 1939), 279; TS to G. Stanley Hall, July 2, 1906, box 7, f. 1,

TSP. Schroeder was moving between Redfield, South Dakota, and Madison, Wisconsin, in late 1902 (trying to settle his father's estate). Though he had visited New York on prior business, it appears that he did not relocate there until January 1903. He was definitely not involved in the agitation surrounding Craddock's final round of trials in 1902.

15. TS, '*Obscene' Literature and Constitutional Law* (New York: n.p., 1911), 58–61.

16. TS, "Ida's Theomania," box 5, f. 29, ICP; TS, "Puritanism through Erotomania to Nymphomania"; TS, "Philosophy and Moral Theology of an Erotomaniac," box 5, f. 32; TS, "The Philosophy of an Erotomaniac," box 5, f. 22, ICP; TS, Outlines for Volumes on Religion and Sex, box 6, f. 1-3, ICP and box 60, f. 2, TSP. For the mistaken byline, see *Alienist and Neurologist* 38 (1917): 288.

17. TS, "Phallic Worship to a Secularized Sex," *Journal of Sexology and Psychanalysis* 1 (1923): 73–75; TS, "Revivals, Sex and Holy Ghost," *Journal of Abnormal Psychology* 14 (1919): 34–47; TS, "The Erotogenesis of Religion," *Alienist and Neurologist* 28 (1907): 338–339. For broad statements of his theory, see TS, "Outline for a Study of the Erotogenesis of Religion," *Journal of Religious Psychology* 5 (1912): 394–401; TS, "The Erotogenesis of Religion: Developing a Working Hypothesis," *Alienist and Neurologist* 34 (1913): 444–476; and TS, "The Psychoanalytic Approach to Religious Experience," *Psychoanalytic Review* 16 (1929): 361–376.

18. TS, "Revivals, Sex and Holy Ghost," 46–47; TS, "Phallic Worship," 75–78, 83–86.

19. "Is Sex the Basis of Religion?" *New York Times Magazine*, April 4, 1915, box 4, f. 2, TSP. Van Teslaar directly credits Schroeder in the *Times* article itself, but see also J. S. Van Teslaar, "Religion and Sex: An Account of the Erotogenetic Theory of Religion as Formulated by Theodore Schroeder," *Psychoanalytic Review* 2 (1915): 81–92. The critics could say what they wanted about his scientific naturalism, but Schroeder thought that all too many American psychologists, including William James and George Coe, displayed a failure of scientific nerve when it came to religion. See TS, "Some Difficulties and Problems of the Psychologists of Religion," *Psyche and Eros* 3 (1922): 159–168.

20. SML, 1–4.

21. Ibid., 4; DPE, second part, 12. She did mention a dream about their time together as friends in San Francisco, but it was not a sex dream (DPE, second part, 12).

22. SML, 3–4; Richard B. Westbrook to EBF, Feb. 14, 1894; Henrietta Westbrook to IC, Feb. 15, 1902, box 1, f. 1, ICP.

23. IC, "Miscellaneous Notes," box 6, f. 7, ICP; SML, 3.

24. WTS to Philander Knox, Sept. 24, 1902, box 2, f. 2, RGP; WTS to TS, March 10, 1906; TS to WTS, March 24, 1906; WTS to TS, Nov. 12, 1907; TS to Estelle Stead, Sept. 26, 1913; Estelle Stead to TS, July 28, 1914; TS to Estelle Stead, Dec. 17, 1918, box 1, f. 4, ICP. Schroeder had been collecting Craddock materials—

pamphlets, letters, and manuscripts—from any and all sources. He already had a lot of material by 1915, but the Stead collection was the lodestone.

25. TS, "One Religio-Sexual Maniac," 26–28.

26. Ibid., 30–31; SML, 3.

27. TS, "One Religio-Sexual Maniac," 31–32; IC to Katie Wood, Dec. 8, 1887, box 1, f. 1, ICP.

28. TS, "One Religio-Sexual Maniac," 32. Westbrook shared some of Craddock's interests in marriage reform. That was particularly true when it came to the liberalization of divorce laws, but he made the case less on the grounds of the idealized love of soul mates than on the secularist principle that the churches should not set the terms of a civil contract. See Richard B. Westbrook, *Marriage and Divorce* (Philadelphia: Lippincott, 1883).

29. TS, "One Religio-Sexual Maniac," 33–35; TS, "Ida's Theomania," 3–4.

30. TS, "One Religio-Sexual Maniac," 34, 45.

31. SML, 5–7; DPE, second part, 16.

32. DPE, 33, 39, 118, 207, 225. I have put an emphasis on the ordinary dimensions of Craddock's fantasized relationship with Soph in order to indicate that her experiences were not exclusively sexual but complexly imaginative—autoerotic in the broadest sense of Havelock Ellis's term. At times, I have left somewhat more to the reader's imagination than Craddock's private diary did. These experiences with Soph were sacred intimacies to her, and it seems crucial—as Stead also intuited in trying to keep the journal out of Schroeder's hands—to handle her diary with great care. Where that interpretive discretion becomes its own form of censorship is not at all a simple line to draw. My aim has been to give a full sense of Craddock's psychical love life without lapsing into voyeuristic detail.

33. Ibid., 182; second part, 29.

34. Ibid., 44, 68.

35. Ibid., 74, 77–78, 199, 210; second part, 35, 52, 54.

36. Ibid., 52–54, 64, 74, 77, 140–141, 189, 202.

37. TS, "'Spiritualizing' Sexual Insanity: Diary of Ida C.," box 6, f. 2 ICP; DPE, 140.

38. DPE, second part, 46.

39. WTS to IC, Sept. 24, 1902; WTS to Knox, Sept. 24, 1902, box 2, f. 2, RGP.

40. DPE, second part, 24; WTS to IC, Sept. 24, 1902; George Du Maurier, *Peter Ibbetson* (New York: Harper, 1891), 233, 366–367, 417.

41. IC to Katie Wood, Dec. 9, 1898, box 1, f. 1, ICP; DPE, second part, 8, 11–12. In her diary Craddock occasionally spelled Ibbetson as Ibbetsen; I have silently corrected it in those cases.

42. DPE, 61, 81, 89. For a superb commentary and exhibition on spirit photographs, see Clément Chéroux, Andreas Fischer, Pierre Apraxine, Denis Canguilhem,

and Sophie Schmit, *The Perfect Medium: Photography and the Occult* (New Haven: Yale University Press, 2005).

43. DPE, 48, 57.

44. "Bouguereau Dead at 80," *New York Times*, Aug. 21, 1905, 7.

45. "Work of a Crazy Censor," *Omaha World Herald*, Dec. 16, 1890, 2.

46. IC, "Marriage Relation," 44–45, box 3, f.3, ICP. The cultural politics surrounding Bouguereau's nudes, especially his *Nymphs and Satyr* (1873), are well analyzed in David Scobey, "Nymphs and Satyrs: Sex and the Bourgeois Public Sphere in Victorian New York," *Winterthur Portfolio* 37 (2002): 43–66.

47. IC to WTS, Sept. 10, 1901; DPE, second part, 25; "Psyche and Love, by Bouguereau," in *Paris Exposition Reproduced from the Official Photographs* (New York: Peale, 1900), n.p. Bouguereau took up Cupid and Psyche as subjects a number of times, including a rendering of them as infants. See the catalogue *William Bouguereau, 1825–1905* (Montreal: Montreal Museum of Fine Arts, 1984), 246–248, 252. In addition to the 1889 and 1895 paintings, Bouguereau also displayed another version of the pair, similarly posed in flight, at the Paris Exposition of 1900 (see the photographic volume on that exposition cited above). Which of the renderings Craddock had in mind is unclear: *The Abduction of Psyche* was described under the title "Psyche and Cupid" in contemporary accounts, which matches up with Craddock's usage (see "American Art in Paris," *New York Times*, April 29, 1895, 5), but the heavenward pointing arm of Eros in the 1889 version better connects with her description of Bouguereau's figure. The artist, including his American reception, has received a modest amount of renewed attention in the last two decades. See Fronia E. Wissman, *Bouguereau* (San Francisco: Pomegranate Artbooks, 1996); Eric M. Zafran, "William Bouguereau in America: A Roller-Coaster Reputation," in James F. Peck, ed., *In the Studios of Paris: William Bouguereau and his American Students* (Tulsa: Philbrook Museum of Art, 2006), 17–44.

48. DPE, 48, 91; second part, 11. For her miscellaneous research notes for the project, see box 6, f. 7 and box 7, f. 5, ICP. Craddock highlighted this longer history of heavenly conjugality rather than the work of more recent visionaries such as Andrew Jackson Davis, Thomas Lake Harris, and Paschal Beverly Randolph. Their own religio-sexual absorptions make clear that Craddock had significant occultist company in her explorations of angelic unions, though their immediate influence on her appears negligible. See John Patrick Deveney, *Paschal Beverly Randolph: A Nineteenth-Century Black American Spiritualist, Rosicrucian, and Sex Magician* (Albany: State University of New York Press, 1997), esp. 28–29, 224–225, 304–305, 382, 393, 484–491, 541–543.

49. TS, ed., "Heavenly Bridegrooms," *Alienist and Neurologist* 36 (1915): 435, 439. Craddock was right about the substantial concern in Christian commentary with the question of such divine-human congress. On the widespread theological theorizing of the problem of whether (and how) angels and demons, as spirits, could

copulate, see Walter Stephens, *Demon Lovers: Witchcraft, Sex, and the Crisis of Belief* (Chicago: University of Chicago Press, 2002).

50. TS, ed., "Heavenly Bridegrooms," *Alienist and Neurologist* 38 (1917): 123; Richard von Krafft-Ebing, *Psychopathia Sexualis*, trans. Charles Gilbert Chaddock (Philadelphia: Davis, 1893), 5.

51. TS, ed., "Heavenly Bridegrooms," *Alienist and Neurologist* 37 (1916): 219; 38 (1917): 295–301. Craddock's monograph survives in two typescripts in box 4, f. 1 and f. 4 in ICP.

52. Ibid., 37 (1916): 220.

53. IC, "Marriage Relation," 26.

54. Baphomet [Aleister Crowley], Review of "Heavenly Bridegrooms," *Equinox* 3 (1919): 280–281; [Michaels Whitty], Review of "Heavenly Bridegrooms," *Azoth* 3 (1918): 300–301. Not surprisingly, a review in the *Truth Seeker* took the opposite position and heralded Schroeder's discoveries. See H. Tullsen, "Sex in Religious Origins," *Truth Seeker*, Nov. 23, 1918, 740. Crowley's notice of Craddock in 1919 has led in the last decade to a freshet of interest in her work in occult circles. She has now been inducted posthumously into the Order of the Eagle within the U.S. Grand Lodge of the Ordo Templi Orientis, a group that has set up a Web site in her honor (www.idacraddock.org). See Vere Chappell, "Ida Craddock: Sexual Mystic and Martyr for Freedom," in Richard Metzger, ed., *Book of Lies: The Disinformation Guide to Magick and the Occult (Being an Alchemical Formula to Rip a Hole in the Fabric of Reality)* (New York: Disinformation, 2003), 212–217, and, for this group's place in the sexual history of occultism, see Hugh Urban, "The Yoga of Sex: Tantra, Orientalism, and Sex Magic in the Ordo Templi Orientis," in Wouter J. Hanegraaff and Jeffrey J. Kripal, eds., *Hidden Intercourse: Eros and Sexuality in the History of Western Esotericism* (Leiden: Brill, 2008), 401–443. As suggested by the date on the Crowley review, Craddock's adoption is a posthumous repositioning. While she clearly breathed the occultist air of her day, she was during her lifetime outside the organizational matrices of fraternal lodges, hermetic orders, and secret societies. Crowley himself came to learn of her only belatedly through Schroeder's edited volume of 1918. For esoteric fascinations within the history of religions as a field of inquiry, see especially Steven M. Wasserstrom, *Religion after Religion: Gershom Scholem, Mircea Eliade, and Henry Corbin at Eranos* (Princeton: Princeton University Press, 1999). For the particular uses that women could put this form of "higher learning," see Alex Owen, *The Place of Enchantment: British Occultism and the Culture of the Modern* (Chicago: University of Chicago Press, 2004), 36–37, 90–91.

55. DPE, 129–130, 202–203.

56. Ibid., second part, 55–56.

57. Ibid. One more indication of just how complicated questions of voice are: This final diary entry asserting her "queen of myself" autonomy actually echoed a

passage that Craddock had excerpted in her research notes from Robert Greer, *Lecture Delivered before the West Chicago Philosophical Society July 12, 1880, at Castle Hall, Chicago, on the Horrors of Modern Matrimony as Viewed from a Moral and Sanitary Standpoint* (Chicago: n.p., 1892), 11–12. Craddock's extract from Greer's lecture includes a quotation from an unmarried woman to this effect: "I do not wish to lose my identity in others. I wish to be independent and to retain my own individuality and to reign as queen over my own person." Any individuality of voice remains within an echo chamber of voices—internal, textual, and spoken. See IC, "Miscellaneous Notes," box 5, f. 14, ICP.

Epilogue

1. Julianna Baggott, *Lizzie Borden in Love: Poems in Women's Voices* (Carbondale: Southern Illinois University Press, 2006), 41–42.

2. Margaret Sanger, *An Autobiography* (New York: Cooper Square Press, 1999), 111–12, 171; William J. Robinson, "Pioneer of the Birth Control Movement in America," *Medico-Pharmaceutical Critic and Guide* 18 (1915): 321–323.

3. Raymond A Sokolov, "Nonfiction in Brief," *New York Times*, Oct. 28, 1979, Book Review, 4. Twentieth-century sexology, despite the conservative polemics against it, was not a uniformly secular, anti-religious enterprise; Alfred Kinsey, for example, actively courted religious liberals. See R. Marie Griffith, "The Religious Encounters of Alfred C. Kinsey," *Journal of American History* 95 (2008): 349–377. On the ways in which religion has often been cut out of the history of women's rights, see Ann Braude's introduction to the new edition of *Radical Spirits: Spiritualism and Women's Rights in Nineteenth-Century America*, 2nd ed. (Bloomington: Indiana University Press, 2001), xx–xxiv, and Kathi Kern, *Mrs. Stanton's Bible* (Ithaca: Cornell University Press, 2001), 10–13.

4. Edward W. Said, *Representations of the Intellectual* (New York: Random House, 1994), 74, 83.

5. On the recent growth of an evangelical sex-manual industry, see Amy DeRogatis, "What Would Jesus Do? Sexuality and Salvation in Protestant Evangelical Sex Manuals, 1950s to the Present," *Church History* 74 (2005): 97–137.

6. For the contemporary debate on pornography, feminism, and censorship, see Catharine A. MacKinnon, *Only Words* (Cambridge, MA: Harvard University Press, 1993); Catharine A. MacKinnon and Andrea Dworkin, eds., *In Harm's Way: The Pornography Civil Rights Hearings* (Cambridge, MA: Harvard University Press, 1997), and Nadine Strossen, *Defending Pornography: Free Speech, Sex, and the Fight for Women's Rights* (New York: New York University Press, 2000). Craddock's case has been invoked on the Strossen side of this contemporary free-expression debate about pornography (mostly for its symbolic value for dramatizing the evils of censorship). See especially Edward de Grazia's use of Craddock's story in his *Girls Lean Back Everywhere: The Law of Obscenity and the Assault on Genius* (New York:

Random House, 1992), 3–6. The focal concerns of MacKinnon and Andrea Dworkin with misogyny, harassment, and sexual violence are clearly echoed in Craddock's case as well, though. Nineteenth-century marriage reformers shared many of Comstock's concerns about the commercialization of sex, even as they argued against the censorship of frank works on human sexuality that aimed at educational uplift and women's emancipation.

7. "Sex and Yoga: They're Good for the Soul," *Yoga Journal*, Aug. 2006, cover. The Christian adaptation of yoga is rapidly becoming its own niche in the fitness industry. See, for example, Susan Bordenkircher, *Yoga for Christians* (Nashville: Nelson, 2006).

ACKNOWLEDGMENTS

Books are written in the gloom of the failings and doubts of their authors. Why don't chapters, or even mere paragraphs and sentences, come together more easily or eloquently? Will the patient search of sources be rewarded with unexpected disclosures or founder on evidential gaps? Will the book actually be read, should it ever get done in the first place? Will it matter? To the usual specters, I have added this time the failure of others. Would my efforts be as unrequited as those of my predecessors?

The lawyer and psychoanalyst Theodore Schroeder was the first inquirer to plot out a book on Craddock, and by 1920 he had amassed a remarkable archive of her materials. Over the next two decades Schroeder shuffled around chapter outlines, drafted and redrafted various sections, and sent out numerous feelers to different editors, but he never finished his multi-volume study on religion and sex in which Craddock was slated to play the leading role. Despite Schroeder's failure to bring his own work to closure, he remained a free-speech advocate to the last: More than a century after her death, Craddock can still have her say in large part because of Schroeder's resolve to preserve her writings from oblivion. Without his labor as the self-appointed curator of Craddock's papers, this book could not have been written.

Ralph Ginzburg, a leading free-speech agitator of the 1950s and 1960s, was the next figure to take up Craddock's life in the context of his own larger explorations of American censorship. Publisher of an artsy quarterly called *Eros*, Ginzburg was charged with obscenity in 1962 under the same Comstock law that had vexed Craddock sixty years earlier. The case eventually wound its way to the Supreme Court where Ginzburg lost on a 5–4 decision in 1966, ultimately serving eight months in prison and becoming something of a countercultural hero. When not taunting his opponents with his libidinous ventures—he tried, for example, to get *Eros* mailed from Intercourse, Pennsylvania, before settling on Middlesex, New Jersey—Ginzburg made plans to write a book-length exposé of the New York Society for the Suppression of Vice. To that end, he began research on many of Comstock's old thorns, including Craddock, but he, too, failed to see his project into print and ended up with only a ream of clippings, notes, and rough chapters. Without his foresight, though, crucial pieces of Schroeder's original collection of Craddock manuscripts would have been lost. In its small way, this book offers a vindication of the failed designs of Schroeder and Ginzburg, particularly their confidence in the significance of Craddock's story.

Most of Theodore Schroeder's papers, including his Craddock assemblage, came to rest in the Special Collections Research Center at Southern Illinois University in Carbondale. I owe the manuscript curators, librarians, and assistants there an immense debt for their professionalism and patience as I made all too many requests for archive boxes and photocopies. Ralph Ginzburg's papers are housed at the Wisconsin Historical Society in Madison, and the staff members there were likewise extremely helpful and supportive. The stewards of other research collections also played essential parts, including those at the New York Public Library, the National Archives and Records Administration, the Library Company of Philadelphia, the University of Pennsylvania, the Philadelphia City Archives, Princeton University, the University of Michigan, the Library of Congress, the Chicago History Museum, the Andover-Harvard Theological Library, the Friends Historical Library at Swarthmore College, the Wagner Free Institute of Science, and the British Museum. I extend a special thanks to Denise Morris for personally searching the records of Friends' Central School for material on Craddock's attendance there. Finally, I offer my appreciation to Frederick R. Koch for his generosity in inviting me to view his art collection, particularly William Bouguereau's *Le ravissement de Psyché*.

Rebecca Davis, Cynthia Eller, Jonathan Gold, Kathryn Lofton, and Jon Pahl offered incisive commentary when I premiered chapter drafts among colleagues at Princeton. Anne Boylan at the University of Delaware, Sarah Iles Johnston at Ohio State University, and Hussein Ali Agrama at the University of Chicago welcomed presentations from this project on the sexual history of religion. Bradford Verter provoked my initial interest in the writers on "phallicism" who so engrossed Craddock, and I have over the years learned much else besides from his esoteric learning. Ann Braude, accomplished historian of the broader religious and political world Craddock inhabited, provided critical feedback and scholarly encouragement. Rachel Lindsey supplied valuable research assistance in the early stages of the book's development, while Kip Richardson did the same in its final preparation for press. Finally, Lara Heimert, Giles Anderson, Alex Littlefield, and Sandy Chapman furnished wise editorial and literary counsel along the way.

John Merrill, a tried-and-true friend since graduate school, accompanied me on my first trip to Carbondale. During the day he pursued his art, photographing (in this case) Midwestern outbuildings; in the evening over beers, he assured me that what I was finding in the archives sounded like it had potential. My standard question to him after the library's closing time: "Was it a good day for the arts?" His return query: "Was it a good day for the humanities?" Both were flourishing for us in that midland meeting point.

Acknowledgments

R. Marie Griffith is a far better historian of women, gender, and sexuality than I will ever be. I thank her for indulging my trespass onto her scholarly terrain. I thank her, too, for all the spirited banter about Craddock's ideas and experiences. I have no doubt that she heard a little bit more about this project over the last five years than she found necessary or enlightening. Craddock never said right marital living would be easy. The book dedication is not recompense; it is gratitude and admiration.

INDEX

IC stands for Ida Craddock.
Page numbers in italics indicate photographs.